Palgrave Studies in Liter

CW00832547

Series Editors
Deborah Reed-Danahay
Department of Anthropology
The State University of New York at Buffalo
Buffalo, NY, USA

Helena Wulff
Department of Social Anthropology
Stockholm University
Stockholm, Sweden

This book series aims to publish explorations of new ethnographic objects and emerging genres of writing at the intersection of literary and anthropological studies. Books in this series will be grounded in ethnographic perspectives and the broader cross-cultural lens that anthropology brings to the study of reading and writing. The series will explore the ethnography of fiction, ethnographic fiction, narrative ethnography, creative nonfiction, memoir, autoethnography, and the connections between travel literature and ethnographic writing.

More information about this series at
http://www.palgrave.com/gp/series/15120

Máiréad Nic Craith

# The Vanishing World of *The Islandman*

## Narrative and Nostalgia

Máiréad Nic Craith
Heriot-Watt University
Edinburgh, UK

Palgrave Studies in Literary Anthropology
ISBN 978-3-030-25774-3      ISBN 978-3-030-25775-0   (eBook)
https://doi.org/10.1007/978-3-030-25775-0

© The Editor(s) (if applicable) and The Author(s), under exclusive licence to Springer Nature Switzerland AG 2020
This work is subject to copyright. All rights are solely and exclusively licensed by the Publisher, whether the whole or part of the material is concerned, specifically the rights of translation, reprinting, reuse of illustrations, recitation, broadcasting, reproduction on microfilms or in any other physical way, and transmission or information storage and retrieval, electronic adaptation, computer software, or by similar or dissimilar methodology now known or hereafter developed.
The use of general descriptive names, registered names, trademarks, service marks, etc. in this publication does not imply, even in the absence of a specific statement, that such names are exempt from the relevant protective laws and regulations and therefore free for general use.
The publisher, the authors and the editors are safe to assume that the advice and information in this book are believed to be true and accurate at the date of publication. Neither the publisher nor the authors or the editors give a warranty, express or implied, with respect to the material contained herein or for any errors or omissions that may have been made. The publisher remains neutral with regard to jurisdictional claims in published maps and institutional affiliations.

Cover illustration: GeoStock / Stockbyte / Getty Images

This Palgrave Macmillan imprint is published by the registered company Springer Nature Switzerland AG
The registered company address is: Gewerbestrasse 11, 6330 Cham, Switzerland

# Series Preface

*Palgrave Studies in Literary Anthropology* publishes explorations of new ethnographic objects and emerging genres of writing at the intersection of literary and anthropological studies. Books in this series are grounded in ethnographic perspectives and the broader cross-cultural lens that anthropology brings to the study of reading and writing. By introducing work that applies an anthropological approach to literature, whether drawing on ethnography or other materials in relation to anthropological and literary theory, this series moves the conversation forward not only in literary anthropology, but in general anthropology, literary studies, cultural studies, sociology, ethnographic writing and creative writing. The "literary turn" in anthropology and critical research on world literatures shares a comparable sensibility regarding global perspectives.

Fiction and autobiography have connections to ethnography that underscore the idea of the author as ethnographer and the ethnographer as author. Literary works are frequently included in anthropological research and writing, as well as in studies that do not focus specifically on literature. Anthropologists take an interest in fiction and memoir set in their field locations, and produced by "native" writers, in order to further their insights into the cultures and contexts they research. Experimental genres in anthropology have benefited from the style and structure of fiction and autoethnography, as well as by other expressive forms ranging from film and performance art to technology, especially the internet and social media. There are renowned fiction writers who trained as anthropologists, but moved on to a literary career. Their anthropologically inspired work is a common sounding board in literary anthropology. In the endeavour to foster writing skills in different genres, there are now courses on ethnographic writing, anthropological writing genres, experimental writing, and even creative writing taught by anthropologists. And increasingly, literary and reading communities are attracting anthropological attention, including an engagement with issues of how to reach a wider audience.

*Palgrave Studies in Literary Anthropology* publishes scholarship on the ethnography of fiction and other writing genres, the connections between travel literature and ethnographic writing, and internet writing. It also publishes creative work such as ethnographic fiction, narrative ethnography, creative non-fiction, memoir and autoethnography. Books in the series include monographs and edited collections, as well as shorter works that appear as Palgrave Pivots. This series aims to reach a broad audience among scholars, students and a general readership.

Deborah Reed-Danahay and Helena Wulff
Co-Editors, Palgrave Studies in Literary Anthropology

**Advisory Board**
Ruth Behar, University of Michigan
Don Brenneis, University of California, Santa Cruz
Regina Bendix, University of Göttingen
Mary Gallagher, University College Dublin
Kirin Narayan, Australian National University
Nigel Rapport, University of St Andrews
Ato Quayson, University of Toronto
Julia Watson, Ohio State University

# ACKNOWLEDGEMENTS

There are many institutions and individuals who should be thanked for making this book possible. In the first instance, I wish to thank the Department of Celtic Studies at Harvard University, who hosted me as a visiting scholar in Spring 2018. Catherine McKenna, Joseph Falaky Nagy and Natasha Sumner offered very interesting insights into the Irish cultural context at the time that Tomás wrote his memoir, while Mary Violette ensured access to numerous resources. A number of academics gave generously of their time during my trips to Massachusetts. These include Brian Frykenberg, Philip Deloria and Michael D. Jackson (all at Harvard University).

At Boston College, I had fruitful conversations with James H. Murphy, Richard Kearney and Phillip O'Leary. Christian Dupont Burns (also at Boston College) provided me with an original scan of Flann O'Brien's personal copy of *An tOileánach*, while the bookseller Stephen Griffin gifted me with many useful books. A trip to the Irish Cultural Center of Western New England afforded the opportunity to meet with Gerald Costello, Thomas Moriarty and Sean F. Cahillane and to experience the importance of an American-Irish cultural institution for descendants of the islanders in Holyoke.

Inevitably, much of this research was conducted in Ireland. Seán Ó Coileáin, emeritus Professor at the National University of Ireland (Cork), gave generously of his time on several occasions to encourage and support the idea for this book. A number of individuals on the Dingle Peninsula gave advice. These include Mícheál de Mórdha and Daithí de Mórdha, former staff at the Blasket Interpretative Centre, creative artists Lone Beiter (pottery), Maria Simonds-Gooding (artist) and Antonio Fazio (sculptor). In Dublin, Pat Cooke (National University of Ireland) was helpful in providing insights into the establishment of the Interpretive Centre. Anne O'Connor of RTÉ (Dublin) facilitated access to archival material, while Garry Bannister (translator) generously gave of his time to talk to me through the translation process of the latest edition of *An tOileánach*. Mary Sorensen, Librarian at Cork City Council, tracked down a number of useful newspaper articles of relevance, while staff at the National University of Ireland Galway (Maureen Linnane, Morag Kelly and Geraldine Lyons) were helpful in accessing library material there.

A key dimension to this book has been its reception on Continental Europe. Academics such as Regina Bendix (Göttingen University), Michaele Fenske (Würzburg University) and Orvar Löfgren (Lund University) offered advice and insights into issues of authenticity and nostalgia. Writing this book has meant accessing sources and researching in several languages (Danish, French, Galician, German, Italian, Russian, Spanish and Swedish). For their help with this research, I would particularly like to thank Angela Robinson (Sweden), Angelika Diez (Germany), Victoria Walters (England), Lone Beiter (Ireland), Laura Saura (Spain), Marc Romano (Scotland) and Chiara Cocco (Scotland).

In Scotland, I have had the benefit of advice on literary anthropology from Nigel Rapport, University of St. Andrews. Academics at my own institution (Heriot-Watt University) deserve credit for their support for this research. In particular, I wish to thank Tom Farrington, Isabelle Perez and Vitalija Stepušaitytė. A very special thank you to Cristina Clopot at the University of Hull. The study has benefited from thoughtful responses to papers I have presented at the University of Göttingen, University of St Andrews, Cambridge University, Harvard University and Stockholm University. I have had useful e-mail communications with a range of people in different locations including Margaret Humberston (Springfield Museums), Robert Kanigel (Baltimore), Christopher C. Fennell (University of Illinois), Brian Ó Conchubhair (University of Notre Dame) and Joern Wilhelm, translator (Germany), Lorcán Ó Cinnéide (Blasket Interpretative Centre) and Muireann Maguire (University of Exeter, UK).

This book has been through a rigorous peer review process. I would like to thank a number of "critical friends" who generously critiqued individual chapters. These include Hastings Donnan (Queen's University, Belfast), Seán Ó Coileáin (University College, Cork) Nigel Rapport (St Andrews), Pat Cooke (University College, Dublin), Emma Hill (Edinburgh University), Cristina Clopot (Hull University), Claudia Angelleli, Tom

Farrington and Ullrich Kockel (all at Heriot-Watt university). Palgrave has ensured that both the initial proposal and the final manuscript were sent for external review. I would also like to thank the editors Deborah Reed-Danahay (University at Buffalo) and Helena Wulff (University of Stockholm) and all the staff at Springer who patiently dealt with my queries.

Finally to my mother Máiréad, my father Tom and my brothers Dónal and Mícheál—thank you for all your love and support over the years. To my sister Máire and my brother Tom—I am sorry that you did not live to celebrate this book with me. This book is dedicated to my husband Ullrich Kockel, who first requested that I write it some twenty-five years ago—I hope the wait was worth it!

# Praise for *The Vanishing World of* The Islandman

"In tracing the journey of a memoir from the sparsely populated Blasket Islands into the world, Nic Craith chronicles the acquisition of literary ambitions, editorial interventions and translational transformations. The originality of this contribution to literary anthropology resides in the skilled and surprising combination of angles through which we witness both the memoirist and those who have appropriated him."
—Regina F. Bendix, *Professor of Cultural Anthropology/European Ethnology,*
*University of Göttingen, Germany*

"The book represents an innovative work at the intersection of cultural analysis, literary anthropology heritage and island studies. It avoids the traps of previous approaches to islands as isolated spots stuck in the past. Nic Craith's islands are places of living cultures, products of cultural policies and literary narratives, niches of transnational connections. This remarkable book will find readers among heritage experts, students of European cultures, but also all those interested in island imaginaries."
—Dr. Nevena Škrbić Alempijević, *President of SIEF, Department of Ethnology*
*and Cultural Anthropology, University of Zagreb, Croatia*

"Like all seminal works of literature, Tomás Ó Criomhthain's autobiography is an inexhaustible resource, in which every generation and individual finds new meaning. In this work of sweeping comparative research, Máiréad Nic Craith demonstrates its continuing relevance equally to the world of the primitive and of the modern, as well as its centrality to the cultural values of the new Irish State."
—Seán Ó Coileáin, *Emeritus Professor of Modern Irish, University College Cork,*
*Member of the Royal Irish Academy, Ireland*

"The beauty of this book, crafted by Máiréad Nic Craith with sensitivity and dedication, is the insight provided into *The Islandman* (and its ilk) without claiming definitive answers or finally disambiguating its mysteries. It is a remarkable literary journey between island and world, tradition and modernity, materiality and nostalgia."
—Nigel Rapport, *Professor of Anthropological and Philosophical Studies,*
*University of St Andrews, UK*

"Ninety years after its first publication, Máiréad Nic Craith offers a welcome reex-amination of Tomás Ó Criomhthain's Blasket Island autobiography *An tOileán-ach*. Situating it within the wider contexts of early twentieth-century ethnographies and ethnographic theory, translation studies, the interface of orality and literacy, and the history of the book, Nic Craith shows how Ó Criomhthain's book fits into the history of twentieth-century Western anthropology and literature."
—Catherine McKenna, *Margaret Brooks Robinson Professor of Celtic Languages and Literatures, Harvard University, USA*

# CONTENTS

# PREVIOUSLY PUBLISHED BOOKS
# BY MÁIRÉAD NIC CRAITH

## MONOGRAPHS

*Narratives of Place, Belonging and Language: An Intercultural Perspective*, 2012.

*Europe and the Politics of Language: Citizens, Migrants, Outsiders*, 2006.

*Culture and Identity Politics in Northern Ireland*, 2003.

*Plural Identities: Singular Narratives—the Case of Northern Ireland*, 2002.

*Malartú Teanga: An Ghaeilge i gCorcaigh sa Naoú hAois Déag*, 1993.

*An tOileánach Léannta*, 1988.

## EDITED BOOKS (CONTRIBUTING EDITOR)

*Heritage and Festivals in Europe* (with Ullrich Kockel, Cristina Clopot and Baiba Tjarve), 2019.

*Companion to Heritage Studies* (with William Logan and Ullrich Kockel), 2015.

*Companion to the Anthropology of Europe* (with Ullrich Kockel and Jonas Frykman), 2012.

*Cultural Diversity, Heritage and Human Rights: Intersections in Theory and Practice* (with Michele Langfield and William Logan), 2010.

*Everyday Cultures in Europe: Approaches and Methodologies* (with Ullrich Kockel and Reinhard Johler), 2008.

*Language, Power and Identity Politics*, 2007.
*Cultural Heritages as Reflexive Traditions* (with Ullrich Kockel), 2007.
*Communicating Cultures* (with Ullrich Kockel), 2004.
*Watching One's Tongue: Issues in Language Planning*, 1996.
*Watching One's Tongue: Aspects of Romance and Celtic Languages*, 1996.

# PROLOGUE

My first trip to the Dingle Peninsula on the south-west coast of Ireland was in 1977. As a young student learning the Irish language, my course required that I spend a month living with an Irish-speaking family in the *Gaeltacht* (Irish-speaking region). Although the Great Blasket Island was constantly on the horizon during that visit, it was some years later before I actually visited it for the first time. That visit sparked a life-long interest in a traditional way of life that has effectively disappeared. Later, as an undergraduate in University College Cork, *An tOileánach* (*The Islandman*), the first memoir written by a Blasket Islander, was a core reading for my Arts degree (Ó Criomhthain 1929). I could hardly have anticipated how that book would journey with me over a lifetime.

When subsequently, under the supervision of Prof. Seán Ó Coileáin at University College Cork, I focused on this memoir for my master's degree (by thesis only), I began a love-affair with an island that has not diminished over time. A revised version of that thesis was published as *An tOileánach Léannta* (*The Learned Islandman*), (Nic Craith 1988), and for a time was one of the best-selling Irish-language books in Ireland. The research questions of that first book focused on Tomás Ó Criomhthain, the first island author.

In my early academic career, I was especially interested in the portrayal of peasant writers across Europe as unlettered and uneducated. I explored Tomás's schooling and informal education on the Great Blasket Island as well as his literary skills in Irish and in English. I was keen to ascertain Tomás's reading material and debunk the myth that writers such as Tomás were unfamiliar with international newspapers and literature. The primary methodology was archival and involved considerable research on the original book manuscript in the National Library and on various letters at the National Folklore archives in Dublin that Tomás had written in both Irish and English.

Since that time, my interest in memoirs has emerged regularly in my publications, most notably in my previous monograph, which focused on contemporary multilingual writers and their intercultural memoirs on the experience of living in between two or more languages (Nic Craith 2012). Unlike my first book, archival research did not feature at all in that volume and the work drew substantially on life-story interviews as a methodology. While some Irish writers such as Hugo Hamilton and Ciaran Carson featured in that book, the focus was primarily on continental European authors such as Marica Bodrožić and Natasha Wodin.

The present book returns to *An tOileánach* but with an anthropological rather than an archival perspective. Instead of the author, my research questions focus on the book and its reception nationally and internationally. I ask how and why a peasant memoir might appeal not only to a national but also to an international audience. In a sense, the locality of the work may be part of the appeal. In his poem "Epic," the Irish poet Patrick Kavanagh reflects on a simple row that took place between two Irish farmers at a time when larger altercations were casting a shadow over pre-Second World War continental Europe (McAuliffe 2009). As the Munich Agreement of 1938 ceded the Sudetenland of western Czechoslovakia to Germany, the ghost of Homer came whispering to Kavanagh's parochial ear:

He said: I made the Iliad from such
A local row. Gods make their own importance (Kavanagh 1974, 286).

Every book aims to achieve something new and original. My key aim with this book has been to bring the work of a historical, indigenous Irish-language writer to a contemporary anthropological audience on an international scale. With few exceptions, the memoir has been critiqued primarily in an Irish (language) context and within an Irish cultural framework. Given the interdisciplinary nature of my own research career, I felt it entirely appropriate to revisit the volume and set it in a new context that is global and anthropological, and located in literary anthropology, which is the focus of this series.

Dealing with written texts is hardly a new practice for anthropologists (Nic Craith 2012). In 1973, Clifford Geertz compared the process of doing ethnography to reading a manuscript—although not in the conventional sense. In *Writing Culture* (Clifford and Marcus 1986), James Clifford (and others) reflected on the notion of culture as text. Many of the techniques of reading more commonly associated with literary criticism were applied to the practice of ethnographic writing in that volume. Since its publication in 1986, the collection has generated a number of mixed responses (Behar and Gordon 1995; James et al. 1997; Waterston and Vesperi 2009; Barton and Papen 2010).

Despite the emerging canon, the concept of "literary anthropology" continues to be contested. One of the key points of criticism is the lack of a field in the Malinowskian tradition. Sometimes this branch of anthropology is criticised as "armchair anthropology." However, as Ulf Hannerz (2016, 4) notes: "Yet past, and present, anthropology is dotted with people whose main scholarly contributions have been from the armchair or the desk." A key resource for literary anthropology is the text, and critics tend to assume a sole reliance or over-reliance on the text. However, the process of anthropological engagement with a text involves substantial fieldwork. Sometimes it involves travelling in time as well as space, deploying participant observation by interpreting other "voices" from different sources.

In order to focus deeply on the local, the methodology for this book has been ethnological—drawing reflexively on participant observation, interviews and what Helena Wulff has called "yo-yo fieldwork", and which she describes as "increasingly common" (Wulff 2003, 139). While an extended stay in the field was common practice among anthropologists in the past, contemporary fieldwork sometimes involves a different sort of engagement across both time and space. I conducted many journeys to and from Edinburgh to Dingle, Cork, Galway and Dublin. My research involved short as well as extended stays in the Boston area. Interviews were conducted with people in continental Europe, especially Germany, France and Denmark, but also in the US. My informants were relatives of former islanders, curators, translators, editors, academics and artists. This might be considered what Hannerz (1998) has called studying sideways. My informants were professionals, fellow intellectuals living parallel lives.

As the field of literary anthropology emerges and consolidates, it is being redefined. In 2012, Nigel Rapport identified two branches of literary anthropology. His first branch focuses on literature itself and the role it plays in our social and individual lives. "This sub-field considers historical writers such as Chekov, Dickens and Eliot and their endeavour to describe life authentically through social realist fiction" (Rapport 1994, 17). Rapport himself had ventured on such a journey and had conducted fieldwork in a rural village in Northern England (Rapport 1993). His fieldwork focused on social relations between particular people and their wide-ranging worldviews. This methodology was used by Helena Wulff (2017) in her research on Irish writers (in English). She has described the process as changing "the role of the anthropologist in relation to the people we study" (Wulff 2014, 148).

Engaging with the diversity of personal beliefs and the disarray of our social reality, Rapport (1994) argues that this confusion was also inherent in the writings of E.M. Forster. The combination of fieldwork and texts was necessary to deliver a rounded picture of British culture and society at a particular point in time (Nic Craith and Kockel 2014). In a similar vein, Handler and Segal were attracted to Jane Austen's fiction. Although Austen was not a professional anthropologist, Handler and Segal (1999) regarded her novels as anthropological, since they offered significant insights into nineteenth-century English culture and society.

Rapport's second branch of anthropology explores the discipline itself and the role of writing in the emerging canon of anthropological knowledge. This branch queries the relationship between writing itself and anthropology and asks whether anthropologists can be writers and whether anthropology can be expressed in different literary genre. It considers the role of the literary in the dissemination of anthropology and the nature of the creative experience for anthropologists (Geertz 1988).

More recently, Ellen Wiles (2018) has argued for a three-pronged division of the field of literary anthropology. The first of these (often used by historical anthropologists) mines literary texts as ethnographic source material; the second focuses on literary approaches to writing ethnography, while the third explores literary creativity from an anthropological perspective. Given that I am exploring the social life of *An tOileánach* and the reaction to the book in human, literary and artistic terms, this book is more akin to the Wiles's third branch—although the boundaries are hardly clear-cut.

As my book was being written, the theme of nostalgia emerged as a "thread" uniting many of the chapters. Nostalgia is hardly a new theme for anthropologists (see, e.g. Berliner 2015; Cashman 2006; Rosaldo 1989). To set the context, I begin with an exploration of the exo-nostalgia that prevailed in the field of anthropology a century ago and the interest of (primarily American) anthropologists in "vanishing races" (frequently Native

American). This nostalgia was hardly confined to anthropologists who were intrigued with vanishing races in the US, and some Harvard anthropologists came to Ireland in search of the vanishing Celtic people. As noted in the first chapter of this book, these anthropologists were aware of Tomás's memoir but didn't travel to the Great Blasket Island where it was written. However, many European folklorists subsequently followed in their footsteps to research the folklore and language of a disappearing way of life.

In many instances, literary anthropologists tend to focus on fiction (albeit social realist fiction), whereas mine specifically deals with a memoir. One could argue that memoir is a more "factual" resource than fiction, but as I have argued elsewhere, this is hardly the case, as writers of memoirs themselves engage in a process of selectivity when deciding what to highlight and what to omit in their writing (Nic Craith 2012). In Chap. 2 of this book, I debunk the myth that Tomás Ó Criomhthain (like many "peasant writers") was unlettered and investigate the influence of European literary giants such as Pierre Loti, Knut Hamsun and Maxim Gorky on Ó Criomhthain. I explore Tomás's handwriting of the memoir and query the representative nature of the published text. I also look at the denial of agency to an island author who was moving from oral to literary expressions of his stories.

In the following chapter, I query the extent to which Tomás's memoir presents a "thick description" (Geertz 1973) of life on an Irish island. I explore the attempts to portray Tomás as the representative voice of a community rather than an individual islander with agency. The debate regarding individual or folk narrative applies widely in oral literature, and in the case of Tomás, I explore the censure-ship of his authorial voice in order to ensure adherence with standards of the time which prohibited any sexual nuances or unseemly behaviour.

At the time of the publication of Tomás's memoir, the Irish state had newly emerged from many centuries under British rule. As an independent state, a chief aspiration of the Irish government was the restoration of the Irish-speaking, Catholic, peasant idealisation of Ireland's precolonial past. This could be regarded as a form of restorative nostalgia. Along with the promotion of Irish language, a native Irish literature and a national system of education, Tomás's original Irish-language memoir and its English translation were very useful tools in promoting Irish ideals and an authentic peasant lifestyle.

The craft of translation can take many forms—from one language to another, and generally from one medium to another. Chapter 4 begins with the "translation" of the Irish landscape of *An tOileánach* into visual images by the artist Maria Simonds-Gooding for the second Irish-language edition. I subsequently explore the translation of the book from Irish into English, raising questions regarding power relationships between the two languages. While the translation of the memoir into English introduced the work to a large English-speaking audience, it also had implications for conceptual mapping and the development of a sense of place.

Given that anthropologists and folklorists were involved in salvage ethnology, they were keen to give voice to indigenous peoples and to ensure a written record of what they perceived as vanishing worlds. In Chap. 5, I take the opportunity to deepen a comparison between Tomás and Black Elk, a renowned Oglala Lakota medicine man, who had collaborated with John Neihardt on the publication of a memoir entitled *Black Elk Speaks* (Black Elk and Neihardt 2000 [1932]). Both Tomás and Black Elk were regarded as pioneers in developing a literary heritage for their respective peoples. In both instances, the original, authorial "voice" has been overlaid with "helpful" and sometimes critical, editorial voices, and the original authentic voice is not easy to discern. For this reason, I primarily engage with the most recent editions of the text (Ó Criomhthain 2002; O'Crohan 2012) rather than earlier ones. Unlike previous editions, these newer ones have endeavoured to present Tomás's memoir as it was originally written by the fisherman himself.

The appeal of a simple, peasant lifestyle, which was disappearing in the wake of industrialisation and urbanisation, prompted European contemporaries of Tomás such as Knut Hamsun and Hermann Hesse to write novels highlighting the relationship between man and the natural environment (see Chap. 6). This continental nostalgia for a pre-industrial society may have sparked the European interest in Tomás's memoir, which has since been translated into English, Swedish, Danish, French, German, Italian and (partly) Spanish (O'Crohan 1937, 1949, 1983, 1989, 1991; Ó Criomhthain 1996).

At the beginning of the twenty-first century, contemporary interest in the sublime motivates visitors today to visit the Blasket Interpretative Centre in the Dingle Peninsula, which has recently been designated part of Ireland's "Wild Atlantic Way." This centre highlights the material culture prevalent during Tomás's lifestyle as well as some artistic responses to excerpts from the book. In Chap. 7, I explore the curatorial vision that inspired the original initiative as well as the significance of *The Islandman* for the museum exhibition. This centre, which is located at the edge of

Europe, highlights the interfaces represented in *An tOileánach*—between tradition and modernity, between literary and visual, and between the local and global.

Some of the visitors to the Blasket Centre include descendants of islanders now living in the US. Although living in a new homeland, these Irish-Americans maintain a strong connection with the island and are proud of its literary heritage (see Chap. 8). While they are nostalgic for the way of life on the island, this form of nostalgia is more reflective than restorative, and there is no longing to return to a way of life that was distinctly difficult and challenging. However, the literary tradition continues, and one could regard contemporary American-Irish diaspora narratives in Holyoke, Springfield and Cape Cod as part of the legacy of Tomás's original book.

At the beginning of this research process, I was intrigued by the continuing interest in this fisherman's memoir of island life at the turn of the nineteenth and twentieth centuries. It is possible that this can also be explained by people's ongoing fascination with islands. Modern social anthropology was established on an island in the Trobriand archipelago (Eriksen 1993). "Island fascination is age-old" notes Lowenthal (2007, 202) as he points to the prominence of islands in literature, from Homer's *Odyssey* to Golding's *The Lord of the Flies*. The reference to Greek civilisation is appropriate in this context, as many visiting folklorists regarded life on the Great Blasket Island as Homeric—a theme that will feature prominently in this book. The remoteness of an island can evoke a strong sense of nostalgia. "Remoteness is to space what nostalgia is to time. Nostalgia is longing for a time out of time, based on some really historical event, but so idealised as to bear none of the scars that history inflicts" (Gillis 2001, 56).

There is a strong tradition of fascination with islands in Ireland's cultural memory. In pre-Christian Ireland, the "promised land" was located across the sea to the west. An Irish literary genre known as the *Immrama* frequently featured holy men undertaking sea-voyages in a quest to get closer to the Divine. Of particular fame was the legend of St. Brendan, as recorded in the ninth-century *Navagatio Brendani*, which has been variously perceived as fictional account or factual pilgrimage (Anderson 1988; Burgess 2002; MacCana 1980). This story served as the catalyst for islands of the imagination in the Atlantic. Of particular fame is Hy Brazil, a Gaelic blessed island, which "wanders across the medieval charts between the west coast of Ireland and the Azores until it settled in the Gulf of St Lawrence, where it is 'found' in 1481 by two Bristol ships that almost certainly made landfall, in what is now Newfoundland" (Smith 2017, 23).

A fascination with islands was hardly confined to Ireland. Geography often determines that a journey to an island is a voyage to the wild or the remote—and the excursion itself becomes a ritual. "Like a pilgrimage, an island journey is circular, a cultural practice dependent as much on going as coming, on the possibility of eternal return. The sacredness of the island itself, its perceived distance from the profane, everyday world" (Gillis 2001, 52). Although modernity has impacted on our concepts of space and time, islands are often regarded as having escaped the vestiges of modernity, which makes them ideal locations for the emergence of nostalgia in all its forms.

The fact that the Blaskets were a group of islands undoubtedly enhanced their appeal as a mythical heartland and inspired the Irish imagination. A Galician photographer, Placido Castro (2013 [1932], 41), once described them as "the spellbound islands of the Irish legends and not the gloomy ones of Synge's dramas" (Castro 1933, 41, translation from original Galician). While the Blasket Islands were not Ireland, they were useful as a metaphor for the larger island of Ireland. Their remoteness and isolation would ensure that here was a distinct place in which authentic Irishness could be maintained apart from the rest of the country. Along with the Aran Islands on the west coast, the Blasket Islands had an "aura of pre-history" (O'Toole 1997, 102). The island signalled unity—something which the larger mother Ireland was lacking. John Wilson Foster remarked that the western island "came to represent Ireland's mythic unity before the chaos of conquest; there at once were the vestige and the symbolic entirety of an undivided nation" (Foster 1987, 96).

With the publication of *An tOileánach* in 1929, a literary journey began that still continues today. Given that almost a century has passed since the original publication of the memoir, it is interesting to consider why an ordinary life story written by an ordinary fisherman on a small island off the west coast of Ireland in a language that is not widely spoken outside of Ireland still has appeal in the early decades of the twenty-first century. This is not simply a "history of a book," but more what Michael Jackson (2013, 227) calls "the social life of stories." This book focuses on the literary journey of a memoir from the west coast of Ireland into a wider world that reaches from the US to Continental Europe (and beyond). This book is one dimension of that literary journey—and somehow I feel, the story will continue for some time to come. As Caputo (2013, 220) says: "No book is ever closed. It will always be necessary to say something about the future, to keep the book open on the future, to expose the book to the future."

# LIST OF ILLUSTRATIONS

# CHAPTER 1

# The Lure of the Primitive

When Tomás Ó Criomhthain penned his memoir in the early twentieth century, he could hardly have imagined the worldwide impact of his life story. Tomás Ó Criomhthain (anglicised O'Crohan) was born in April 1855 (possibly 1856) as the last of eight children to Dónal Ó Criomhthain and Cáit Ní Shé. He was an ordinary, everyday fisherman and small farmer who lived on a small island off the western seaboard coast of Ireland. People on the Great Blasket Island lived unremarkable lives and communicated with one another in a language that was not the mainstream in the wider world. Tomás had not witnessed any particularly extraordinary events. In fact, his was a regular lifestyle, and his life story was that of an everyday Irish-Gaelic islander.

Yet, it was that very ordinariness that was to capture the imagination on an international scale. When retelling this story, Kanigel (2012, 7–8) said: "The Blasket story, I came to realize, wasn't only about one little corner of Ireland. In telling it, I could get at a bigger, more urgent story, as central to this century as to the last, about how we live now, what we've left behind, and at what cost." A well-told life story can shed light on a society far beyond the experiences of that individual (See, e.g. Shostak's (1983 (1981)) biography of a hunter-gatherer woman or Oakdale and Course's volume (2014) on lowland South America). Tomás's story is a universal one. People worldwide can empathise with a way of life that was being wiped out by the unremittent progress of Western civilisation. The fact that it was a Celtic story located on a small Irish island enhanced its appeal.

© The Author(s) 2020

M. Nic Craith, *The Vanishing World of* The Islandman,
Palgrave Studies in Literary Anthropology,
https://doi.org/10.1007/978-3-030-25775-0_1

This was a story that needed to be told. The likes of these islanders would not be there again. Here were traditions that needed to be salvaged before extinction.

## SALVAGE ETHNOGRAPHY

Salvage ethnography is commonly associated with Franz Boas and his academic colleagues who engaged in a quest to collect the languages and the lore of "vanishing" Indian tribes. Clifford (2002) outlines some of the ideological conceptions that lay behind salvage ethnography in general. The first of these was a particular concept of time and space. Evolutionist theory commonly assumed that history was linear, and that as Western civilisation progressed, some "primitive" cultures were doomed to extinction. "There is no going back, no return, at least in the realm of the real" (Clifford 2002, 160). The impending death of a way of life was not just inevitable, nor simply a consequence of marginalisation. It was a result of primitive people's incompatibility with modernity. While white people might progress from barbarity to civilisation in a linear manner, that was not the destiny of people like the American Indian. The stereotypical perspective was that the American Indian "cannot be himself and be civilized; he fades away and dies. Cultivation such as the white man would give him deprives him of his identity. Education, strange as it may appear, seems to weaken rather than strengthen his intellect" (Custer 2009 [1876], 17).

It is commonly assumed that anthropologists were complicit in reenforcing this hierarchical framework of cultures and peoples. Indeed, anthropology has frequently been accused of aiding colonial encounters (Asad 1973; Said 1978, 1989; Deloria 1969; Fabian 1983). Anthropologists have been reproached for "othering" colonised peoples, thereby aiding the process of subjugation. Stasch (2014, 200) suggests: "In doctrines of social evolution elaborated by anthropological thinkers of the 19th century, for example, the primitive other is unambiguously inferior to the civilized self." Yet they also retained something that the modern was felt to have lost—authenticity. Those at the bottom of the evolutionary ladder were an authentic people whose way of life was about to disappear—hence, there was a need to record their lifestyle before it completely expired.

If one returns to the original publications of anthropologists engaged in salvage ethnography, one finds a more nuanced perspective. In 1871 (the year when Darwin's *Descent of Man* was published), *Primitive Culture* by the anthropologist Edward P. Tylor was also published. While Darwin's thesis emerged from a biological perspective, Tylor was analysing the cumulative heritage of human knowledge that was passed on from one generation to the next. His title was deliberately provocative, since it implied that even primitive people have culture and his definition of culture was wide ranging. (This was possibly a reaction against Mathew Arnold's (1869) *Culture and Anarchy*, which focused primarily on high culture or what one might call "theatre culture.") Given that Tylor was working within the context of Victorian anthropology, which was evolutionary in its outlook, his work had enormous impact. Tylor is regarded as the first to use the term survival to explain seemingly irrational practices and customs, which had evolved from earlier rational habits.

Boas brought an anti-evolutionary perspective to bear on the concept of culture. He proposed that differences between peoples were not a consequence of progress in one place and arrested development in another. Instead, the local conditions and context were hugely influential in the emergence of particular customs or habits. He argued: "the term 'primitive' has a double meaning. It applies to both bodily form and culture. We are accustomed to speak both of primitive races and primitive cultures as though the two were necessarily related" (Boas 1938 [1911], 3). This message was re-enforced in his volume *The Mind of the Primitive Man*, in which he reasoned: "Our globe is inhabited by many races, and a great diversity of cultural forms exists. The term 'primitive' should not be applied indiscriminately to bodily build and to culture as though both belonged together by necessity" (Boas 1938 [1911], 31).

Boas noted that while some peoples had been led to civilisation, it could not be assumed that this was because they were more gifted than others who remained in a state of primitivism. Indeed, he was convinced that the gap between the "civilised" and the "primitive" was not that wide. He wrote: "Some Europeans live in a way not so very different from that of simpler people, for the mode of life of the agricultural Indians of North America at the time of Columbus, or that of some agricultural Negro tribes, is, so far as nutrition and occupation are concerned, quite similar to theirs" (Boas 1938 [1911], 87). Many of the differences between civilised and primitive peoples were "more apparent than real." It was social conditions in the Western that gave "the impression that the mind of primitive man acts in a way quite different from ours, while in reality the fundamental traits of the mind are the same" (Boas 1938 [1911], 137).

While originally Boas was deeply involved with the collection of material artefacts for the American Museum of Natural History, his significance in the field of anthropology is due to his analysis of languages and oral traditions, which he regarded as the most critical data for issues concerning culture (Cruikshank 2000, 101). He did not view the languages of Native Americans as primitive or simple. On the contrary, he argued:

> Many primitive languages are complex. Minute differences in point of view are given expression by means of grammatical forms; and the grammatical categories of Latin, and still more so those of modern English, seem crude when compared to the complexity of psychological or logical forms which primitive languages recognize, but which in our speech are disregarded. (Boas 1938 [1911], 172)

Boas rejected cultural evolutionism—that is, a linear view of evolution that placed the primitive at the beginning of the process or at least much further behind than their "civilised counterparts." This theory of "parallel development ... would require that among all branches of mankind the steps of invention should have followed, at least approximately, in the same order, and that no important gaps should be found" (Boas 1938 [1911], 179). He concluded that nothing in science has supported this perspective. People who regarded the primitive as "lower down" or "further behind" on the evolutionary ladder were engaging in ethnocentrism and imposing the standard of one cultural framework onto another. They were "using their own society as a standard for human evolution and were thus ranking other societies and cultures from a vantage-point which was deeply ideologically-biased, and which made no explanatory sense" (Eriksen 1993, 137). They did not recognise that other cultural traditions could be different but no less complex or valuable than the mainstream.

It was not "race" or "genetic inheritance" that determined one's behaviour. Instead, one reacted from cultural experience. Where people participated in a common cultural framework, their reactions were similar.

> Experience has shown that members of most races placed in a certain culture can participate in it. In America men like Juarez, President of Mexico, or the highly educated Indians in North and South America are examples. In Asia, the modern history of Japan and China; in America the successes of educated Negroes as scientists, physicians, lawyers, economists are ample proof showing that the racial position of an individual does not hinder his participation in modern civilization. (Boas 1938 [1911], 179)

In fact, were one to endeavour "to select the best of mankind .... all races and all nationalities would be represented" (Boas 1938 [1911], 272). All languages and cultures were to be treasured—hence the need to document those that were disappearing.

The imminent disappearance of Native Americans motivated Boas and his colleagues to collect and record as much data as possible from Native Americans. Although the peoples themselves would not survive, a record of their languages and oral traditions would be available for future generations. Boas's students "sought to record Indian lives in print as part of the great and urgent project of 'ethnographic salvage' that sought to preserve, in the museum or the library, traces of lives and cultures that could not (so it was then believed) have a continuing existence anywhere else" (Swann and Krupat 2005, xi).

The work of professional anthropologists was reinforced visually by others such as the painter George Catlin, who decided to rescue "from oblivion the looks and customs of the vanishing races of native man in America" (Krupat 1989, 38). The photographer Edward Curtis also captured images of the vanishing race. He sought "to document all aspects of a marvellous culture which was being inexorably destroyed, in such a way as to retain the spirits of the culture and keep it alive" (Krupat 1989, 38). Salvage ethnography in the US was driven by changes that were happening across the country. Legislation had determined that Native Americans living in the eastern US would be relocated to west of the Mississippi River (Krupat 1989, 38). Their departure enhanced the impression that these tribes were *en route* to extinction. However, the mission of salvaging the past was not confined to the Native Americans or to the US.

## ANTHROPOLOGICAL EXO-NOSTALGIA

Social change in the US was contemporaneous with extraordinary social change in the west of Ireland. There too, it prompted feverish activity, seeking out the true Irish race and its Gaelic language, lore and lifestyle. Between 1891 and 1903, an Irish ethnographic survey was conducted in rural Ireland. With a grant from the Royal Irish Academy in Dublin, Alfred Cort Haddon and Charles R. Brown set up the Anthropometry laboratory. The surveyors visited 426 different localities and travelled more than 45,000 miles. They took detailed measurements of 10,000 adult men right throughout the country. They focused primarily on rural rather than urban settings, since the country folk were "less likely to be mixed with recent foreign blood than would be the city dwellers" (Hooton et al. 1955, 8). They undertook a survey in each place and published reports with separate sections covering the landscape (coastline and surface), the people, the "lifestyle" (houses, transport and customs) and "antiquities" (Walsh 2013, 17).

However, the west of Ireland was also drawing the attention of anthropologists and linguists internationally. In 1892, Jeremiah Curtin (a Harvard-trained linguist from Milwaukee) visited west Kerry in search of folklore and made it to the Great Blasket—although his trip was not very successful. In his memoirs, Curtin noted the following conversation on the island: "I asked a man on crutches if he knew any Gaelic myths. His answer was: 'I care more about getting the price of a bottle of whiskey than old stories.' Another man said: 'If you'll give me the price of a bottle of whiskey, I'll talk about stories. I got no stories" (Curtin 1940, 455).

Donnan (2017) traces the birth of modern Irish anthropology to the arrival of William Lloyd Warner in Ireland in 1931. Although Warner was not the first anthropologist to conduct research in Ireland, "he was the first to promote there (and arguably in Europe as a whole) the systematic application to 'modern social life' of the methods and perspectives of anthropology that had developed in the study of societies overseas" (Donnan 2017, 21). Directed by Warner and assisted by Conrad Arensberg and Solon Kimball, the Harvard Irish Study (as it is commonly known) was carried out on the west coast of Ireland between 1932 and 1936. The choice of location was subsequently explained by Arensberg: "Literature has taught us to look for this land in the barren moors and rugged mountains of the west, among the tiny white cabins of Connemara and along the misty headlands of Kerry and West Cork. It is the Ireland of Aran and the Blaskets" (Arensberg 1988 [1937], 31). These locations were attractive, given their link with the Celtic past: "This people preserves an unbroken ancient tradition that goes back, perhaps long into pre-Christian times. Their variant of Celtic culture and language is lost in prehistory" (Arensberg 1988 [1937], 33). From the perspective of these American anthropologists, the isolation of the west coast had preserved its authenticity as an "outpost of western Europe" which had wider implications, given the Celtic past on the continent (Arensberg 1988, 33).

The Harvard anthropologists were impressed with the range and quality of archaic material still available. "The ethnographer finds primitive tools and house-forms, even a wooden plough of Bronze-age days, still in use in remote Waterford or Connemara mountains" (Arensberg 1988, 34). They complimented the commitment of the recently established Irish Free State to the preservation of Irish folklore (see Chap. 4). However, even more impressive were the oral traditions which the anthropologists encountered in their research. Despite the rurality and isolation of the location, local oral tales had clearly adapted strong international tropes.

"International tales like those Grimm recorded first in Germany, traceable from India and Siberia to the remotest Irish coasts, can still be heard, regarbed in a traditional Gaelic dress" (Arensberg 1988, 164). It is interesting to note that although Arensberg and Kimball did not actually visit the Blasket Island, they were aware of the memoir (*An tOileánach*), and Arensberg (1988 [1937], 74–5) actually referenced it.

On completion of his fieldwork in Ireland, Arensberg obtained a position at Harvard University (from 1934 to 1938). During those years he delivered a set of lectures which formed the material for a short volume entitled *The Irish Countryman* (Arensberg 1988 [1937]). This book was later followed by *Family and Community in Ireland* (Arensberg and Kimball 1940). Byrne et al. (2001, 24) suggest that the book "provides an account of Irish rural ways of life in the 1930s, describing customs, folklore and beliefs, work on the farm, family, kinship, matchmaking, marriage, the connection of the rural family with land, the position of older people in the community and the world of shops, pubs and fairs." There is also a concluding chapter dealing with religion, fairy lore and social values. In the preface to the second edition (1968), Arensberg locates *The Irish Countryman* within the "pioneering" tradition of community studies. Byrne et al. (2001, 47) suggest that this puts the volume on a par with "Warner's Yankee City and Deep South studies" such as the Lynd's studies of Middletown (Lynd and Lynd 1943) and Robert Redfield's work in Mexico (Redfield 1930). However, Arensberg and Kimball's representation of rural Ireland has since been challenged (see Gibbon 1973).

The motivation behind the Harvard Survey could hardly have been the notion of a vanishing Irish race. In fact, these anthropologists seem to have been more concerned with establishing functionalism as a paradigm than with any romantic notions of a Celtic people. However, it may also have been driven by the desire to record a disappearing Gaelic daily life on the rural, west coast of Ireland. More significantly, the iconic status of this work ensured that the "West of Ireland" became a symbol for authentic Ireland. Donnan (2017, 22) says:

> Ethnographically, 'Ireland' was thereby firmly placed in the west of Ireland and located within a particular constellation of substantive themes and issues that focused on family and community, a 'localizing strategy' that privileged certain lines of inquiry and shaped subsequent fieldworkers who situated themselves within the same geographical and theoretical contexts that Arensberg and Kimball had championed.

There is a question as to whether, in their quest to study Irish rural life, the American anthropologists regarded the rural Irish as "primitive"—and were placing them on a par with Native American indigenous peoples (see Chap. 5). In undertaking an anthropological study of the west of Ireland, Arensberg and Kimball were crossing into European territory—a point noted with pride by Arensberg himself. He observed that the two texts, *The Irish Countryman* and *Family and Community in Ireland*, were distinctive in that they "were the first of the cultural-anthropological studies, now so widely distributed, to cross the ocean to the Old World of Europe and high civilisation" (Arensberg [1968] 1988, 10).

To study Europeans rather than Native Americans could be understood as "othering" the native Irish and, in the Irish context, there was an added complication. Although the American anthropologists may not have regarded the Celt as a separate race, opposition between the Celt and the Anglo-Saxon had been strongly racialised during the previous century (See Nic Craith 2002). There had been deliberate attempts to present the Irish as sub-human in the media. In 1862, a typical cartoon from the periodical *Punch* suggested that "a creature manifestly between the gorilla and the negro is to be met with in some of the lowest districts of London and Liverpool." The creature "belongs to a tribe of Irish savages" who spoke a language other than English "a sort of gibberish" (Anon. 1862, 165; Nic Craith and Leyland 1997).

Arensberg himself (in a manner similar to Boas) was keen to deny any demotion of the Irish people, arguing: "Whatever we may think of her, we cannot include Ireland among the primitive and barbarous peoples." He added (perhaps unhelpfully): "If we go on to relate primitive survivals to the way of life of the Irish country-people, we certainly do not condemn them wholesale as barbarians, nor can we rightfully regard them as primitive" (Arensberg 1988 [1937], 22–31). However, subsequent anthropological investigations in Ireland identified the west as a society in decline, beset by alcohol-related problems, a high-rate of mental illness and a sexuality that was constantly repressed by the Catholic Church (Brody 1973; Messenger 1969; and Scheper-Hughes 2001 [1979]).

## In Search of Folklore

As with Boas's research among Native Americans, the motivation behind academic visits to the Blaskets at the turn of the twentieth century was language and folklore. Folklorists (rather than anthropologists) from

Scandinavia, England, Germany and France were keen to salvage the Irish language and its rich oral traditions that were still alive on this tiny island. They were also interested in the lifestyle of the islanders who spoke the ancient Irish language and passed on its oral traditions. "The work of these men was most similar to that of Arensberg and Kimball, since in order to learn Irish they came to live in the West of Ireland, many in the Blasket Islands" (Mac Conghail 1987, 136).

Many of the visitors were not especially interested in Tomás Ó Criomhthain at first. Instead, they were interested in the whole island community with its rich tradition of Irish folklore, but there were a number of factors that made Tomás a clear choice as a tutor. Tomás was married to the king's sister and was a regular visitor to the king's "guesthouse" in which the visitors stayed. Tomás's literary skills in both Irish and English were a strong advantage from the perspective of the visitors. It was this combination of assets that marked Tomás as an appropriate mentor for visitors who wanted to learn Irish (Nic Craith 2019) (Illustration 1.1).

**Illustration 1.1**   Great Blasket Island. (© Máiréad Nic Craith)

*Carl Marstrander*

One of the most significant scholars from the perspective of Tomás's literary journey was the Norwegian academic Carl Marstrander, who set out
for Kerry in the summer of 1907 (Nic Craith 1988). Marstrander stopped
in Ballyferriter, where he stayed with a Mr Long. "He was very pleased
with his place in Mr Long's. He is himself a 'native speaker' and his house
is by far the best in this place" (Ó Lúing 1984, 109). Although enjoying
the local environment, Marstrander "thought the Irish spoken there had
too large an admixture of English" (Ó Lúing 1984, 109). In his quest to
find the purest Irish possible, Marstrander ventured out to the Blasket
Islands. The island king (who also operated as an island postman) accompanied him on his journey. On a Sunday in early July, Marstrander set foot
on the island. At that point, his command of modern Irish was not very
strong, as is evidenced by the following narrative:

> In later years, he used to relate a story, which he may have embellished a
> little, about his reception on the Island by the King, Pádraig Ó Catháin,
> who greeted him with a speech by way of civic ceremony. Marstrander did
> not understand a word of what the King said but, nothing daunted, he
> delivered in reply a prepared speech of his own, composed in archaic Irish,
> the only kind he then knew, to which the puzzled King made the courteous
> observation that the Norwegian was a fine language indeed! (Ó Lúing
> 1984, 109)

Marstrander took lodging in the island king's house and began his relationship with the local people. He sent the following letter on 6 August
1907, describing his progress to date and makes his linguistic intentions
clear (his interest in Irish was possibly motivated by his belief that the origin of many Norwegian words was to be found in Ireland):

> As you can see, I am now on the Blasket Island, and will certainly stay here
> for the coming months. Ballyferriter was a wonderful place, but the speech
> seemed to me too undisciplined. I made up my mind very quickly, and left
> Ballyferriter yesterday, with all my belongings. I have installed myself here in
> Mr. Patrick Keane's house, with whom I have evidently as good lodgings as
> I found in Ballyferriter. I am not quite sure yet how long I will remain here,
> perhaps two, perhaps four months. The dialect seems very interesting. With
> my best wishes to you and your wife (cited in Ó Lúing 1984, 109).

Before long, Marstrander had integrated himself into the community. "Marstrander, for his part, found himself in total harmony with Blasket life. The Irish spoken there he considered the purest he had ever encountered. He enjoyed the good company and happy relaxed air of the island, mixing with the people as one of themselves, which was, he thought, the best way of acquiring the language" (Ó Lúing 1984, 109). In part, the welcome the islanders had for Marstrander was due to his exceptional physical strength. Marstrander was an expert long-jumper and he sought to teach these same skills to the island youth. At night, Marstrander used to read to the islanders. He had brought with him a copy of a novel by Peader Ua Laoghaire entitled *Niamh* (Ua Laoghaire 1898). This book would have huge influence on the Irish literary tradition for many decades. As Mac Conghail puts it: "It was a happy coincidence that Ó Criomhthain should be introduced both at the same time to the young Norwegian scholar and to the work of a writer in Irish who was to establish the direction for prose in modern Irish" (Mac Conghail 1987, 135).

Although well integrated with all of the islanders, Marstrander struck up a special relationship with Tomás. Tomás describes how the island king initiated their language classes: "He [Marstrander] asked the King who would be the best person to teach the language to him. The King decided that I would be the best one, because I was able to read it, and because I had fine stylish Gaelic even before I had learnt how to read it" (O'Crohan 2012, 269). Marstrander was very content with Tomás's Irish literary skills but he needed to know about his proficiency in English also. Marstrander noted: "You are good, but do you speak English?" "I haven't great English, Sir," I replied. "That's fine," says he. "But you wouldn't be able to do the job without a little English" (O'Crohan 2012, 269–70). "The master" was an affectionate term that Marstrander gave Tomás, and initially, they spent two or three hours together every evening in the king's house—with Tomás mentoring the Norwegian academic in reading and writing Irish.

Marstrander had initially intended spending a very extended period on the island—but before the year was out he received news that he should return home. In consequence, he doubled his daily schedule with Tomás for the final fortnight. He departed the Great Blasket before Christmas. While they did not meet again, the correspondence between the two continued, with the Norwegian scholar occasionally rewarding Tomás for his efforts with a pipe or a small fee. Marstrander had actually intended returning to the island, but the First World War impacted on the correspondence between them.

Soon after his departure from the island in December 1907, Marstrander sent Tomás a parcel full of blank paper, requesting him to write down the name of every bird in the sky, every fish in the sea and the names of all the herbs growing on the island. Marstrander asked Tomás to write down these terms as he spoke them and not to worry about "correct" spelling. Tomás agreed to the request although he didn't heed the advice to work independently. Instead he sought the help of Tadhg Ó Ceallaigh, a temporary dance teacher who ran a dance school on the island for a short period. Contrary to Marstrander's request, Tomás was concerned that he wouldn't spell the terms correctly. Moreover, he had little experience of actually writing in Irish at this time. Tadhg was glad to help and both he and Tomás worked together on the document until the task was complete.

The document was written in Tomás's own handwriting. It contained a lists of birds, insects, plants and so on, as requested. On occasions the list was a simple translation from Irish into English—that is, *leantóg* (nettles), *sgeach* (briar), *spúnc* (colts-foot). Unsurprisingly, there were occasions where neither Tomás nor Tadhg had knowledge of an English translation. On these occasions, Tomás would give an extended explanation of the term. *Splincín* was described as "a wide greenish fish, resembling the *luitheóg* but different in as much that it swims about, whereas the *luitheóg* keeps to the bottom of the sea." Another example is *Cráinn dubh*, which is explained as "a smaller kind of whale – very plentiful here some years ago – used to annoy the fisherman very much. She always used to keep around the shoals of mackerel" (Ms Catalogue of terms, Oslo). When the task was complete, Tomás dispatched the catalogue to Marstrander, who subsequently edited the manuscript and ordered it alphabetically. It appears that Marstrander had originally intended to construct a study of the dialect. However, that document was never completed. Marstrander returned to Ireland in 1910 to take up a position at the School of Celtic Studies in Dublin but never returned to the Great Blasket.

### Robin Flower

Although he himself did not return to the island, Marstrander's lectures in Old and Middle Irish at the School of Celtic Studies sufficiently sparked the interest of a young Oxford scholar, Robin Flower, to make the journey from the British Museum to the Great Blasket. This is how Marstrander related the tale (note his reference to the daughter of the island king as "princess"):

I am lecturing twice a week in the University for two students. One of them is very clever and has decided to give all his time to Celtic Studies. I will secure him a scholarship next year and send him off to the Blaskets to my old friend Thomás Ó 'Crithin – providing the Princess is not there; she might disturb the piece [*sic*] of his heart, which according to his friends is of a very soft material (Ms *Seanchus ón Oileán Tiar*, 29.4.11).

Since his proficiency was inadequate to complete the cataloguing of Irish manuscripts in the British Museum. Robin Flower accepted Marstrander's advice and left for the Blaskets. Like the Norwegian, he settled in the king's house and it was not long before he met Tomás, whom he described in the following terms: "A slight but confident figure. The face takes your attention at once and holds it. This face is dark and thin, and there look out of it two quick and living eyes, the vivid witnesses of a fine and self-sufficing intelligence" (Flower 1944, 12). Flower mixed well with all the islanders, working on the island quay with them, rather than engaging in non-participant observation.

However, his primary motivation in visiting the island was to learn the language, thereby enhancing his career opportunities. For this he needed lessons from Tomás: "We have to discuss what form my lessons are to take. I want to practise myself in writing down the language from his lips. What is he to give me, isolated words and sentences, or tales and poems? The verdict falls for the tales" (Flower 1944, 16). From then on Tomás and Flower used to spend a couple of sessions together every single day. Flower paints a picture of both scholars working together, one dictating and the other transcribing: "And so, he sitting on one side of the table, rolling a savoury sprig of dillisk round and round in his mouth to lend a salt flavour to his speech, and I diligently writing on the other side, the picture of the Island's past grew from day to day under our hands" (Flower 1944, 16).

The following March, Flower married Íde Máire Streeter and brought his newly-wed wife to spend their honeymoon on the Blaskets. In August of that year he described their time on the island in the following terms to Richard Irvine Best:

Yes, we are just back from the Blasquets [sic]. We had a glorious time there… I got to be able to speak and understand pretty well. I feel now as though I couldn't speak a word, but I suppose if I went back, I should be able to get along all right. My wife enjoyed herself thoroughly and did some rather nice sketches of the Island. (Ms 11,000, National Library of Ireland).

Flower was a regular visitor to the Blaskets in the pre-War years. Initially Flower focused on learning Irish from Tomás, and (like Marstrander before him) he wrote down short anecdotes from "the master." As his Irish improved, Flower began to record Tomás's folklore. Together, he and *the Islandman* made good progress:

> Tomás and I have been working on the book of stories and it is getting into reasonably good order. I hope to start printing soon after I get back. It is a fascinating collection with the whole life of the Island in the past generation in it and talking over the tales again and again with Tomás, I have reached a fair understanding of that life which might too stand me in good stead in editing the collection (Ms 11,000, National Library of Ireland).

Unfortunately, this visit was interrupted by the First World War and Flower was obliged to return to London. It would be five years before he could return to his island haven. However, the correspondence between Flower and Tomás continued in the intervening years—with Tomás mentioning personal life-details as well as the struggles of the islanders more widely in his letters to Flower.

In 1925, Flower returned to the Blaskets, and over the following years made a number of visits to the island. His whole family accompanied him on these occasions. In April 1929, he wrote about his daughters:

> They are having the time of their lives here running about and dozing and picking up bits of Irish. The weather has been wonderful this last fortnight and now with the sun all day and a full moon over the Island at night it is a heaven to be here (Ms 11,000 23.4.29, National Library of Ireland).

During these later visits Flower perfected the record of Irish tales he had salvaged from Tomás. These would not be published for some decades (Ó Criomhthain 1956). Tomás described the book as follows:

> The book will be a description about every misery, big or small, that occurred around the Blaskets, and the hardship that befell some island people. It will describe the way in which some of them lived on the small islands for a while, their appearance and their way of life. It will deal with a shipwreck, as well as the fairy voices, and other visions that often used to appear to them —that is, if they are to be believed (O'Crohan 2012, 288).

In 1929, Tomás's memoir was published in Irish (Ó Criomhthain 1929). That year also, Flower was promoted to the position of Deputy Keeper of

Manuscripts at the British Museum. He was subsequently to publish a number of volumes that emerged from his Blasket sojourns. These included an English translation of Tomás's memoir in 1937 (O'Crohan 1937) as well as *The Western Ireland; or the Great Blasket Island* (1944). (That volume was illustrated by Flower's wife, Ida Mary Streeter). Flower also published a collection of essays entitled *The Irish Tradition* in 1947 (Flower 1947).

Under Flower's influence a number of other British scholars (e.g. George Thomson and Kenneth Jackson) visited the Blaskets in a quest to further salvage authentic Irish folklore. Like Flower, these "foreign scholars sat at the feet of the local inhabitants and took instruction in the rich culture handed down to them. Like Arensberg and Kimball, they were trying to learn about a society by living within its everyday habits and rhythms" (Byrne et al. 2001, 14–15). A number of continental folklorists also visited the island, such as the French scholar Marie-Louise Sjoestedt (1900–1940), the Galician photographer and researcher Plácido Castro (1902–1967), and the Swedish folklorist Carl Wilhelm von Sydow (1878–1952).

### Brian Ó Ceallaigh

It was an Irish visitor, however, that had the most significant influence on Tomás's literary journey. Pádraig Ó Siochfhradha (more commonly known as An Seabhac meaning the Hawk) first introduced Brian Ó Ceallaigh to the Irish language. Brian (or Bryan Albert Kelly) was born in Killarney in 1889. His family was comfortable, being in the hotel and drapery trade. Brian had a law degree from Trinity. Although Brian could speak several European languages, he had not learned any Irish in school but had subsequently developed an interest in the language. The Seabhac recommended that if he wished to perfect his language, Brian should spend some time on the Great Blasket. In 1917, Brian arrived on the island and soon adopted Tomás as his mentor. They practised oral and written Irish regularly in the king's house (Nic Craith 1988).

Initially, Tomás and Brian read *Séadna* by Fr Peadar Ua Laoghaire together as a mutually beneficial exercise. It introduced Tomás to new writing in Irish while consolidating Brian's language skills. Sometimes they read the book in the island king's house. On other occasions, Brian sat on a rock dubbed 'Brian's chair' in a field and both enjoyed the book together. Given the simplicity of style in *Séadna*, it was an appropriate choice of reading for both master and pupil. The author, Fr Peadar Ua

Laoghaire, was explicit about his writing style in Irish: "Throughout the entire story there is not a single word, nor a single turn of expression, which has not been got directly from the mouths of living people 'who knew no English'. There has been no 'word-building'. Not a single phrase has been either 'invented' or 'introduced from any outside source'. The reader can rest assured that while reading the story he is reading the 'actual speech of living Irish people who knew no English'." (Ua Laoghaire 1898, 1).

Douglas Hyde (Ireland's first president) said of the volume that it brought 'the language of the people into modern literature with a sureness and lightness of touch that has never been surpassed, and that elevated it at once into a classic' (Hyde 1920, 299). This appeal to the use of unadulterated Irish impressed Tomás, who was subsequently criticised for using "difficult" Irish to tell his own story—a claim which Tomás rejected. "Nothing has distressed Tomás more than the suggestion that his book contains 'hard Irish': 'There isn't one word in it', he said to me at our second meeting, 'that wouldn't be understood by every child on the Island'" (Binchy 1934, 552).

Brian remained several months on the island—departing briefly in November and returning again in December. On the last day of 1917, he left the island for Valentia, a nearby island on the Atlantic seaboard. It is not clear whether Tomás and Brian met again, but they maintained a regular correspondence over the years. As with the letters to Flower, Tomás described the heart-break of the death of his children in personal tones, which is absent from the memoir. He regularly described also the hardship of living on the island. Their correspondence continued until 1925 when Brian left Ireland never to return.

Brian and all of the other visitors were aware of the European significance of the Blasket Islands, which had become "a mythic terrain, a place where Odysseus and Nestor still walked the earth and older verities remained true" (O'Toole 1997). For many of these scholars, a number of factors (in addition to the language and folklore), made it a place of significant value. "In the rural society of the West of Ireland, they saw the ideal life, the image of the Ireland that they wished to fashion: a rural society led by a new aristocracy, the aristocracy of the mind" (Ó Giolláin 2000, 145). The island was a place where one could re-visit (albeit temporarily) a past that was untainted by modern materialism. The Industrial Revolution and an increasingly urbanised Europe had sparked a desire to visit a haven where: "In contrast 'time stands still' in the periphery, in the backwaters, in the lost corners" (Leerssen 1994, 4).

The visitors were not disappointed. Many of them found the "primitive" on the Blaskets that had disappeared from continental Europe. In Europe, the concept of the Noble Savage had captured the imagination a century before Boas (see Chap. 6). Ashcroft et al. (2000, 192–3) argued that the concept had arisen in the eighteenth century, "as a European nostalgia for a simple, pure, idyllic state of the natural, posed against rising industrialism and the notion of overcomplications and sophistications of European urban society." Primitive man was much happier than his modern Western counterpart, who had been trapped by social institutions. Modern man was corrupted, unlike the Savage who was free from this corruption since he had not been tainted by Western society. However, like the vanishing Indian, the Noble Savage concept was "deeply rooted in an idealized past – the utopia of a Golden Age, a time and place of happiness, moral purity and the absence of priesthood and governmental rule" (Lindberg 2013, 18).

Visiting folklorists appear to have found this vanishing utopia on the Great Blasket Island. Of George Thomson, Kanigel (2012, 97) notes: "When, later, he'd come to compare Ireland to the ancient world of the Greeks, George Thomson would liken the Blaskets to Ithaca, which Odysseus endorsed as 'a rough place, but a fine nurse of men'." This reaction was true of many of the European folklorists and linguists who had visited the island. John Eastlake wryly comments: "Visitors to the Great Blasket island had a remarkable habit of finding what they were looking for: Synge discovered a pre-capitalistic society, George Thomson discovered a window into the poetry of Homeric Greece, E.M. Forster thought it the Neolithic Age, and Robin Flower found the world of medieval Europe" (Eastlake 2009b, 244). With these comments, the visitors were attributing a particular culture to a clearly-defined territory without recognising that culture is fluid and mobile.

These academics had found a society that was linked with ancient traditions in Europe. However, like Curtis, it may be that these visitors did not see (or preferred not to see) the interconnectedness of the Blaskets with other cultures on continental Europe (see Chap. 6)—and with the US in particular (see Chap. 8). Like other Europeans, Blasket men and women were being led into the world of modernity and its associated materialism. As the Blasket Islanders saw little prospects of survival on their tiny island, their way of life was indeed vanishing—but not because these people were incapable of adapting to modernity. Instead, they embraced it through the alternative route of migration. "Every now and then, a voice in the wilderness claims that the folk have not gone away, but that, instead, we might have had the discursive wool pulled over our eyes" (Kockel 2008, 12). Many of the islanders emigrated to the US (see Chap. 8), while others stayed closer to home—within view of their beloved island but from the relative safety of the mainland.

# CHAPTER 2

# Writing the Past

It is commonly assumed that Tomás was unlettered—or at least that his literary experience was very minimalist. "Great efforts are made to de-emphasize the multiple mediations which have taken place in the process of production of the book" (O'Sullivan 2006, 388). Indeed, this unlettered image was deliberately projected by some of the visiting folklorists and by Robin Flower in particular. In the forward to his English translation, Flower noted that Tomás was "practically uneducated in the modern sense, though highly trained in the tradition of an ancient folk culture" (Flower 1978 [1937], v). In emphasising Tomás's inheritance of the "strong literary tradition among the Munster peasantry" and their "considerable corpus both of folk-song and of the more elaborate poetry of the eighteenth century," Flower (1978 [1937], viii) was demoting the impact of published literature on the Islandman. However, the reality is that Tomás may have been familiar with some European literary giants—and in particular with the writings of Pierre Loti, Knut Hamsun and Maxim Gorky.

## European Literary Influences

In Tomás's library, one finds a copy of Hamsun's two-volume *Growth of the Soil* (1917). Written by the first Norwegian Nobel Laureate, it is regarded as his literary masterpiece. Knut Hamsun was the pen name of Knud Pedersen (1859–1952). Many of his later publications focused on the lifestyle in small communities in rural Norway. In the Hamsun novel,

© The Author(s) 2020
M. Nic Craith, *The Vanishing World of* The Islandman,
Palgrave Studies in Literary Anthropology,
https://doi.org/10.1007/978-3-030-25775-0_2

the chief protagonist is Isakhan or Isak, an everyday peasant who resists industrialisation and lives in the Norwegian wilderness. He is joined in his endeavour by Inger, a Sámi woman with a hare-lip who bears him a number of children. When one of these is born with a hare-lip, she secretly kills it. Her crime is subsequently discovered, and she is sentenced to eight years in prison.

When Inger returns home from prison, it is clear that great changes have occurred. Her hare-lip has been surgically removed and she has acquired new skills as a seamstress and for a time there is a clash between her "civilised" prison-manners and Isak's rural, peasant demeanour. In the final part of book, one sees the unlettered peasant Isak failing to put together the new farm moving machine until his educated son Eleseus reads the instructions. The clash between the literate and non-literate worlds takes place in front of the neighbours and is a cause of great shame to the illiterate father. Book Two replicates many of the incidents in the first and family fortunes. In the final stages, one son decides to emigrate to America and the other is unable to persuade him to change his mind. Ultimately, the barren land that was once tilled by Isak is filled with rich settlers.

*An Iceland Fisherman* (the English translation of *Pêcheur d'Islande*), published in 1896, was a gift from Brian Ó Ceallaigh to Tomás. Pierre Loti was the pseudonym of a French naval officer by the name of Louis-Marie-Julien Viaud (1850–1923). As part of his training, the author served in Tahiti and Northern Vietnam and visited places such as British India and China. Over his lifetime, he published a range of material drawing on his experience of the exotic. His *Pêcheur d'Islande* was rooted in the lifestyle of Breton fishermen, living in circumstances similar to the Blasket Islanders.

Brian Ó Ceallaigh also introduced two of Gorky's three-volume autobiography to Tomás. The first volume, *My Childhood* (Gorky 1915), covers the early years of the author's life, beginning with his father's funeral and ending with his mother's death. At the end of the first volume, the child is told by his grandfather, in no uncertain terms, that it is time to fend for himself and earn a living. The second volume, *In the World* (Gorky 1917), describes the youth's meagre existence in a range of jobs from working on ships on the Volga, in a bakery and for an iconographer.

It is interesting to think about why these particular volumes were selected for Tomás. In conversation with me, Seán Ó Coileáin suggests:

It is unknown to what extent Tomás really did heed books like *the Growth of the Soil* by Knut Hamsun, or *An Iceland fisherman* by Pierre Loti. The fact that he was given these books shows what the editors were after and where they were coming from, how they visualised these possibilities and therefore moulded them, at least to some extent, from the outside, even before Tomás had begun to write at all. That's an example of editing in advance of the book being written. (Interview with Ó Coileáin, July 2017)

The choice of Hamsun may have been determined by the rural setting of the volume as well as its strong engagement with nature. Certain characteristics of the volume may also have felt appropriate. One reviewer has described several characters in the Hamsun volume as Homeric. Lyngstad (2005) argues that the central character Isak is epic and the embodiment of Hamsun's concept of the national ideal. Like Tomás, he is native to the soil. Like Tomás, Isak has also battled with elements of the natural environment. However, there is not much to indicate that Tomás actually read the volume.

The Loti book had found favour with significant Irish figures at this time. The Irish playwright J.M. Synge read Loti's volume in 1898 and brought it with him on his journey to the Aran Islands. He subsequently acknowledged that the general plan of his volume on the Aran Islands was "largely borrowed from Pierre Loti" (see Skelton 1971, 25). Foster (1987, 334–35) speculates that it was for "the documentary value in Loti's novelistic account of the Breton cod-fishermen" that Loti seemed an appropriate choice for Tomás but doubts that it had any significant influence on the island author. Foster does underline the primitive nature of the book choice, arguing: "It is revealing of revival thinking, however, that O'Kelly should read a sophisticated primitivist author to Ó Crohan from whom he wished to solicit a primitive account" (Foster 1987, 334–5).

Brian Ó Ceallaigh possibly had another reason for selecting this Loti volume for Tomás. When his diary *Allagar na hInise* (1928) (*Island Cross-Talk* 1986) was almost complete, Brian requested Tomás to write a short story in Irish. The story that Brian had "planned" for Tomás was essentially one where a young girl arrives on the Blasket Island with her wealthy father. She is his only daughter. She remains on the island to learn Irish and becomes enraptured with a young handsome Blasket Islander. He falls in love with her but, given the gap in their social status and material circumstances, initially fails to tell her. Eventually they do get married (see Nic Craith 1988).

The Loti story is quite similar in plot. In that novel, a young girl named Gaud comes with her father to live in Paimpol. Her father is a fairly wealthy man. After some time, she falls in love with a local fisherman named Yann. Given the discrepancy in circumstances, he is far too shy to reveal his love for her and avoids her. Eventually her father dies, and Gaud is left in impoverished circumstances. She and the fisherman subsequently marry. The similarity in plot can only lead one to assume that Brian had given the volume to Tomás in an effort to persuade him to compose a similar narrative. However, Tomás was not impressed. This "story" was fiction and shouldn't be associated with the Blasket Islands. Tomás did not wish to use a creative plot. He was more interested in writing non-fiction.

Gorky's writings were well known among Irish-language activists and writers. The first Irish president, Douglas Hyde, regarded "the revelation of the Russian temperament" by Russian authors as "perhaps the chief event of nineteenth century literature" (O'Leary 1994, 82). Pádraig Pearse felt that Irish literature would best be served by an approach that blended an appreciation of foreign models such as Gorky with a recognition of the riches of its own cultural past (O'Leary 1994, 80). Máirtín Ó Cadhain (1969, 26) describes his experience of reading Maxim Gorky as being on a par with St. Paul's conversion on the road to Damascus. When Ó Cadhain read a French translation of some of Gorky's work, he jumped up in surprise and joy. He had never read anything like this before. Why had no one told him that stories like this existed? His instant reaction (like that of Tomás) was that he could write in a similar vein. The subject-matter was mirrored among his own community—only the names were different. According to his son Seán, Tomás was similarly excited by Gorky's volumes and recognised the potential for penning a volume that would be similar thematically. Upon reading Gorky and Hamsun, Tomás was persuaded to begin his memoir—noting that if these authors were prepared to make fools of themselves, Tomás could perform the same feat! (Ó Criomhthain 1988, 114).

An obvious reason for Brian's choice of the Gorky volumes relates to the biography of the Russian author, whose real name was Alexei Maximovich Peshkov. Gorky was the first "unlettered peasant" in Russia to put pen to paper. According to Hingley, "Gorky, another social upstart, came of a poor family and worked in his youth as a shop-boy, baker, washer-up on a Volga steamship and so on, thus graduating as the first major writer closely associated with the Russian proletariat. From the largest and most humble social class, the peasantry, literature had few recruits"

(Hingley 1967, 24). Gourfinkel makes a similar observation: "Gorky, an artist, a subjective person, had emerged from the very depths of the common people, from an illiterate background. Several months spent in a parish school was all he had of academic training. Self-taught, he owed his vast but disorganized knowledge to his enormous reading" (Gourfinkel 1975, 66–67). Tomás's reaction to the Gorky volume was emphatic.

Although the precise influence of Gorky on Tomás cannot be determined, the two authors had much in common. Levin notes: "But between Gorky's story – that of the first Russian of a common class who dared and was artistically able to write in depth of his childhood – and those of the Irish and American commoners, there is an immediate likeness. The figures, their pains and joys and problems, are the same. It is an internationally recognizable land" (Levin 1967, 21). Gorky's autobiography was a clear catalyst for Tomás to write the memoir. It is also possible that its influence went further and that in selecting particular episodes for inclusion in the memoir, Tomás had been influenced by Gorky's volume. As Tolton writes of the French author Gide:

> To point out these parallels in novels familiar to Gide is not to say that these passages had strongly or even directly influenced our author's creative processes... Moreover, a close comparison of all the related passages would inevitably reveal glaring differences in the purpose, detail, and style. What one sees here is merely that in selecting material from his life for transmittal to his autobiography, Gide often chose the "stuff" of successful fiction... He could indeed have been inspired to choose some episodes over other possibilities because of some vague but agreeable literary recollections stored in the recesses of his memory. (Tolton 1975, 71–72)

The Gorky, Loti and Hamsun books describe grim, primitive lifestyles. However, there is also a sense of hope and belief emerging in these volumes. Cambon (2014) notes the nobility of the Breton peasant in the Loti volume. "The Breton soul bears an imprint of Armorica's primitive soil: it is melancholy and noble. There is an undefinable charm about those arid lands and those sod-flanked hills of granite, whose sole horizon is the far-stretching sea. Europe ends here, and beyond remains only the broad expanse of the ocean" (Cambon 2014, 9–10). Hamsun's volume endorses engagement with the earth. "Its dominant note is one of patient strength and simplicity; the mainstay of its working is the tacit, stern, yet loving alliance between Nature and the Man who faces her himself, trusting to

himself and her for the physical means of life, and the spiritual content-
ment with life which she must grant if he be worthy" (Worster 2013, 2).

The Hamsun volume was not just about "breaking new land." It has
been described as a "gospel of the soil," published at the time of the First
World War and designed to give people something to believe in (Larsen
2012). Žagar (2011, 40) suggests that the book "offers a somewhat comparable hope that mankind might be saved through hard work on the soil
and such efforts as settling the wilderness." The book has been described
as "regressive utopian" (Žagar 2011, 15)—as searching "for the re-
establishment of a new-primitive society that would re-embrace patriar-
chal values and expresses a primitivist nostalgia which is articulated most
clearly for women: a return to nature and natural cycles and a turn away
from progress and modern lifestyles" (Rossi 2013, 409). (However, several decades after Ó Ceallaigh's gift of the Hamsun volume to Tomás,
Hamsun's political sympathies and his moral support of the Nazis were
condemned by the Norwegian people, and Hamsun was heavily fined and
vilified by his countrymen.)

All three authors (Loti, Hamsun and Gorky) focus on the rural rather
than the urban. Although geographically close, the people represented
therein are somehow "foreign" or "exotic" for cosmopolitan readers. It is
as if the authors deliberately depicted the primitive other within European
territories. "Loti seeks his heroes and heroines among the antique races of
Europe which have survived all conquests, and which have preserved with
their native tongue, the individuality of their character" (Cambon 2014,
9). Loti's earlier works had emerged from his travel experiences in Africa,
Asia and the Pacific Islands, but his Breton characters were equally foreign
to the Parisians. "Our Breton sailors and our Basque mountaineers were
not less foreign to the Parisian drawing-room than was Azuyade or the
little Rahahu" (Cambon 2014, 6). The same could be observed of the
Blasket books in Ireland. Of these people, Binchy (1934, 558) observes:

> I have often wondered about the nature of the difference, at once so subtle
> and so infinite, between the people of the Gaoltacht and the bulk of their
> compatriots whose mother tongue is English.... in reality, they belong to
> quite a different world. Tralee, Cork and Dublin are almost as "foreign" to
> the Blasket Islander as London or Glasgow.

While Gorky's story was not necessarily "foreign," it did represent a voice
in literature that had not been previously heard. Gorky's voice was the first

Russian proletariat to be heard in a literature-scape that was previously dominated by aristocrats. Tomás was the first published author from the Blasket Islands, which was steeped in oral traditions.

## THE PHENOMENOLOGY OF WRITING

Although Tomás's memoir was written in his middle-age, one should not assume that Tomás began writing solely at the behest of the visitors. There is an important incident in Tomás's life story, which relates to his youth when, as a young man, his day's work was interrupted by the island poet. Since they had not much dry turf in storage, Tomás had gone to cut turf in the hills. He had only begun working when the poet Seán Dunleavy arrived with a spade to cut turf for himself. Upon seeing Tomás, he invited him to sit down and wait with him until the day became a little cooler. Tomás was not very happy but agreed to the poet's request. (The following excerpt illustrates the power of the poet in Irish society):

> I wasn't too pleased with his banter, but I felt awkward about not sitting down beside him. Of course, I also realised that unless the poet were pleased with me he could easily write a satire about me, which wouldn't be helpful, especially as at this time I was a young man just starting out in life. So, I sat down beside him, as I could see he wanted me to do something. (O'Crohan 2012, 96–7)

Having a captive audience, the poet took the opportunity to recite the first poem he had ever written, "The Black-Headed Sheep." On completion, Tomás praised the quality of the poem very highly. The poet's reaction was to request that the recitation would be written down. "'The song will be lost,' says he, 'unless you record it. Have you a pencil in your pocket or a scrap of paper?'." Although not yet skilled in writing, certainly not in Irish, Tomás obliged. In so far as writing had been taught in the national school on the Blasket, it related only to English. (This would have been true on the mainland also):

> Well, it wasn't for the good of the poet that I took pencil and paper out of my pocket, but for fear that he'd turn on me with the rough side of his tongue. So, I began jotting down whatever came out of his mouth. I wasn't writing in Irish because I wasn't proficient at it then, and I was only so-so in English. I didn't enjoy doing this work one little bit. (O'Crohan 2012, 96–7)

This excerpt is important for a number of reasons—demonstrating in the first instance, that even before learning to write formally in Irish, Tomás was already writing phonetically in his native tongue. It also shows that as a young man Tomás was carrying pen and pencil while going to the hill to do a day's physical labour. It's real significance however, is noted by Muiris Mac Conghail (1987b, 158) who argues that:

> Ó Criomhthain chose to "create" or "record" this event and place it in his autobiography well out of reach of the later associations with scholars, including Robin Flower, his particular friendship with Brian Ó Ceallaigh, who brought his creative narrative prose into being and ultimately to the publication of his two books *An tOileánach, The Islandman,* and *Allagar na hInse, Island Conversations* [i.e. *Island Cross-Talk*]. Ó Criomhthain was saying, "I didn't stumble on this writing business – I choose to write."

It is not certain when Tomás began writing his autobiography. He himself notes that he began in June 1922, but this is unlikely to be correct since the first date on the manuscript is 4.2.1923. It also seems possible that Tomás continued completing his journal *Allagar na hInise* (1928) (*Island Cross-Talk*, 1986) while beginning his life story. In writing the memoir, Tomás narrates a linear story, beginning with his birth in 1856 (a disputed date) saying: "I can remember being at my mother's breast; I wasn't weaned until I was four years old. You might call me the dregs of the little jug, the last of the brood. That's why I was left so long feeding on my mother's breast" (O'Crohan 2012, 1). He ends with his pleasure in having set out his story and offers a blessing for all his potential readers: "To anyone who takes my books into their hand, however much they have paid for them, may God grant that they may receive their value sevenfold in wealth and in health! And may He make room for all of us in His Blessed Kingdom! The End, 3 March 1926, Tomás O'Crohan, The Great Blasket" (O'Crohan 2012, 293).

The original version of the first chapter of the memoir is unavailable today. It is unclear whether the current version was edited by Brian Ó Ceallaigh or whether Brian wrote it down orally from Tomás, but the text is quite problematic—with missing and clearly misspelt words. This raises the question of whether Brian Ó Ceallaigh returned to the island in 1922/1924 in an endeavour to persuade Tomás to begin a new writing venture. Was it during a subsequent visit that Brian brought Loti and Gorky with him to read extracts (in Irish) to Tomás? Is it possible that in persuading Tomás to pen his memoir, of which the first chapter was a collaborative effort, with Tomás narrating his early childhood and Brian putting it on paper? (Seán Ó Coileáin (2002, xviii) notes that Brian seemed to be writing according to the sound rather than the meaning of the word.) Although there is no clear evidence to suggest that Brian returned to the island at this time, An Seabhac does suggest that Brian paid more than one visit to the island (Ó Siochfhradha 1937, 27). If true, this hypothesis would explain many of the issues relating to the "missing" first chapter (including the date that it was begun as well as the misspelt words). It would also explain the method by which Tomás "read" Gorky and/or Loti.

The rest of the manuscript, which totals 94 larger-sized bifoliate foolscap and one single foolscap page, is in Tomás's own clear neat handwriting. According to Tomás, he wrote his life story for the sake of the language. "That's why I'm writing this book in Gaelic because, as I have already mentioned, I would never allow the language to die out if I could help it" (O'Crohan 2012, 37). He wanted to write in the vernacular language of his fellow people. He described the movement of the pen in his hand as being like water running in a river that does not stop. The words were flowing through him as if in a stream of consciousness (Ms 15,785 no date).

Tomás's son Seán gives us a vivid pen picture of the ritual of writing that took place in the evening:

> In those days the people on the Blaskets used to have their tea in the evening. They didn't call it an evening meal but evening tea. That was between seven and eight o'clock, and we used to go out after it. There was a table here in the corner at the right-hand side of the fire-place. Tomás would pull up the table. There was a lamp high on the wall with a mirror on it behind the globe and two wicks, each of them as big as a light-house. Tomás would draw up to the fire. His pipe was always on the hob along with his tobacco. He'd smoke a fine blast of the pipe and then turn around, get his foolscap ready and set to work with his pen, a beautiful one which he had got from one of the visitors. (Ó Criomhthain 1988, 113)

The pen was a gift from Brian Ó Ceallaigh and was treated almost as a sacred object by *the Islandman*. It can still be viewed at the Blasket Interpretive Centre in Dún Chaoin (see Chap. 7). Seán continues:

> It was a Waterman's fountain pen, and every night when finished with it he'd dry it with a piece of cloth and a bit of paper and put it away. If a

butterfly or a cricket in the corner as much as touched it he'd nearly kill them. Not a hand was to be laid on the pen in case it might be damaged. (Ó Criomhthain 1988, 113)

Apparently, Tomás spent several hours writing every night: "He used to write depending on how long the house was quiet, and according as thoughts occurred to him he'd put the finishing touches to them, and he was often writing when I came home. It might be ten o'clock or half-past ten and Tomás would still be on the pen" (Ó Criomhthain 1988, 113).

While nowadays we might regard the process of handwriting a book as laborious or cumbersome, the anthropologist Tim Ingold defends writing by hand as a "gestural movement, with all the care, feeling and elevation that goes into it." He compares the flow of handwriting with that of playing a cello, and the writer to a hunter in search of an idea. He says: "A hunter who followed a bee-line from a point of departure to a predetermined destination would never catch prey. To hunt you have to be alert for clues and ready to follow trails wherever they may lead. Thoughtful writers need to be good hunters" (Ingold n.d.).

Tomás was clearly an expert hunter and throughout the book, he describes various characters in the island community. Principal characters include the old woman next door, his school teacher, his father, "Bald Tom" and the island king. The events recounted are typical of island life at that time and range from schooldays to marriages and funerals. Tomás describes gathering seaweed, killing seals, hunting rabbits and visiting ships. Various seasons such as Christmas and Lent are described in the book—and all of the activities take place locally—either on one of the islands or on the nearby mainland in Dingle. Not all of the events described in the book occurred during Tomás's lifetime, and occasionally he tells a tale from the past.

As Tomás wrote the book, he sent the handwritten pages to Brian in the post. It is highly likely that when Tomás began his book, he didn't envision a publication. Instead he jotted down memories for the enhancement of Brian Ó Ceallaigh's language skills. This is clearly not an ideal way to write a book—as Tomás never had the occasion to review what was already written before continuing his narrative. "This method of composition accounts for the book's haphazard quality, a quality which, as it happens, reflects a way of life that was full of surprises and incidents, governed as much by serendipity as by predictable simplicity" (Foster 1987, 324). Moreover, it appears that Tomás didn't get feedback from Brian as to how the work was shaping up. In one letter, he complains that he has no idea how much he has written—nor has he had any communication from Brian for some time (LN Ms. 15,785 no date).

Tomás worked on the memoir for eighteen months. The last date on the manuscript is 1.6.1924, and this appears to be the last section that was dispatched to Brian in the post. Brian held onto the manuscript for a period of two years and desperately sought publishers who might be persuaded to publish the volume. He showed the manuscript to people in Paris and to the Irish Texts Society in London, but they were not interested. He also took the manuscript to Eoin Mac Néill, the then Minister for Education in Ireland, but to no avail (Mac Conghail 1987b, 161). Having decided to leave Ireland for good, a despondent Brian approached An Seabhac. Brian asked An Seabhac to take the control of the manuscript. An Seabhac agreed as long as Tomás was content with the new arrangement. An Seabhac also requested full editorial control over the text. It was not long before Tomás sent a letter indicating that he was satisfied with the new arrangement.

## EDITORIAL INCARNATIONS

### An Seabhac

An Seabhac set about organising Tomás's handwritten pages in a logical manner into 25 chapters with titles such as "My Childhood" or "My Manhood" or "The Troubles of Life." Each chapter was subdivided into several subsections. It appears that the title of the book was An Seabhac's decision. It is possible that the Scottish Gaelic book *An tEileanach* by John MacFayden (1921) may have been the inspiration behind the title *An tOileánach* (*The Islandman*). As editor, An Seabhac felt that a lot of changes were needed, and he began advising Tomás on revisions to the manuscript at the end of 1925. There was a mammoth task ahead. One of these related to the language in which the book was written.

Given that Tomás's spelling was greatly influenced by the phonology of the spoken dialect of West Kerry (Sjoestedt 1937, 1938), An Seabhac deemed it necessary to rewrite the entire text in an official, standardised language (An Fear Eagair 1929, 5). An Seabhac removed any loan words in Irish that he considered too Anglicised. These included words such as *lumpaí* (lumps) or *compás* (compass). The editor also removed terms that he considered vulgar. And so, for example, he removed an entire passage that contained the term *mún* (urine). An Seabhac replaced the word *bleader* (bladder) with the more palatable *bolg* (belly). He refrained from including the word *smuga* (mucus, snot). Although it was not possible to remove the word *tóin* (backside, bottom) entirely from the text, he reduced the number of times it was used (see Lucchitti 2009, 129).

As editor, An Seabhac felt there was too much repetition of events that were largely similar in plot—too many storms, too many drownings, too many visits to Dingle on the mainland, too many killings of seals and too many bouts of drinking. For this reason, he discarded incidents that he considered repetitive. However, repetition may not have been the sole motivation in expunging these elements. Stewart (1976, 235) argues that many of "the cuts listed were made to save face rather than space, because, mistakenly, they were believed to show the Islanders as either too punchy, too sexy, too sly or too slanderous."

It appears that An Seabhac was determined to remove any incidents that might portray the islanders in a negative light. Women fighting over eggs or men quarrelling over a pot were not deemed appropriate for inclusion. Some of Tomás's harsh remarks about his neighbours were excluded as well as his critical opinion of Father Clune, who had published a volume of folklore without acknowledgement of Tomás's substantial input into the publication. Such changes were designed to "whitewash" the image of the islanders and present them as a people without the full spectrum of human emotions (Lucchitti 2009, 128).

An Seabhac also omitted an incident which appeared to show Tomás breaking with tradition for the sake of love. This concerns a young lady from the Blasket Island (a relative of Tomás) who travels to the mainland for her arranged wedding. However, she changes her mind at the last moment and returns to the island to the man she loves and is married to him a few days later. Rather than criticise her decision to desert the groom that had been arranged for her, Tomás applauds her saying: "I was closely related to the girl, and I wouldn't be the one to blame her for what she did, because 'life is only worth living when you have the freedom to choose', as someone said long ago, and there's a great deal of truth in that saying" (O'Crohan 2012, 172). In a culture of arranged marriages, Tomás's comments could have been considered highly controversial. This is particularly the case since Tomás subsequently proceeded with his own arranged marriage, despite his affection for a girl from the neighbouring island of Inishvickillane. That remark never appeared in the initial Irish-language edition (Shea 2014, 100).

One significant feature that An Seabhac omitted from the first Irish edition was the many songs that Tomás had included in his original memoir. Perhaps An Seabhac deemed the songs as an expression of emotion that was not appropriate for the image of the islanders. Shea (2014, 99) points to a nine-page deleted story of a few days on Inishvickillane filled with singing and dancing. These were days also filled with the emotion of young love as Tomás declares, "it wasn't unheard of for me to spend a week amongst the young women over there, as one of them was dearer to me at that time than any other woman in Ireland" (O'Crohan 2012, 162).

This omission of songs is noteworthy, given the strength of that oral tradition on the Blaskets. Moreover, these songs were not just emotional insights; they were social documents containing multiple references to folklore and history. Given that Blasket life was a song culture, and Tomás himself a songwriter, the decision is difficult to defend (see Ó Coileáin 1998, 247). Tomás himself questions this decision (O'Crohan 2012, 247). Mac Conghail (1987b, 162) says: "The omission of these songs distorts the Ó Criomthain autobiography, not only because of their documentary value, but also because of what they tell us about the author himself; a singer of tales."

As well as clipping the text, An Seabhac felt that some details were missing from the original manuscript and he asked Tomás to add in new sections. These included an entirely new chapter on the island houses. In conversation with me, Ó Coileáin notes:

> Clearly it would never have occurred to Tomás to describe these houses. These were the houses he had grown up in and the only houses he had known, in any real sense. He would have observed other houses in Dingle but this was the natural state of affairs. It wouldn't have occurred to An *tOileánach* to describe them as somehow unnatural, or something that needed to be explained to an outsider, but An Seabhac, an insider-outsider, was clearly aware of the need to do so. (Interview with Ó Coileáin, July 2017)

Following An Seabhac's request, Tomás gave a detailed description of the houses in which the islanders lived. "Those houses used to be made out of stones and clay-mortar. Most of them weren't in too great a shape because they used to be built in a hurry, with everyone lending a helping hand. The roof was made of rushes or reeds, with sturdy thick layers of turf underneath" (O'Crohan 2012, 301). Tomás did not confine his remarks to the materiality of the houses. Instead we received further insights into the people that lived in them.

> The bed near the fire was for the old people. They'd have a stump of a clay pipe going. If there were two of them they'd both be puffing away. There'd be a good fire of top sods glowing away until morning. Every time they woke up they used to shove in a twisted wisp of straw that they used as a spill, and then take a puff out of the pipe. If the man had an old woman with him, he'd stretch over towards her and stick the wisp into the pipe. Then smoke from the two stumps would curl up the chimney, and when they were at full blast the couple's bed looked like a steamship going at full blast. (O'Crohan 2012, 301)

Animals also lived in the houses at night:

> There might be two or three dogs lying at the foot of the bed. Any cows would be below them, with their heads turned to the wall. Calves usually had the run of the kitchen, with their snouts to the fire. The donkey used to be tied to the other side of the house, opposite the cows; and the cat, and perhaps a couple of kittens, would be lying by the hob. (O'Crohan 2012, 301)

In requesting this chapter, An Seabhac was recognising the importance of material objects—as part of the island cultural experience. "Humans do not live in an immaterial world of pure ideas; rather, we are embodied persons ourselves and interact with each other's bodies – and with material things in the course of social action" (Eller 2016, 28).

The most significant addition that An Seabhac requested was a new ending to the memoir. In 1926, Tomás finished the volume for the first time. The original ending was very traditional with Tomás noting: "As the storyteller used to say long ago after telling his story: 'That's my story and if there's a lie in it, let it be. Here is my story and there is no lie in it, only the bare truth'" (O'Crohan 2012, 294). Tomás didn't neglect to mention the financial aspect of his work either—adding "to anyone who takes my books into their hand, however much they have paid for them, may God grant that they may receive their value sevenfold in wealth and in health!" (O'Crohan 2012, 294). The concluding chapter was dated 3 March 1926.

However, An Seabhac was not convinced that this was an appropriate conclusion and he requested that Tomás write a fresh ending. The new final chapter reinforces the simplicity of life on the island but also the hardship that it entailed. Tomás describes the Great Blasket as "a rock in the middle of the sea, and very often the foaming sea rises up with the full strength of the wind, so that you couldn't stick your head out, any more than a rabbit could, crouching down in its burrow while outside the sea raged and the rain swept down" (O'Crohan, 296). The hardship of the fishing life is highlighted. "We'd spend long, cold, stormy nights struggling with the sea, very often without much to show for it, often yearning for God's help. It was seldom that we used to catch what we needed, and so we used to have to cut the nets and to let them go – both the fish and the net; the net being a very expensive item for us to purchase" (O'Crohan 2012, 297).

The new final chapter with its reference to his being at his mother's breast as a young child makes a clear link with the beginning of the book. It also contains reflections on the vanishing lifestyle of the islanders. "One day the Blasket will be without any of the people I have mentioned in this book, or anyone who will remember us" (O'Crohan 2012, 298). Tomás expresses pride as the author who had achieved the transition from oral to literary on the island. "Since the first fire was lit on this Island, no one has written about their life here. I'm proud to be the one who did it. This book will tell how the Islanders got on in old times" (O'Crohan 2012, 299). Finally, Tomás steps away from the world represented in the book with the memorable phrase: "*Ní bheidh ár leithéidí arís ann*" (our likes will never be here again) (Ó Criomhthain 2002, 329; O'Crohan 2012, 298). It is almost as though in recreating that world in literary form he had destroyed it. The additional chapter also contains a hint of impatience on behalf of Tomás who noted the following of the memoir as a whole: "Perhaps it hasn't got a short tail on it now! If there is a sentence there that you don't like, leave it out" (O'Crohan 2012, 299).

The Irish-language memoir was published in 1929. Tomás seems to have been happy with the published product. In a letter to An Seabhac dated 6-10-1929, Tomás wrote that since the book hadn't sent anyone to the madhouse, no one should complain about it. From his own perspective, Tomás neither praised nor condemned it—if for no other reason that self-praise is not praise (Collection, Dingle Library, Kerry). Tomás was paid for his efforts and was grateful to both An Seabhac and to Brian Ó Ceallaigh for their input into the process of publishing the book.

## *Pádraig Ua Maoileoin*

The first edition of *An tOileánach* was published in 1929. More than four decades later, a second Irish-language edition emerged. On this occasion, the new editor was Pádraig Ua Maoileoin, a grandson of Tomás. Pádraig Ua Maoileoin was "a man of the *Gaeltacht* (Irish-speaking community) but very much also the urban Irishman of the present day" (Cruise O'Brien 1977, 35). Mary Cruise O'Brien (1977, 35) suggests: "There is basically not a great deal to choose between the two versions." However, there are significant differences between them.

The most obvious of these are visual differences since the new edition contained 11 illustrations of island life by local artist Maria Simonds-Gooding (see Chap. 4). Another notable difference is the print form—*An Cló Gaelach* (Gaelic type), a variant of the Latin alphabet that had previously been in use for decades for Irish-language printed material but had subsequently been abandoned. Moreover, the language had been standardised since the late 1950s, which involved spelling reform and specific grammar standards.

While Ua Maoileoin revised the language of the book with official standards in mind, he didn't adhere slavishly to these standards. In his introduction to the second edition, Ua Maoileoin gave a brief description of his methodology, but whether he was successful in dealing with the language of the book is debatable. In conversation with me, Seán Ó Coileáin argued the following:

> Pádraig Ua Maoileoin had an unsurpassed knowledge of the spoken Irish of the Gaeltacht. He had, of course, as I had access to the manuscript, and worked from the manuscript, but unfortunately, he fell between two stools. He couldn't decide, it seems to me, whether he was producing a school or university textbook of *An tOileánach* (with standardisation of verbal and other forms and so on) or whether he was trying to represent what Tomás wrote. Indeed, he states in the introduction, that he himself had to choose, as he puts it, what to include and what to omit. So, this becomes a kind of a dangerous game. (Interview with Ó Coileáin, July 2017)

Ó Coileáin continues:

> Pádraig Ua Maoileoin was ideally positioned as editor. He knew every twist and turn of the Blasket Island culture. His mother was Tomás's daughter. She was the one who survived the day of the drowning, and while he was

then two generations removed from Tomás, and while the Irish of his generation wasn't quite the Irish of the Island, nevertheless it was as close as one could humanly get, to island culture, in terms of the language. But instead of using that as a strength, Ua Maoileoin rejected it, in favour of a doubtful compromise. (Interview with Ó Coileáin, July 2017)

Ó Coileáin was not implying that Ua Maoileoin rejected Tomás's Irish. Instead he is concerned about the lack of clarity in the purpose of Ua Maoileoin's edition.

I'm not saying he was rejecting Tomás's Irish, but it seems that the purpose of the book was never clear to him. It seems to me, that he basically set out to do the same as an Seabhac—even though An Seabhac would have been much more faithful to the verbal forms, to the language of the book, than Ua Maoileoin was. Ua Maoileoin essentially set out the terms of his editing and omissions. He was attempting to standardise the language here and there or applying standard forms to Tomás's forms. In terms of the editing process, he did broadly speaking what An Seabhac had done but without the excuse that An Seabhac had or without the purpose that An Seabhac had. (Interview with Ó Coileáin, July 2017)

As was the case with An Seabhac, the new editor went through the manuscript to decide what should be included/excluded. As a rule of thumb, Ua Maoileoin verified the original material and any material in the old version that does not appear in this second edition is absent because he could not find it in the original manuscript. Any new material he supplied was not in order to give an element of novelty to the book but because he felt it enhanced the narrative as a piece of literature and as a social document. It also gives additional insights into the character of the author as well as a broader perspective on the community in which he lived (Ua Maoileoin 1992, 150).

One omission made by An Seabhac that was included by Ua Maoileoin in the second edition relates to the sequence regarding Tomás's first love for the girl on the neighbouring island (Inishvickillane). This narrative "is told almost entirely in terms of songs sung when they met at fair or fireside, songs with names like these: *Ar Éirinn ní 'neosfainn cé hí, Ré-chnoc Mná Duibhe, An Clár Bog Déil, Aitheantas Bháb na gCraobh*. All of them are intensely passionate and basically unhappy songs, as was the fashion" (Cruise O'Brien 1977, 35). Given the emphasis on the song tradition on the Island, this was an appropriate editorial decision.

Ultimately Tomás's bride was chosen for him by his family and the arranged match was not with the bride of his choice. In *An tOileánach*, Tomás does not express resentment at this. However, he did write that he sang a sad song (the only one he sang) concerning unrequited love at his wedding gathering. An Seabhac had removed the reference to this song from the first edition—possibly because it might be perceived as a betrayal of Tomás's wife. Ua Maoileoin reinstated the song. Cruise O'Brien (1977, 35) notes: "The second editor, Tomás's grandson, has restored it and, very beautifully, it finishes the account of an idyll." Despite reinstating this and a number of small number of incidents that were omitted in the first edition, Ua Maoileoin continued to omit major portions of the manuscript that he considered boring/repetitive.

Although Ua Maoileoin endeavoured to verify all the original material in the manuscript, he failed to locate the original chapter concerning the houses. Despite the lack of an original text, he included the "house chapter" in the second edition since (in his opinion) it was one of the best in the book. He believed the level of detail was extraordinary and was impressed by the fluent, sparse language in which it was written. Sometimes he felt that Tomás's style was almost poetic (Ua Maoileoin 1992, 151).

Overall the second edition made few changes of real significance. However, as Ó Coileáin argues, in the intervening decades between the publications of the first versus the second volume, the audience reading the book had changed. The time factor was also noted by the second editor. In the preface to the second edition, he notes his intention to represent *An tOileánach* in a way that was relevant for the 1970s rather than the 1930s. There had been many changes in Ireland since the first edition was published in 1929. One of the most notable changes was the evacuation of the Great Blasket Island in 1953.

There was also a change of mindset in Ireland. Between the two Irish editions, 1929 and 1973, it was believed that the Gaelic utopia could still be realised—although it was also recognised that it was going into rapid decline. The book was part of the vision of a Gaelic Ireland (see Chap. 4). "We understood that it was not a particular individual or community that was speaking to us in this book but a people and that we were that people. It was a kind of mythology that came down to us over the centuries – vision that like every vision was needed in the current times but would never be realized" (Ó Coileáin 2002, 26). From that perspective, even if the wording were the same—time had moved on. The understanding of the Irish people has changed and the Irish mentality had changed. Inevitably, the response of the reader to the book was different (Ó Coileáin 2002, 26).

## *Seán Ó Coileáin*

The third edition of *An tOileánach* (*The Islandman*) was a labour of love that over a number of decades. The editor of that edition is Seán Ó Coileáin, emeritus professor of Irish at University College, Cork and probably the greatest living expert on *An tOileánach*. When I asked Seán why he felt the need to publish a new edition, he made the following response:

> There are inaccuracies in the original edition. These were deliberate inaccuracies. Obviously, An Seabhac was steeped in this culture, and knew it far better than I could ever know it in that immediate sense. At the same time, he clearly didn't feel bound as a modern scholar would, as it were, to follow Tomás's exemplar. (Interview with Ó Coileáin, July 2017)

Ó Coileáin points to An Seabhac's request for a chapter on the houses on the island as a dimension that Tomás would not himself have written. He also points to Tomás's portrayal of the king as having been censored.

> Consider, for example, Tomás's description of his schoolmate, the king to be, who of course wouldn't be island king for many years yet, but even now was pointing out such unsavoury scenes such as the young boy who had a big yellow snot (as Tomás describes it) hanging from his nose. The king is being represented here as already standing apart from and above his fellows. When the girls come upon him and Tomás stark naked after swimming, we are told that the king immediately made to cover a certain part of his anatomy with his hands. Tomás stands his ground and accosts the more daring of the girls of whose forwardness he clearly disapproves, noting that a child was later born to her out of wedlock. (Interview with Ó Coileáin, July 2017)

The editor felt the need to improve Tomás's text. Seán Ó Coileáin observes:

> In An Seabhac's edition the big yellow snot becomes an unblown nose, as though an island child of the period might be expected to keep a handkerchief about his person. The episode of the encounter with the girls is omitted altogether. This is not so much official censorship as self-censorship on the part of An Seabhac. We might partially ascribe this to his being close to

people of the island and not wishing to cause offence, but we should also remember that the book was being produced in the very early years of the State and that Gaelic culture, the restoration of which figured so largely in the mythology of that State, still in the course of creation, could not be perceived as barbarous or uncouth. Indeed, *An tOileánach* would emerge as a seminal exemplar of a heroic, self-sufficient community, unadulterated by foreign language or ways, as though it were a state in microcosm. (Interview with Ó Coileáin, July 2017)

The notion of authenticity strongly influenced this final Irish-language edition, as the editor sought to present a text that was as close as possible to the original set of documents written by Tomás. For this reason, Ó Coileáin removed the chapter titles that An Seabhac had composed to give structure to the text. However, Ó Coileáin retained the chapter structure partly in deference to the first editor, but also to help interested readers compare the different editions. As with the previous two editors, the issue of language was also challenging. In his introduction to the new edition, Ó Coileáin explains the rationale for updating the language in the text—a process which has been lauded as "diplomatic" by one reviewer (Ó Sé 2006, 128).

Ó Coileáin reinstated a number of passages that had been either curtailed or deleted from previous editions. "Some passages in the original manuscript appear to have been omitted on grounds of literary taste; almost invariably, it seems to me, the author's judgement is to be preferred to that of his first editor and they have been restored in the 2002 edition" (Ó Coileáin 2012, xiii). Many of the restored passages change the tone of the volume. Shea (2014, 94) says: "The reinstated passages afford … a more complex and intriguing rendition of Tomás O'Crohan, the man and the writer." Shea points to passages concerning the romance between Tomás and Cáit Daly (the girl from Inishvickillane). He notes: "We get a better feel for the spirit of invigorating liberation and piquant stimulation that the Islanders embraced on trips beyond their usual pale" (Shea 2014, 109).

Ó Coileáin's edition restored passages that present much more "rounded" personalities on the island. One of the restored passages concerns the antics of three Blasket men in Caherciveen. In the original edition, the episode is presented briefly, but the final edition expands the sense of fun both in the incident itself but also in Tomás's remembering of it. In the shortened narrative, some Blasket men are *en route* to a guesthouse for the night when three women approach them in search of some company. One of them a red-haired woman speaks to one of the men saying, "Come along, Blashket man, won't you have a drink?" He is frightened (red-haired women were sometimes associated with bad-luck in the Irish tradition). She spoke to him in English—a language he was barely familiar with. As he tries to escape her, "she gripped him by the back-piece of his vest and tore away that piece from top to bottom" (O'Crohan 1937, 157). The three men dashed to the guesthouse only to find that the ladies have followed them, since the red-haired woman wishes to return his torn vest.

In the first edition, the redhead is described as follows: "The redheaded woman who was speaking to us was a good six feet high. She had a shock of hair, and was a fine woman" (O'Crohan 1937, 157). The final edition presents a much more interesting character. "One of the women, with bright red hair, who was the one doing most of the talking, was a clean six foot in height and with the finest head of hair you ever did see — the same colour as this very fancy lamp I have on my table, which the gentleman from the Kelly family sent me" (O'Crohan 2012, 188) (Shea 2014, 102).

Another episode that Ó Coileáin restored concerns a nightmare that Tomás experienced, which featured a rough encounter between himself and a seal. Tomás was so frightened by the dream that he called out in the night, prompting his mother to rush to him to soothe the child. Tomás describes the dream as follows:

> I'd just managed to doze off when I had a nightmare. I screamed out so loud that my mother had to get out of bed and come to me. I caused her a lot of trouble before I settled down. Eventually, I dropped off again, but I didn't have a proper rest because another rather unpleasant dream robbed me of any decent sleep. This was my dream. I thought that I was on the strand and that a fine cow-seal encountered me at the high-water mark. As I had nothing to kill it, she got away from me. In the morning my mother told me that I let out three more screams in the middle of the night, which was probably when the seal went away. (O'Crohan 2012, 80)

The following day, Tomás had a genuinely rough battle with a seal which left him severely injured. Ironically, part of a different seal's flesh was used to heal his wound. Previous editors omitted the dream narrative but retained the real-life battle. In contrast, Ó Coileáin (1998, 33) restored the dream narrative since there was a direct connection between the dream and the battle and that connection was relevant for the reader. From my perspective, there is a further dimension here in that the dream could be interpreted as a "premonition" or foresight, which was very strong in the Irish tradition.

Another restored passage concerns the astonishment of the Blasket *Islandmen* when they see a massive cable house for the first time. Tomás describes their surprise in the following terms:

> On the other side of the hill we saw a huge mast, with as many ropes tied to it as found in any vessel that ever sailed the seas. There were many gadgets tied to that mast; you'd have been blinded if you looked at them in the sunlight. It was the mast that carries the large cable bringing messages from Newfoundland to Ireland. A dozen experts are in charge of that mast. (O'Crohan 2012, 197–98)

The cable-house in question linked Europe with North America. Given that Tomás had never travelled beyond Kerry, he very effectively describes the sense of wonder and surprise engendered by the mast. "We can only speculate what 'wild surmise' (to use Keats's phrase about the Spanish explorers' first glimpse of the Pacific Ocean) may have run through Tomás O'Crohan's mind when his own inquiring eyes stared at the telegraph station of the first transatlantic cable" (Shea 2014, 105–6). More significantly, Shea speculates whether the sight of the transatlantic cable may have encouraged Tomás to consider the possibility of communicating with the wider world. "Did the concept of messages traversing an ocean set O'Crohan pondering the possibility of communicating himself among a wider world? Did this startling sight that completely enthralled Tomás spur a notion of a wide audience – a notion destined to lay dormant until the turn of the century?" (Shea 2014, 105–6)

Apart from this and other reinstated passages in the volume, Ó Coileáin restored the original order of the text. The "houses chapter" that An Seabhac requested after the completion of the original volume and was sequenced as the third chapter in the first two editions, appears as an appendix in the final edition. This also applies to a number of episodes which were originally written at the request of the editor—rather than emerging during the original process of writing. In total, there are five appendices in this final version. The first of these is the chapter describing the houses, while the final one concerns a woman who was out early in the morning on the island. She noticed a motor-boar at the white strand. Not knowing why they were there, she became alarmed.

She had good reason for being alarmed because notices for rents, tax and dogs had come from the Government, and not one of them had been complied with. And so she thought that they were a search party from the Government that had come secretly to take all the men with them, or all the women, whichever they happened to choose. (O'Crohan 2012, 313–4)

She woke the sleeping islanders who were not very happy, since it transpired: "The reason for the hullabaloo with the boats was that one of them had been there two days earlier and had caught thirty pounds worth of fish and fifteen pounds worth on the second day. The first boat had done this unbeknownst to the others" (O'Crohan 2012, 313–4). This piece was relegated as an appendix because its format was much closer to Tomás's diary volume than to his memoir. Moreover a shortened version of it had already appeared in Tomás's previous volume, *Island Cross-Talk*.

One final matter that needs to be taken into account regarding the final edition is the time factor. Ó Coileáin had previously noted the changes in Ireland between the first and second editions. However, there were equally remarkable changes between 1973 and 2002, the date of publication of the final edition—most notably Ireland's membership of the European Union and the decline in numbers of Irish-speakers in Gaelic-speaking regions. This era also witnessed more obvious indications of interest in Tomás's work and the Blasket heritage more generally from descendants of Blasket Islanders in the US (see Chap. 8).

Tomás did not live the see either the second or third edition of his memoir. After the completion of the original manuscript, he undertook no further major tome. He did continue writing short pieces, but gradually ill health impeded further writing. In July 1935, he told An Seabhac that the hand that had written *An tOileánach* could no longer put food in his mouth or close a button. Tomás had not been well for thirteen months and could only get out of the bed with help. He felt that he was unlikely to even pick up a pen again—but perhaps he shouldn't complain (Dingle Library Collection). Within two years, Tomás was dead. However, his reputation spread through the Island of Ireland. Subsequently, his memoir would be published in a range of European languages (see Chap. 6). Tomás had initiated a literary tradition that continues to this day in Boston, Massachusetts (see Chap. 8).

CHAPTER 3

# Narrative and Voice

Once published, Tomás's life story was highly acclaimed. However, the
high regard in which it was held may have had more to do with the subject
matter of the memoir, rather than with the author or his literary style. It
was widely held that *An tOileánach* presented a "thick description"
(Geertz 1973) of a vanishing Irish-Gaelic way of life on the Great Blasket
Island. Tomás was the medium through which the Irish community was
given voice. Such assumptions were not untypical of reactions to writings
of peasant authors at the time—it was presumed that a peasant narrative
was at once the story of an individual and his or her homogeneous community. There were no tensions between an individual author and the
community from which s/he emerged. This assumption is also evident in
the reaction to the publication of Tomás's memoir.

One cannot underestimate the significance of the "voice question."
Deborah Reed-Danahay 1997b, 3) notes that: "Who speaks on behalf of
whom are vital questions to ask of all ethnographic and autobiographical
writing. Who represents whose life?" Inevitably there are tensions between
the individual voice and those that this voice is destined to represent.
Smith and Watson describe such tensions in terms of commonality with
and difference from the wider community. They suggest (2010, 38) that
"any autobiographical act involves making oneself known by acts of iden-
tification and difference, and by implication, differentiation."

In her anthropological field work on the island of Corsica, Jaffe (1997,
151) noted the similar conflation not just of the individual narrative with

© The Author(s) 2020                                          43
M. Nic Craith, *The Vanishing World of* The Islandman,
Palgrave Studies in Literary Anthropology,
https://doi.org/10.1007/978-3-030-25775-0_3

that of the community but also with that of the island itself. She writes that: "you can't write the 'I' without that 'I' being read as 'Isle' as a representation of a collective cultural identity." In fact, she proposes a strong pressure on Corsican authors to resist complexity and depict an unrealistic hegemony and uniformity across the island. The dialectical relationship between the writer of a memoir and the society from which s/he emerges has been critiqued by many (e.g. Luchitti 2009, 186).

## INDIVIDUAL OR COLLECTIVE NARRATIVE

A key question in any memoir is that of voice, but what is meant by voice? In one sense, it's the physicality of the voice. What did Tomás's voice actually sound like? We can imagine how it sounded, but we do not really know. We "hear" a voice in the text, which Alan Titley (2012, vii) describes as: "a voice without buckles, without posies, without flowers, without fancies. It is a voice that cuts through all the crap, and gets right down to it beyond yea or nay, or neigh or bay." However, voice is much more than tone.

Voice is also about identity—and sometimes even the concealment of that identity. Rapport (2014, 118) says that: "The relationship between voice and individual identity is always an ambiguous one, complex and partial. One might speak of disjuncture or fracture between the two." Rapport points to the fact that sometimes an individual may "put on" or "perform" a voice. "How often is it the case that the individual will 'perform' a voice that is not essentially his or her own for the purpose of playing a role?" (Rapport 2014, 120).

Voice is also about having permission to speak and being heard. Who is allowed to speak for whom is not a neutral process but reflects sociohistorical norms in which it is produced. Spivak (1998 [1973]) has framed this debate in terms of the subaltern who has not had permission to speak. When Ireland was part of the British Empire, the Gaels were a subaltern community, often without voice. In postcolonial Ireland, the Gaelic-speaking peasant had permission to make his or her voice heard, but there were limitations on what s/he was permitted to say, and that voice was edited incorporated into the greater state narrative (see Chap. 4). Tomás was seen as representative, because he was framed as "everyman."

For many decades, the common reaction to Ó Criomhthain's volume was to deny him a personal voice in favour of a collective one. There was a sense in which the value of the life story rested on its bearing the "imprimatur of a community" (Jackson 2013, 77). As Franz Boas asserted, folk narratives like myths "present in a way an autobiography of the tribe" (1916, 393). This was not an uncommon perspective at the time. Narayan and George (2003, 452) note of folklore more generally: "Folk narratives have tended to be so analytically yoked to communities that many collections and analyses have rarely mentioned tellers, or have alluded to them only by name – as though their existence is important only because they serve as conduits of traditional knowledge." This was the position that academics and the state also took in relation to *An tOileánach*, arguing that it gave voice to a homogeneous community with little cultural differences. One could argue that postcolonial Ireland was now treating its Irish-language citizens as its "Other" or "exotic" within. Like Native Americans (see Chap. 5), Irish-speakers were not autonomous individuals. Instead they were reduced to a stereotype.

### Collective Voice

The original editor of *An tOileánach*, An Seabhac, was keen to represent Tomás as a medium—not just for the community of his time—but also for previous generations of Blasket Islanders. Given the precarious nature of existence on the island, Tomás was giving voice to dead generations and the final generation alike (Luchitti 2009, 119). Tomás's writings were the medium through which the last of the islanders would not be forgotten. His was the voice—not only of past generations—but also of absent future ones. While giving some credence to the personal dimension of Tomás's voice, Jacquin (1998) hears Tomás as giving voice to a "mute" peasantry—to a subaltern group that had not previously been heard. Jacquin proposes that Tomás is keen to portray the material circumstances of life on the Great Blasket rather than revealing his own personal sentiments.

Many academics concur with this perspective. Seán Ó Tuama (1995, 205) asserts that *An tOileánach*, "is more the biography of an Island community than of a single Islander." He evidences this with reference to the speech of the author. "The language the author uses throughout – rich, immediate, incisive – has little of his own personal stamp: it is the colloquially common language" (Ó Tuama 1995, 205). John McGahern, the Irish writer, reinforces the same point. He argues that Tomás's "view of reality is at no time a personal view and it is never at variance with the values of his society as a whole. In fact, we find him boasting that never once in a whole lifetime did he break a custom, and custom was the only law of that civilization" (McGahern 1987, 7–8). There is general agreement that the memoir narrates the communal values and traditions of the island, rather than that of a particular individual. In the words of Lucchitti (2009, 199), "Tomás gave his coaxers what they asked for and satisfied the thirst for the material facts of the culture and society within which he lived."

In part, the presumption of a collective voice is due to Tomás himself. In the final chapter of his memoir, he articulates a strong desire to represent the life of the community. He notes: "I wrote in detail about a lot of all our goings-on so that there'd be some recollection somewhere about them, and I have tried to describe the character of the people who were around me so that there might be an account of them after we're gone, because our likes will never be here again" (O'Crohan 2012, 298). Was Tomás influenced by his reading of Gorky (see Chap. 2) who expressed a similar purpose and asks: "When I try to recall those vile abominations of that barbarous life in Russia, at times I find myself asking the question: is it worth recording them? . . . yes, because that was the real loathsome truth and to this day it is still valid" (Gorky 1966, 217).

Statements such as these imply that such memoirs are social rather than personal documents, and at the time of publication of Tomás's memoir, the postcolonial Irish state was "adopting" classic social documents of Irish-speaking communities. Gorky's work was similarly valuable to the Soviet Union. Habermann says that Gorky's autobiography, "provides a valuable document of the political and cultural history of czarist Russia, recounting the sufferings, the wisdom, and the strength of the Russian people" (Habermann 1971, 76). Hare concurs: "The most arresting feature common to all these autobiographical books is their deliberate self-effacement... Unique in their absence of self-absorption, they excel in authentic pictures of his Russian environment and the many strange people he had met in it" (Hare 1978 [1962], 87–88). Alan Harrison (2001, 492) writes that "above all it, it is a social document that gives us an almost anthropological insight into a way of life that has now vanished."

If the memoir had been written to represent community life, some voices one might have expected to hear are "missing" from the text. Quigley (2013, 50) notes: "Absence haunts Ó Criomhthain's text. Over the course of the book, this sense of absence builds from all that Ó Criomhthain does not say and all that he cannot say." This particularly applies to the voices of close-family women. While Tomás praises the fine appearance of his mother, we rarely actually hear her voice. We hear her words indirectly, and her indirect speech can give an impression of a lack of agency. Of his mother, Tomás says: "My mother was easily as tall as a policeman. She was beautiful, vigorous, strong blonde, but by the time I was at her breast there was no nourishment left in her milk" (O'Crohan 2012, 1). While we occasionally hear her speak, it is a rare occurrence.

Similarly, his sister Maura's voice is generally reported rather than heard. When she hears that a marriage has been arranged for Tomás, she interferes to prevent it going ahead—since she feels the proposed marriage will not benefit family fortunes in the long-term. She has another bride in mind. In the following excerpt, we can infer the authority and forcefulness of Maura's voice—but we don't actually hear the words that are spoken. "She herself had in mind a well-educated girl with relatives in the township, who could help us whenever necessary. She began to explain this to us, like a priest reading the litany, until there was no fight left in us" (O'Crohan 2012, 175). Tomás was married within a week of his sister's intervention. Although the couple had many children, we do not hear their voices either.

### Individual Voice

The literary critic John Wilson Foster was possibly one of the first to challenge the collectivity of voice in *An tOileánach,* suggesting that such a perspective "is only half the story" (Foster 1987, 327). He bases his hypothesis in part on Tomás as "a man set apart from his fellows." With this argument, he is highlighting the traits of commonality and difference inherent in storytelling as noted by Smith and Watson (2010). Tomás was a member of the island community—but he was also a little different from them. Foster takes an intermediate position between personal and collective voice. Interestingly, he makes some comparisons between Tomás and the character of Robinson Crusoe. Taking the example of Tomás's combat with the seal (see Chap. 2), Foster observes that the fight recalls not just an ancient Celtic collective folk narrative but also the individuality of Robinson Crusoe. He makes an important point in saying:

> Both books glorify self-sufficiency. Both heroes dislike idleness and ingratitude. Neither Crusoe nor Ó Crohan is emotionally forthright and their wives are dismissed in a few sentences. Crusoe and Ó Crohan are kinds of Everyman, yet supreme individualists. Their individuality requires realism

and particularity of expression, a preoccupation with facts and things high-lighted by their similar necessity to beachcomb and salvage.' (Foster 1987, 329)

Perhaps it is the case that a story can never be only personal or collective.

With reference to Hannah Arendt, Michael Jackson (2013, 31) notes that "storytelling is a mode of purposeful action (praxis) that simultane-ously discloses our subjective uniqueness and our intersubjective connect-edness to others, as well as the environmental forces to which we are all subject." Every story lies somewhere on the spectrum between personal meaning and public interest. The location on the spectrum may differ from story to story, but there is no narrative at either extreme end. Jackson himself notes (2013, 46) that "the paradox of human plurality, by which she [Arendt] meant that every person is at once a singular being and someone who shares common traits with every member of his or her spe-cies, class or kind."

Tomás himself signals agency with the use of the pronoun "I" and this occurs right at the beginning of the book. He begins:

> I can remember being at my mother's breast; I wasn't weaned until I was four years old. You might call me dregs of the little jug, the last of the brood. That's why I was left so long feeding on my mother's breast. I was also the family pet. I had four sisters, each of them putting morsels of food into my mouth as if I were their own fledgling bird. (O'Crohan 2012, 1)

Lucchitti (2009, 184) argues that each time Tomás uses the personal pro-noun, he is making his own autobiographical intentions explicit and is also entering into a relationship with the reader. While this voice is clearly that of Tomás, it also in some way represents the community. It is both per-sonal and representative, both individual and communal. However, the individuality of that voice has often been lost in the quest to relish the portrait of a simple island community that perfectly addressed a state's needs at a particular point in time (see Chap. 4).

## A Singular Voice?

References to the actual sound of Tomás's voice are rare. Daniel A. Binchy (1934, 547) describes an encounter with Tomás with particular reference to the sound of his voice. He says: "I can still see him as he stood by the hearth in his own kitchen, a trim lithe figure with finely chiselled features and keen bright eyes that seemed to survey the world with friendly and somewhat ironic detachment. His voice still lingers in my ear, clear and musical like a silver bell." Given that most people think of Tomás as an old man, and *An tOileánach* is often flippantly described as "an old man's book," the notion that Tomás's voice is like a "silver bell" is unexpected and intriguing. Binchy also comments on the singularity of voice that we hear in Tomás's book—arguing that "although every child may understand it, nobody except Tomás could have written it." More significantly, Binchy argues that Tomás's voice is different from that of his neighbours—that "his mastery of idiom, his effortless vocabulary, his wealth of literary allusion" all set him apart (Binchy 1934, 552).

One major difference between *An tOileánach* and Tomás's previous volume *Island Cross-Talk* (1986) is the diversity of voices that is present in the earlier volume. Dialogue dominated the previous volume, which is hardly surprising given the title! We hear the voices of individual islanders in their dialogue with one another and with Tomás. One could argue that this diversity of voices gives insights into the community—as the mosaic of voices accommodates different ages and perspectives and gives a general sense of community sound. As Lucchitti (2009, 163–164) suggests *Island Cross-Talk* is a "thematic consideration of voice." Voices are the medium through which much of the Island history is archived. Conversation is a celebration of that history. She refers to Bakhtin's theory of polyphony, a metaphor which is drawn from music and accommodates multiple personalities, voices and perspective (Bakhtin 1984). Lucchitti (2009, 165) argues that *Island Cross-Talk* is a polyphonic text in which we hear the voices of multiple islanders and different standpoints. Rather than reporting indirect speech, these islanders are permitted to speak for themselves and the text is presented as an interaction between different characters.

### Personal Voice

This is far from the case in *An tOileánach*—a text in which Tomás's personal voice gradually comes to the fore. As we go through the memoir, there is a silencing of other islander voices and Tomás's personal voice takes centre stage. Tomás is still in dialogue—but it becomes a dialogue with the reader (in the first instance with Brian Ó Ceallaigh) rather than the island community. One could argue that it becomes a dialogue between Tomás as a member from within the community with a reader who is located outside of the community. There is an inside-outside dialectic going in and this (in part) is what makes Tomás's voice so valuable. Mac Conghail (1987a, 163) describes *An tOileánach* as "the work of an artist writer" which "is written from within the Island culture; a tough and at times cold, almost ruthless writer, with an intention to say it all once and well."

This places it in contrast with the writings of the Anglo-Irish dramatist John Millington Synge, who was advised by the Irish poet William Butler Yeats in Paris in 1896 to go to the Aran Islands on the West coast of Ireland, "to express a life that has never found expression" (Synge 1968, 63). The example of Synge constitutes the type of representation criticised by Said in *Orientalism* (1978), which critiques Western hegemonic discourse of the Orient, whose culture is mediated through the lens of an external observer. Said focused on the coloniser-colonised, self-other relationship, which is implicit in Yeats's (albeit well-intentioned) advice. Synge would go to the island and represent those (who like Oriental people) were perceived as being unable to express themselves.

However, there are occasions in which Tomás describes another's voice. Consider, for example, the following excerpt when he tells of his companions in inishvickillane (the company includes the girl he fell in love with): "As I listened to their sweet voices, each more beautiful than the other, I couldn't tell whether they were from this world, or heaven, or from the land of the fairies" (O'Crohan 2012, 164). On another occasion, he feels intensely afraid when he hears the sound of what he thinks are human voices, but his companion re-assures him: "it's easy to see that you've never heard them before this. They [the seals] sound like human voices when there are many of them gathered together on dry land. Look, there's a crowd of them beached on those rocks back there" (O'Crohan 2012, 220). Being a little re-assured, Tomás put his fears to one side but: "Before long I heard the long, soft, sweet singing again. It reminded me of someone singing Éamann Mhágáine, but I just had to keep that idea out of my mind" (O'Crohan 2012, 221). It is clear that voices (whether human or animal) have capacity to spark joy or fear.

Some critics have found Tomás's personal voice incredibly boring (see Chap. 2). In a review of the translation of Seán Ó Coileáin's definitive edition of the volume, Ridgway (2012) argues that the life story reads, "like an exasperating and tiresome chord." This he blames not just on the endless repetitions but also on the undue attention to minor occurrences, which he contrasts with the dearth of attention to major events. It is not just the lack of emotional expression that bothers Ridgway, but also the

3 NARRATIVE AND VOICE

absence of insight into his beliefs, political or religious. However, others suggest that this absence is deliberate. It is explained in part by a lifestyle that was stoic in the face of life's difficulties. And so, for example, Maher (2008, 268) says: "The reaction of Ó Criomhthain to his son's death after a fall from a cliff is revealing of a man who knew that he could not afford to mourn his loss for too long. Tomás notes: 'Well, those that pass cannot feed those that remain, and we, too, had to put out our oars again and drive on'" (O'Crohan 2012, 186). It was characteristic of a lifestyle described by Sheper-Hughes (2001) as absent in emotional expression. People did not openly articulate their sorrow, Instead they simply got on with life.

A more complex explanation of the absence of emotions is forwarded by Quigley (2013), who argues that this absence was a deliberate frustration of the project of autobiographical representation on Tomás's part. He says that, "Ó Criomhthain combines savvy analyses of various efforts to fix and commodify life on the Blaskets with a mode of modest self-presentation in *An tOileánach* that highlights the generic pressures of postcolonial autobiography through his ongoing frustration of the genre's demand for disclosure" (Quigley 2013, 32). From a postcolonial perspective (but with very little evidence), Quigley argues that Tomás is reacting against the self-representation normally expected in an autobiography, and instead of producing a personal memoir, he is writing what Quigley calls, "an autobiography of tradition" (2013, 32). While Quigley (2003) reads this as a refusal to engage with autobiographical representation, I would regard it more as in keeping with the custom of the time.

### Variation in Voice

One interesting dimension of Tomás's voice through the text is its flexibility. Sometimes we hear Tomás speaking as a child. On other occasions, he speaks with the voice of an elder reminiscing on his childhood. At the beginning of the book, he remembers being weaned at his mother's breast. This is the voice of an adult remembering his childhood. However, there are moments in the early chapters that he writes with the voice of a child. Describing his first day in the school classroom, he says:

> I didn't pay much attention until I had munched my apple, and that didn't take me long because I had a fine grinding-mill then, something I can't boast about today. Then I took a good look around the room. I saw books

and papers here and there in little piles, a blackboard hanging on the wall, with white marks jotted all over it as if done with chalk. I was intrigued as to what they meant until I saw the schoolmistress calling the biggest girls to the blackboard. She had a little stick in her hand and was pointing out the marks to them, and it began to dawn on me that she was speaking some kind of nonsense-talk to them. (O'Crohan 2012, 15)

It is possible that Gorky's volume influenced Tomás in his portrayal of a child's voice to a new situation. In his first volume, Gorky describes his reaction to the printed word when his grandfather first gave him a book.

Suddenly, with a loud noise, Grandfather slapped a newish-looking book he'd taken down from somewhere against his palm and called out to me in a lively voice . . . These words were well known to me, but the Slavonic letters didn't correspond to them: the letter 'e' looked like a worm, the letter 'g' made me think of the humpbacked Grigory, and the letter 'ya' reminded me of myself with Grandmother, while Grandfather had something in common with all the letters. (Gorky 1966, 79–80)

The voice of the child takes a comic turn with the visit of the school inspector. It was the first time the island school-children witnessed an individual wearing spectacles. Initially, we hear the child's reaction and then we get the explanation from the perspective of an older person:

"Mary, Mother of God!" whispers the King to me, "he has four eyes." "Yes, and they're lit up," says I. "I never saw anyone like him before," says he. Whenever he turned his head there'd be a gleam in his eyes. Finally, all the big ones in there burst out laughing, while the little ones were screeching with fear. The teacher nearly dropped with shame, and the inspector flew into a rage. "There'll be murder today," says the King in a very low voice, "since I don't imagine anyone has ever seen a person with four eyes in his head before." This was the first person we young ones had ever seen wearing spectacles. (O'Crohan 2012, 31–32)

In the text, Tomás flits back and forth between the present and the past—between the time of writing about the event and when it actually occurred. This technique of going back and forth in time has been noted by Kiberd (2000, 527) who critiques that it is often used in light, humorous situations. And so, for example, when Tomás describes how he elbows a youth as a child, he also makes us aware that this child is now king of the island.

I prodded Pats Micky who was beside me on the bench – this is the same Pats Micky who has been King over us long since, and he's also now the postman for this district. I asked him what sort of gibberish talk was going on between the schoolmistress and the girls around the blackboard. "I haven't the faintest idea," says he, "but I reckon it'll never be understood here." (O'Crohan 2012, 15)

Kiberd is critical of this technique which "can be seen as reasserting time's capacity to heal all wounds, but it runs the risk already noted of removing the suspense from an otherwise gripping story" (Kiberd 2000, 527).

### Folkloric Voice

Throughout *An tOileánach*, one also hears the voice of Tomás as folklorist. Ó Giolláin (2000, 128) says: "all of the Blasket writers are of interest to folklorists and ethnologists through their use of folklore and through their detailed description of the life of a folk society." In the next chapter, I explore further the question of Gorky's impact on Tomás. It may, for example, have introduced Tomás to the place of folklore in biography, since Gorky gives some accounts of storytelling sessions from his grandmother. Gorky integrated this folklore into his memoir in a very natural way and, in so doing, made folklore an integral part of his own life story— note, for example, how Gorky weaves in his grandmother's folklore into the text:

> Grandmother told her stories without a break, each story better than the other. On this occasion Grandmother gave everyone the full benefit of the enormous number of stories she knew – and this was very rare for her. She sat on the edge of the stove, her feet resting on the step, and leant towards her audience, whose faces were lit up by the small tin lamp. When she was in the mood, she always liked to sit up on the stove. She explained this by saying: "I must be high up when I recite, it's much better up there." I sat at her feet, on the wide step, almost directly above the head of just the job. Grandmother started telling the story of Ivan the Warrior and Miron the Hermit; the precise sonorous words would flow rhythmically. (Gorky 1966, 119)

In Tomás's memoir, we hear the story of the Boat of Gortadoo (O'Crohan 2012, 44–46) and of the hunters from the island who were taken to Belfast (O'Crohan 2012, 68–71), as narrated by Bald Tom. The tale of the young gannets on the Skellig is recounted by the poet Seán Ó Duinnshléibhe. In some instances (such as the hunting of tax collectors), Tomás tells the reader that he himself has witnessed the incident. This is a personal touch that was not evident in *Seanchus ón Oileán Tiar* (1956), which consisted of folktales told by Tomás directly to Robin Flower. The folktales in *An tOileánach* are not necessarily new or original stories. However, Tomás is using his artistic licence to link these "memorates" with his own personal life story (Céitinn 1992, 133).

Some suggest that as Tomás advanced in this memoir, he adopted the voice of the anthropologist, in that he consciously began describing island life for the reader. O'Leary (2004, 139) notes that "Ó Criomhthain and the other Blasket writers became amateur anthropologists." Seán Ó Coileáin (2002, xx) points in particular to the "houses" chapter as an example of Tomás as anthropologist. The author is now purposefully describing island material culture in minute detail for an external audience. As noted in Chap. 2, it had not occurred to Tomás to describe the island houses. Islanders and visitors alike had visited and stayed in these houses. Tomás had now become aware of the external reader—the individual who might never visit the island. "The authenticity that is much praised in Blasket literature is thus of an anthropological or ethnographic kind rather than the philosophical, religious or existential authenticity that might be read if the personal quality of the writing had been of more central concern" (Lucchitti 2009, 160).

## NARRATIVE AND AUTHENTICITY

As was the custom with oral traditions on the island, Tomás was keen to emphasise the truthful nature of his narrative. In the original ending to his life story, he says: "As the storyteller used to say long ago after telling his story, 'That's my story and if there's a lie in it, let it be.' Here is my story and there is no lie in it, only the bare truth" (O'Crohan 2012, 294). The second (solicited) ending also emphasises the truthfulness of his account—although in this instance, there are also hints of absent truths.

> Well, I have slithered along to the end of my story. There is nothing in it but the truth. I didn't need to make up anything because over a long life I've gathered a lot of memories – and there are still more in my head, if anyone wants to ask about them. All the same, it was those things that interested me

the most that I jotted down. For ages I'd been mulling over everything I was most interested in. (O'Crohan 2012, 295)

Given Tomás's aversion to writing fiction, it is possible (but by no means certain) that Brian Ó Ceallaigh drew his attention to Gorky's emphasis. Gorky sought a truth that would enable and uplift people from their miserable, sordid lives. He wrote:

The fact is that I hate, with the most sincere hate, the most utter, that truth which, for 99 per cent of the people, is an abomination and a lie… I know that this reality is miserable for fifty million people who make up the mass of the Russian people, and that men have need of another truth which does not debase them but which lifts their energy in toil and creation. (quoted in Levin 1967, 272)

Muchnic (1963, 78) said that for Gorky there was a truth "that saved" and a truth "that killed." Gorky determined to tell the "ugly" truth to ensure that Russian peasants would rise above their miserable circumstances. "As I try to bring the past to life I find it hard to believe that it all really happened. That dreary life was so full of violence that I would even like to question or gloss over much of it. But truth is nobler than self-pity" (Gorky 1966, 25).

Focusing in particular on the context in which Tomás was writing, Cathal Ó hÁinle (1993) makes an important distinction between fiction and untruth. Ó hÁinle (from an etic perspective) argues that as a storyteller of the oral tradition, Tomás would have contrasted truth with fiction rather than with lies. Telling the truth permitted, "artistic licence for the sake of imaginative truth." In the oral tradition from which Tomás emerged, truth was recorded by collective memory rather than a written down record (Lucchitti 2009, 33), and Tomás was at liberty to draw on this memory in a way that would involve creativity in order to improve the story.

But what is truth and how can an author guarantee a truthful account since remembering inevitably involves creativity. Like heritage and nostalgia, storytelling is a selective act. Jackson (2013, 69) notes: "authenticity does not necessarily consist in an exact and objective recollection of a moment in the past that is frozen, as in a photograph, for all time. Rather, the 'truth' of any remembered trauma is both selective and practiced." In one sense, one might talk about a "truth-story" rather than a "true-story" since: "All stories are, in a sense, untrue" (Jackson 2013, 14).

In telling or writing a story, one selects and rearranges experiences depending on the intention and approach. Michael White (2007) describes remembering in terms of re-organisation. One selects and rearranges the most significant people and events in the same way that one "might reorganize the furniture in our homes to create a new and more liveable space" (Jackson 2013, 26–7). The stories one tells are determined by one's journey through life and as one's perspective changes, one's stories may become "fictional" or "counterfactual." This is not that somehow they have become false or have failed to mirror reality. Instead as one uses them to understand the meaning of our lives, one's perspective on these stories may change. One is constantly re-interpreting in the process of remembering. Interpretation is an essential element of the process of remembering, which leads to what James Clifford (1986, 7) terms: "partial truths"—a concept which can be applied in a similar fashion to memoir and ethnography alike. Clifford Geertz noted: "anthropological writings are themselves interpretations, and second and third order ones to boot . . . . They are, thus, fictions; fictions, in the sense that they are 'something made,' 'something fashioned' – the original meaning of $ficti\bar{~}o$ – not that they are false, unfactual, or merely 'as if' thought experiments" (Geertz 1973, 15).

Caputo (2013, 54) puts forward the concept of "literary truth" to describe the truth that emerges from a novel, story or poem which is not expected to be literally true but which in a literary context contains a truth. "Things profoundly 'true' are said in a novel, for example, and even though we don't expect a poem to be literally true, we do know unless we are particularly obtuse readers that they are true with another sort of truth" (2013, 54). This is very different from the concept of objective truth as defined by Kierkegaard, which focuses on objects rather than people. Literary truth is more akin to what Kierkegaard (1992 [1845]) called a "subjective truth," which focuses on the individual who is speaking and the perspective s/he is coming from and their feelings and opinions.

Whatever Tomás's own intentions to "tell the truth," editorial interventions meant that his message was sometimes distorted by the editors of the first two editions in particular. An example of this distortion or "toning down" is Tomás's account of his work with Fr Mac Clúin, who had spent three weeks with him and subsequently published a volume *Réilthíní Óir* (Mac Clúin 1922) without any reference to Tomás's input. In the Flower edition, the narrative is as follows:

This priest spent three weeks with me the first year he visited. We used to have Mass every day from him. He came back and we spent a month together, helping each other correct the whole of *Réilthíní Óir*. We'd have eight hours sitting down together every day, two periods in the day — four hours in the morning and four hours in the afternoon, for a whole month. .... That's the most painful month's work I ever did, on land or sea. (O'Crohan 1951 [1937] 240)

In the final edition, where Tomás is permitted "to speak for himself," his voice is much more bitter.

That month disrupted my fishing and my work on land more severely than any other had ever done. But what infuriated me particularly was when I found out that the person with whom I had worked so hard didn't even mention my help in the work. I suppose that it wouldn't have been so bad if it had been some academic, either in Ireland or abroad, who had done such a thing, and not a member of the church. But wouldn't we have it easy if our road to paradise was a straight one, and not a crooked one! (O'Crohan 2012, 293)

Occasionally, the first and second editors added a comment—apparently to "soften" the tone of Tomás's voice. Ua Maoileoin (1992, 150) noted how being wary of the criticism that Tomás made of the old woman next door, they added a sentence about her good heart as follows:

She was a little, undersized, untidy-haired babbler with a sallow face, not much to look at – a gossip, always hither and thither. She was always saying to my mother that all Ireland couldn't rear an old cow's calf, and I don't think any cow, old or young, ever had a more wretched-looking calf than herself. But all the same, she had a good heart. (O'Crohan 1951 [1937], 2)

The unabridged edition, however, delivers the message as Tomás intended:

This woman was a little scandal-monger, dishevelled, sallow, ugly and shapeless, and she'd go from house to house, gossiping. She often used to say to my mother that Ireland couldn't raise the calf of an old cow. But if you ask me, there never was a cow, old or young in Ireland, that had a calf as miserable as herself. (O'Crohan 2012, 2)

Some incidents were omitted from the first two editions—and so, for example, the following incident, which appears in the unabridged edition, does not feature at all in the first two:

> 1 first saw a shrew of a woman, with a mop of red hair on her head, standing outside a semi-detached cottage. She was going crazy, working herself up into a frenzy. I understood from what she was saying that hens' eggs were the cause of the dispute. "And, you old devil," says she, "you're not satisfied collecting eggs from your own roof but you have to go taking them from mine too." I was amazed that the person she was talking to didn't answer her back, but very soon the woman of the other house came to the door, and peered warily until she had managed to get behind the other woman. Then giving a sudden leap and grabbing her neighbour's red hair, she immediately dragged her to the ground. Well, I didn't blame her for doing that as the red-haired woman deserved to be taken down a peg or two. But she wasn't satisfied even after pulling out tufts of her neighbour's curly red hair, throwing them on the dung yard and digging her knees into her belly. But to make matters worse, the red-haired woman was pregnant. (O'Crohan 2012, 158)

### Censorship

The editorial curtailment on the first two editions was not necessarily ill-intentioned and possibly stemmed from a concern for both author and editor in post-publication decades in postcolonial Ireland (see Chap. 4). For much of the twentieth century, the Irish state and church censored supposedly unlettered and immoral "peasant" accounts of rural life—and these were hardly confined to "peasant" memoirs. "In a country dedicated both to banning books and revering the written word" … any writer learns to "tread lightly and to have a quick exit plan" (Scheper-Hughes 2001 [1983], 7). Consider, for example, the fate of *Tailor and Ansty* (Cross 1942), two Irish peasants whose book was initially lauded but was quickly banned in 1943, following a four-day debate in the Irish Senate—during which both husband and wife were harshly criticised. "The Tailor was condemned as a "sex-obsessed" peasant and his wife, Anastasia (Ansty), was cruelly dismissed as a village moron" (Scheper-Hughes 2001 [1983], 9). At a debate on 18 November 1942 in Seanad Éireann, a member of the senate noted:

This sex-ridden, sex-besotted Tailor speaks of no subject whatsoever without spewing the foulness of his mind concerning sexual relations. The author, Mr. Cross, leaves our Tailor and Ansty to speak out of his own personality, and what do you get? They arrive in Paradise and Ansty does not like the whiskers of St. Peter. Eventually, they are tired of Heaven, because they miss the cow and the neighbours, and "sweet Saint Francis of Assisi" goes down from the joy of the Beatific Vision in Heaven and shares hell with them by preference. I suggest that it is a blasphemous book. (Seanad Éireann debate, 18 Nov 1942)

Prior to that and closer to Tomás's own time, there had been riots in Dublin following the performance of J.M. Synge's *Playboy of the Western World*. Angry that they had been portrayed as a "wild, violent, and lawless white tribe of peripheral Europe," the performers had to be protected by police manning the theatre (Scheper-Hughes 2001 [1983], 9).

An equally negative reaction followed Frank O'Connor's translation of *Cúirt an Mheán Oíche* (The Midnight Court) (Merriman 1961 [1780]). Although the original Irish version was widely available in Ireland, as soon as an English translation was published, it was banned by an Irish Government endeavouring to forge a state of pure, sexless (although fruitful) nationalists. Edna O'Brien's first novel *The Country Girls* (1960) was banned as immoral by the Catholic Church and her parents publicly shamed. Within close range of the Great Blasket, the filming of *Ryan's Daughter* on the Dingle Peninsula was unwelcome. The anthropologist Nancy Scheper-Hughes was more or less "blacklisted" by the local community in nearby Dunquin after the publication of *Saints, Scholars and Schizophrenics* (2001 [1979]).

The Irish did not wish to be the subject of anthropological inquiry (see Chap. 1). Even Conrad Arensberg's volume *The Irish Countryman* (1988 [1937]) considered a fairly sympathetic account of the Irish in the West Coast of Ireland (see Chap. 1) was soon followed by a novel *The Straight and the Narrow* (Tracy 1956), which featured an anthropologist conducting an ethnographic survey in a rural Irish village. Far from being a competent social scientist, the anthropologist is portrayed as a "naïve, bumbling, malicious gossip" (Scheper-Hughes 2001 [1983], xvi). The close network within which people operated is reflected in the proverb "*ar scáth a chéile a mhaireann na daoine,*" the Irish equivalent of "no man is an Island."

Given the small-knit community on the island, Tomás may have felt the need to curtail negativity towards his neighbours. He would have been very aware of the potential reaction of his own community to the publication of the memoir. "Life stories often have less to do with speaking one's mind or sharing one's experiences than with saying what is safest or most expedient to say" (Jackson 2013, 13). The islanders all lived together in a tiny village at one end of the island. This surely would have constrained Tomás in his description of his neighbours. Everyone was interrelated either by blood or by marriage; it would have been impossible for Tomás to speak too frankly in his memoir about his neighbours and then continue to live on the island after its publication.

Ua Maoileoin (1992) remarks that the island community could not have survived without help from one another. They married each other— often close relatives—and living in dire poverty. As neighbours, they were extremely dependent on one another. Fear, hunger and desolation kept them together as a people. The interdependent nature of the community may have been the reason behind the "pallid" nature of some of the characters in the book. Tomás presented a portrait of a community that was poor, and living simply from day to day—a portrait that they themselves may not have recognised (Ua Maoileoin 1992, 153). That did not prevent many of them from reacting negatively to Tomás's portrayal of the island community. Tomás's grandson, Pádraig Ua Maoileoin suggests that this stemmed from jealousy. "The Blasket books generated controversy and debate on the island. Writers were accused of misrepresentation – 'that is not how it happened'; 'all lies and invention,' Much of this criticism was inspired by envy" (Ua Maoileoin 1992, 35).

Before Tomás, there were no Blasket biographies. It is possible that the concept of an individual published life story was largely unknown in this island community until Brian Ó Ceallaigh brought memoirs in Irish and in English to the island (O' Leary 1970). Perhaps his knowledge of these memoirs influenced Tomás in determining what he might or might not say. The concept of an individual memoir was also unknown among indigenous peoples in America. "The biography... does not exist in the Oral Traditions of the Tribes, nor does it exist in any Traditional Native American Literary offspring" (Cook-Lynn 1994, 73).

As with many native figures, Tomás's initial published volume was a collaborative effort and his voice was muted in the first two Irish-language editions. It was not until Seán Ó Coileáin undertook the editorship of the third Irish-language edition that Tomás was given back the voice he had expressed in the original manuscript. By this time, many of the concerns that possibly restrained the first two editors were no longer an issue. Ireland had become much more accepting of books that rejoiced in courtship and featured neighbourly quarrels. While banning of books still continues, many previously banned books are now widely available. Moreover, the Great Blasket island has been evacuated and the original characters featuring in the memoir are largely dead.

CHAPTER 4

# Translating Place

The publication of the first edition of *An tOileánach* in 1929 cannot be separated from its political context. In 1929, the Irish Free State was just seven years in existence. Seven years earlier, the Irish Free State formally withdrew from the United Kingdom under the Anglo-Irish Treaty. The newly established state did not comprise the whole of the island of Ireland. Instead it was made up of 26 of Ireland's 32 counties. The remaining six counties in the north-eastern part of the island of Ireland remained within the United Kingdom. In 1937, the new Constitution of Ireland renamed the 26 county state as Ireland or Éire, and the position of the Irish prime minister, known as "*an Taoiseach*," was established.

More than ten years later, in 1948, the status of the Republic of Ireland was officially recognised by Westminster. Once the Republic of Ireland act was enacted in April 1949, Irish state membership of the British Commonwealth was terminated. While it could have applied for re-admittance to the Commonwealth, the Irish state chose not to. Instead, its political energies were focused on cultivating a fully authentic Irish identity and cultural as well as political independence from its former coloniser. "In the country as a whole, when the new state was set up, the creation of a kind of Irish-speaking, hurling, dancing-at-the-crossroads, leprechaun ridden myth arose from the need to assert and establish a separate identity from England. It was very understandable" (de Mórdha 2017, 95).

© The Author(s) 2020
M. Nic Craith, *The Vanishing World of* The Islandman,
Palgrave Studies in Literary Anthropology,
https://doi.org/10.1007/978-3-030-25775-0_4

The official designation of certain places on the western periphery of Ireland (including the Blasket Islands) as *Gaeltacht* (Irish-speaking) was a key element in Ireland's Government strategy after independence. Although serving as the mythical heartland, the *Gaeltacht* regions were an "atypical part of Ireland" in many ways (Ó Giolláin 2000, 148). Throughout the country, Irish was already in decline (Nic Craith 1993), but the language was still spoken as the primary medium of communication in *Gaeltacht* regions. Other cultural elements, such as folklore and traditional forms of material culture, also survived in these areas. The reclamation of indigenous culture and identity was to be drawn "from the humble cottages of the last living representatives of Celtic purity, the Irish-speaking farm and fisherfolk, and pre-eminently those of the western seaboard" (Shea 2014: 93). However, the land in the *Gaeltacht* was of such poor quality that people living there barely eked out an existence.

Douglas Hyde, Ireland's first president (1938–1945) had long established his commitment to restoring Gaelic Ireland. In a famous speech in 1892 entitled *The de-Anglicization of Ireland* (see Dunleavy and Dunleavy 1991), Hyde argued that the Irish should "strive to cultivate everything that is most racial, most smacking of the soil, most Gaelic, most Irish, because in spite of the little admixture of Saxon blood in the north-east corner, this Island is and will ever remain Celtic at the core, far more Celtic than most people imagine" (Hyde 1892).

Éamon de Valera, Ireland's third president from 1959 to 1984, was formidable in his cultivation of a cultural nationalism that regarded peasants such as Tomás Ó Criomhthain as "a type of aristocrat in disguise" (Ó Crualoaich 1986, 53). This "aristocrat" was Irish-speaking and located on the hallowed ground of the *Gaeltacht*. "Tomás O'Crohan, western man, Islandman, survivor, wittingly or not, provided the Revivalist project with a template of Irishness most useful to the 'imagined community' … under construction" (Lucchitti 2009, 97). The Blasket memoirs were a useful vehicle for reclaiming the indigenous language and identity and the books were instrumentalised as a means of "guarding and perpetuating the Irish language in the face of an increasingly anglicized Ireland" (Ross 2003, 116–7). The imagined community of the 26 counties was a place that was strongly Gaelic.

## FROM PLACE TO IMAGE

Although, there were maps in the first and third editions of *An tOileán-ach*, Pádraig Ua Maoileoin's second edition was exceptional in that it included illustrations of the landscape of the Great Blasket Island. The "translation" of the landscape into visual images was undertaken by a local artist, Maria Simonds-Gooding, who had arrived in Dunquin in the 1960s and immediately identified with the people and the landscape and its isolation. "In that isolated place she read the primordial struggle between the individual and the environment for basic survival and was hooked" (Marshall 2004, unpaginated). Although I have described her as a local artist, Maria was in fact born in India and came to Dunquin in her twenties. Five years later, she made her home there. She purchased a stone cottage that had been built in 1948 by a Blasket Island man Mike "Faight" O Sé, who brought his roof, door and windows with him across the Blasket Sound. Maria's art has taken her to the Greek Islands, New Mexico, to remote regions in India and the Sahara and the Sinai Desert. As an artist, Maria is in search of the universal and the sublime. "The struggle to exist on the land is the same the world over. Farmers sweat to make fields, enclosing them with stone in Dingle, volcanic stone and moisture-retaining black ash in Lanzarote or with water and mud in Rajasthan" (Marshall 2004, unpaginated).

In conversation with Maria, she describes how she was first approached with the request of illustrating the landscape of *An tOileánach*:

> It must have been at Writer's Week in 1970. For the first fifteen years of Writer's Week I participated in the visual arts, but then they largely dropped the art dimension to allow funds for the literary aspect to which it was so widely acclaimed. On the night in question, I was dancing and dancing late into the evening. It was maybe one or two in the morning, when an official looking man came up to me right in the middle of the dance floor. I can just remember this moment. He introduced himself to me as Kevin Etchingham from the Talbot Press. He asked me right there and then if I would like to illustrate the new edition of *An tOileánach*. What a fabulous thing to be asked to do so! I said, "yes" immediately. This was a great challenge which I certainly did not want to turn down. (Interview with Simonds-Gooding, July 2017)

In preparation for her commission, Simonds-Gooding re-read *An tOileán-ach*, to immerse herself in the story, with a view to illustrating it. Her response to the written text was as follows:

> I have had various experiences of storm and the hardship the elements imposed on the island. Sometimes when the islanders went over to shear their sheep for a couple of weeks in the summer they too could get storm bound at that time of year. These experiences helped to give a better under-standing of the hardship of how life was lived in the days of Tomás Ó Criomhthain. (Interview with Simonds-Gooding, July 2017)

As further preparation, Maria decided to spend more time on the island. She asked Patty Dunleavy whether she could stay in his cottage on the island—which he agreed. It was there that she decided that her first illus-tration would feature sheep (see etching 4.1). Sheep have appeared regu-larly in Tomás's *An tOileánach*. Apart from the fact that they feature in most chapters in the context of tax-bailiffs, Christmas, and so on, they were also the subject of the island poet's first poem which Tomás was obliged to transcribe on his way to cut turf (see Chap. 2). Maria comments:

> And then I thought, one of the first things I'm going to illustrate are the sheep. Sheep were a big part of island life. The islanders were never in a hurry and when it came to shearing they had an art of their own. By this time they were getting quite old but they were still very fit. They didn't have to run. They just put an arm out here and there and they spread themselves out. About five men apart rounded the sheep up to shear them. This was some feat since these black faced sheep were very wild, but instinctive at the same time. This all greatly interested me. I started the day going off to look for the sheep. (Interview with Simonds-Gooding, July 2017)

Sketching the sheep was not a straightforward task (Illustration 4.1). However, it was one in which her daschund Sebastian, played a major role. In Maria's own words:

> I had my dog with me and he turned out to be very useful. He was a black and tan standard daschund, he was very close to the ground and very long. Sebastian was his name. There were a lot of visitors on the island at the time and it was disturbing the island life. The sheep took themselves off down the island. When I started going right to the back of the island I found them, but they kept running away. I sat down with my dog beside me to eat

**Illustration 4.1**
"Sheep"; etching by Maria
Simonds-Gooding based
on her book illustrations
for *An tOileánach*, 1972.
(© Maria
Simonds-Gooding)

some sandwiches. But the curiosity of the sheep was too much for them and one by one these black face sheep started appearing closer and closer over the cliff starring at us! Their curiosity was about my dog. I always kept my dog close by my side when there were sheep around. I now had the opportunity to do the drawing I set out for. (Interview with Simonds-Gooding, July 2017)

Seals also featured in Maria's illustration of the memoir (see Illustration 4.2). Unsurprisingly, seals feature frequently in *An tOileánach*. Tomás, for example, recounts his nightmare as a child, when he was attacked by a seal (see Chap. 2). This was some sort of premonition as the following day, a

**Illustration 4.2**
"Seals"; etching by Maria
Simonds-Gooding based
on her book illustrations
for *An tOileánach*,
1972. (© Maria
Simonds-Gooding)

seal genuinely tore a clump out of his leg. The hole was filled by seal flesh.
Simons-Gooding's tells the story of her etching:

> I do know that seals were a big part in the lives of the islanders. There's a
> rocky beach Tráig Eairraí – I don't think you could get down there today,
> the sea has removed part of the cliff. To get there you have to first go to the
> north side overlooking Inis Tuaisceart. It was here also the islanders gath-
> ered their sheep to shear them. When you got down that steep drop and
> walked along by the cliff you would find what looked like a dark cave. This
> was the entrance into a tunnel leading into a small shingly beach enclosed by
> dark high rising cliffs opening into the Atlantic on the west side facing out
> to Inis Tiaracht. Here the seals liked to lie out to bask in the sun. I went

there quietly not to disturb the seals. It was a very hot summer day and I got there early. I sat down surrounded by a family of seals and started to sketch them. What bliss! (Interview with Simonds-Gooding, July 2017)

The final etching of the seals was unusual. Here Simonds-Gooding explains how this came about:

After a while, a grassy sod came swirling down the cliff from up above. It landed not too close but not very far from me either. When I got back to Patty Duleavy's cottage I showed my drawing to the three men who had rowed visitors over that day and who I guessed had thrown the grassy sod, of course it was them. I had drawn two fins on each seal. They looked at my drawing they liked it, but they said the seals should have four hands (they call them hands). So I added two more fins. And that is how it appears in the book. (Interview with Simonds-Gooding, July 2017)

Inevitably, Maria did an illustration of Tomás's house (Illustration 4.3). This was the house that Tomás built on the island as a married man, without help from any of the other islanders. As noted in Chap. 2,

Illustration 4.3   Tomás's house. Pen and ink drawing by Maria Simond-Gooding; original book illustration for *An tOileánach*, 1972. (© Maria Simonds-Gooding)

Tomás took great pride in the finished product, which he claimed would have satisfied even King George!

Overall Maria did 12 illustrations for *An tOileánach* and as she notes herself: "each sketch has a story to tell" (interview with Simonds-Gooding, July 2017). Her pen and ink drawings were in black and white, which she regards as a powerful medium and which reflects the hardship and light in the lives of the islanders. She was placed under considerable pressure to deliver the sketches quickly:

> I was under great pressure when I was asked to give as many drawings as I had ready to one of the boatmen to bring out to the mainland to send to the Talbot Press. This was only when I was half way through. I had no idea I was going to be put under all that pressure. (Interview with Simonds-Gooding, July 2017)

Maria determined to illustrate Tomás's memoir with images of the landscape that do not necessarily coincide with the original text. The absence of any specific extended mention of the landscape has been debated. The artist herself explains it with reference to the challenge of eking out an existence on the land rather than having the leisure-time to admire the landscape. She illustrates this point with reference to a meeting with a shepherd:

> Below Mount Brandon is a very haunting beautiful valley with a river running all along. They used to cut their bogs for turf. The shapes of the cut bog and the stacking of turf became central to my work for some time. The river crosses the road before entering into the valley. It was possible to drive through the river except when there was a heavy fall of rain. For a couple of years I'd go there to paint these bogs. There were few days that I did not go there. One day after torrential rain, the river was too high to drive or walk through. When I got there a sheep farmer with his tractor was adding stones to the river bed to make it passable. I said, "Isn't this a beautiful place". He answered rather sombrely "I take no notice of it". In other words "It's a very hard life. I don't take any notice. And that's how it must have felt for Tomás Ó Criomhthain. It's a very hard life and what you do, you do to survive." (Interview with Simonds-Gooding, July 2017)

There is another possible explanation for the absence of focus on landscape in *An tOileánach*. Tomás had already recounted numerous tales about this island's landscape to Robin Flower. Over a number of years, he had recited stories about the place lore associated with every field on the island. This resulted in *Seanchus ón Oileán Tiar*, which was published in 1956 and which some regard as his best work. Tomás did not necessarily think of his writing his life story as a separate piece of writing. They were all part of a narrative which was later separated into books by editors and visitors.

## TRANSLATION AND ANGLICISATION

### *Flower's Translation*

Although the original *An tOileánach* was published in 1929, a number of years passed before an English translation was published. In the meantime, a second memoir from the island (*Fiche Blian ag Fás*) and its English translation (*Twenty Years A-Growing*) had emerged (Ó Súilleabháin 1933; O'Sullivan 1933). Tomás's son, Seán expressed his dissatisfaction that the English-language translation of *Fiche Blian ag Fás* had been published before that of *An tOileánach*. In a letter in 1933, he wrote:

> According to our book [*An tOileánach*], it was not very successful. Irish [Gaelic] books do not bring much money for Readers are scarce as you ought to know that. The manuscript was given to the Government for £60 and that was all the money my father got for it. There is an English translation in two months' time and it is a wonder that you do not know that from Robin Flower....
>
> You know it should be Published long ago by Jonathan Cape But it took too Long and He gave it up so now it will be published By the Educational Co. of Ireland, Dublin.
>
> It was a great loss for us for O'Sullivan's book *Twenty Years A-Growing* took the market from us and that is the Reason Cape gave it up. Flower should have the translation done within nine months but he was sick and could not Have the work done in time. So it can't Be Helped and We do not Blame any Body. (See Ní Shúilleabháin 1978, 24–25, nonstandard punctuation and capitalisation in original.)

The first English edition of *An tOileánach* was translated by Robin Flower (see Chap. 1). There is no clear explanation as to why Flower translated the volume, but one can possibly infer that his respect for the lifestyle on the island was such that he aimed to bring the memoir to a wider audience. *The Islandman*, the English translation of *An tOileánach*, was initially published in Dublin by Talbot Press, then by Chatto & Windus in 1937 and by Penguin in 1943. The prestigious Oxford University Press (OUP) published *The Islandman* in hardback in 1951. Following several hardback editions, a paperback edition was issued by OUP in 1978 as part of the World's Classics and Oxford Paper Backs series. In 2000, the OUP reissued a complete set of the Blasket Island autobiographies.

Since Tomás's Irish was very rich, translating *An tOileánach* was no easy task (Nic Craith 2019). However, Flower determined that he would adopt a simple style that would be intelligible to every reader. He determined not to use the "*cruadh-Ghaoluinn*," the "cramp-Irish" of the Irish literary tradition (Flower 1978 [1937], ix). Simplicity was his preferred style and he aspired at a "down-to-earth" style that every reader could enjoy. Flower was keenly aware that there would be some loss in translation. "The constant charm of Irish idiom, which is so delightful in the original, must necessarily be lost. But rouge is no substitute for a natural complexion" (Flower 1978 [1934], x).

A key challenge for translators of Tomás's memoir into English is the asymmetry of language between Irish and English. As Alan Titley (2012, ix) notes: "One suspects that languages of Latin origin carry some of the great columns and marble edifices of Rome in their innards and resonances can be more readily shared between them." With regard to Irish and English, Titley (2012, ix) says: "there are vast shelves of libraries and vast cities and practised bureaucracies and marching troops and technical wrestlings which make the gap of feeling immense."

Flower appreciated and acknowledged this challenge. When introducing his English translation, he commented that: "Irish and English are so widely separated in their mode of expression that nothing like a literal rendering from the one language to the other is possible" (Flower 1978 [1934], x). He considered a range of options including the use of "a literary dialect, sometimes used for translation from Irish or for the purpose of giving the effect of Irish speech which in books or on the stage has met with considerable applause" (Flower 1978 [1934], x). However, he declined this option, considering it "slightly artificial" or even "pseudo-poetic" (Flower 1978 [1934], x). He also decided not to use complex English. Instead, he opted for a, "plain, straightforward style, aiming at the language of ordinary men who narrate the common experiences of their life frankly and without any cultivated mannerism" (Flower 1978 [1934], x).

The reaction to the publication of Flower's English translation was mixed. For some, Flower's first translation was very welcome. The Irish-language scholar Pádraig Ó Fiannachta was reasonably positive. He said: "Flower's style is gentle and nostalgic but lacks the taste of salt and the smell of *stuaicín*, and does a little censoring even of An Seabhac's edition" (Ó Fiannachta 1983, 44). Professor D.A. Binchy was more complimentary. He noted: "Dr Flower is the ideal interpreter … he has risen nobly to the occasion, producing a masterly translation in which the sensitiveness of the poet and the accuracy of the scholar are blended in perfect harmony" (Binchy 1934, 549). While John McGahern's assessment was initially negative, the translation subsequently found favour with him:

> When I was first interested in *An tOileánach*, I was always puzzled by the difference between the original and Robin Flower's translation. I was inclined to blame this on the literalness of the translation; and it was only when I tried to translate parts of it myself that I came to realize how good a translation Flower's actually is, and I began gradually to realize that the difficulty was deep in the language itself, in the style. (McGahern 1987, 7)

However, others were less complimentary. In *The Irish Times* on 3 January 1957, Myles na Gopaleen noted of Robin Flower's translation of *An tOileánach*: "A greater parcel of bosh and bunk than Flower's 'man' has rarely been imposed on the unsuspecting public" (na Gopaleen 1957, 6). There was no further English translation until 2012.

### Bannister and Sowby's Translation

When Seán Ó Coileáin's postcolonial edition of *An tOileánach* was published in 2002, two Dublin translators seized the opportunity to produce a new English-language translation of the memoir. They were Garry Bannister who had studied Irish and Russian in Trinity College Dublin before receiving an MA and defending a PhD in comparative linguistics at Moscow State University. Bannister subsequently established the first department of modern Irish at that university. David Sowby, his co-translator, was born in the Lake District in England and was educated in Dublin, where he studied Irish at Trinity. A medical doctor with a prestigious career in Canada, Sowby had previously translated *Cúirt an Mheán Oíche* into English.

Their new translation of *An tOileánach* (*The Islander*) was published in 2012. In the preface, Bannister and Sowby explained that their edition was sparked by the publication of Ó Coileáin's edition of *An tOileánach*, which they greatly admired. In conversation with Bannister, he explained how they carried out the task: "We worked together as a team because we are very different people. I was more the artistic director. I understood how Irish flows and how modern Irish is spoken, whereas he was more a textologist. He was into the text" (interview with Bannister, July 2017).

Bannister and Sowby (2012) faced the same challenges as Flower when translating *An tOileánach*. Originally, they had envisioned a quite literal translation that would serve as a guide for those who might wish to "map" the English translation onto the original Irish text. Their attempt to do this was doomed to failure. "All our best efforts and our dogged adherence to the original only ever resulted in an English translation that was unwieldy, bleak and, for the most part, incomprehensible" (Bannister and Sowby 2012, xx). Bannister explains:

> The translation took us ten years. We wrote it out fourteen times. The first translation that we did of the book was a literal translation. We translated the text almost word for word. At the end of each paragraph we put in notes about the syntactical use of language, the way the ideas were expressed and the mood of the language. (Interview with Bannister, July 2017)

Subsequently, they decided on a different *modus operandi*. They decided to rewrite the first translation which would preserve three critical aspects of the book. "Firstly, although the translation had to be clear and readable, it also, as far as possible, had to reflect the intended meaning of its author. Secondly, the translation needed to convey something of the richness and elegance of O'Crohan's own literary style of expression; thirdly, the language of the English translation was not to lose too much of the essence or feeling of the time in which it was written" (Bannister and Sowby 2012, xx). This is how Bannister describes the process:

> We started trying to get the tone of the piece rather than the exact word for word translation. This was a slow process as we didn't want to lose out on what Tomás was saying. That was very important to us. We made that decision at the beginning that we weren't going to cut anything out. If Tomás

said something, even if we didn't think it important, we wanted it there. (Interview with Bannister, July 2017)

One reaction to the 2012 edition of *The Islander* was negative. The reviewer complained not so much about the quality of the translation, but about the fact that the book was translated at all. From his perspective, the book was a complete and utter bore:

> Here is a man [Tomás] who lives a hard, straightforward life, who "ploughs the sea" and works the land, who grows up and marries and has children, who gets drunk often, and who gets learning in fits and starts but seems to take to it, and who settles into an old age of Gaelic Revival-prompted reminiscences. But there are so many repetitions, so much attention given to minor occurrences and so little to major ones, that it becomes – like the life perhaps – an exasperating and tiresome chore. (Ridgway 2012)

Clearly, this was an inappropriate reviewer who did not appreciate the rich oral tradition that underpinned the memoir—an oral tradition that placed great emphasis on repetition and reflected the cyclical nature of life on the island.

## The Craft of Translation

Translation is a complex process, since a work in translation can transmit images of individual authors or texts as well as of entire communities that the audience assumes to be real. Translation can "invent" an image of an author, a tradition or even a nation (Tymoczko 1999, 18). Translation is never neutral since the process is always selective, involving the loss of some features of the original but also adding in some supplementary ones (Benjamin 1968 [1923]). Translation is not simply a process of translating words. It is also about values, judgements, actions, and so on. In that regard, the ethnographer can also be considered a translator. Core to ethnography is the process of understanding, describing, judging a specific context and then delineating it through the language of social anthropology. "Seen from this point of view, translation ceases to designate only a linguistic technique. It becomes a definition of the core strategy of social anthropology itself. Clearly, translation is a multidimensional phenomenon" (Hanks and Severi 2014, 6).

The impossibility of direct translation has long been recognised in anthropological fields (see De Saussure 2003 [1983]). Having done extensive fieldwork among Native Americans, Franz Boas (2002) concluded that speakers of different languages perceive the world differently. It was not necessarily that the language one speaks limits one's perception of the world, but more a consequence of the routine use of one's native language that framed the worldview in a particular way. Having done fieldwork on a Hopi reservation, Whorf became aware that the Hopi language was structured differently from English. He became convinced that speakers of this language (or any other) tend to view the world through the framework of the grammar of their native tongue. The impact of language on one's worldview was also supported by Sapir following his research on a number of Native American languages.

In referring to the concept of worldview, Whorf and others built the work of the German philosopher, Wilhelm von Humboldt (1767–1835). Underhill claims that Anglophone cultures never really comprehended the concept of worldview as it was expounded by Humboldt. Drawing on Humboldt's original work, Underhill explains *Weltanschauung* as "an individual's or a community's interpretation of the world or the interpretative framework which he or she invokes to help understand the world." He contrasts this with *Weltansicht,* which is "inherent in a language" and "offers the world up for us for interpretation by allowing us to form concepts and exchange ideas about those concepts and the relationships between them" (Underhill 2009, 151, see also Nic Craith 2012).

From the concept of worldview, Sapir and Whorf developed theories of linguistic determinism or linguistic relativity, depending on whether one draws on its strong or weak version. Sapir suggested that human beings are actually "very much at the mercy of the particular language which has become the medium of expression for their society," because the "real world is to a large extent unconsciously built up on the language habits of the group" (Sapir 1985 [1949], 162).

Whorf wrote in a similar vein, arguing that the grammar of a language does not simply reproduce ideas but "is itself the shaper of ideas." He suggested: "We dissect nature along lines laid down by our native languages.... We cut nature up, organize it into concepts, and ascribe significances as we do, largely because we are parties to an agreement to organize it in this way – an agreement that holds throughout our speech community and is codified in the patterns of our language" (Whorf 1956, 212–3).

While anthropologists such as Boas, Sapir and Whorf have defended the impossibility of literal or neutral translation from one language to another, Hanks and Severi (2014, 12) have pointed out that it is also true that different worlds and translation are somehow always translatable into each other. They argue that "no untranslatable language, or culture, has ever existed. The quality of being translatable is inherent in all forms of human communication, as well as in the generation of cultural differences." It was this quality of the "translatable" that Robin Flower captured in his English-language edition of *An tOileánach*. However, the process was far from easy, and personal illness also delayed the task.

In the case of the English translations of *An tOileánach*, the issue was complicated by years of Irish colonial history. For many centuries, Irish was discouraged in the public sphere (Nic Craith 1993). English was the language of influence, authority and officialdom in Ireland. One could argue that translating Irish texts into English is a mark of approval, since it deems the original text to be worthy of translation. However, it can also be a "double-edge sword" because "the English translation then replaces the Irish while appearing to replicate it, insisting it has redeemed the original while suggesting itself as a legitimate substitute" (De Paor 1996, 62). There is considerable irony in a practice that ensures the Blasket voice survives through the language of the former colonial power. From that perspective, the "translators engage in a work of mourning, erecting and marking a memorial site – a linguistic grave of a sort – in acknowledging the unavoidable and irreducible loss of the original splendour and charm of the peasant voice" (Ross 2003, 126).

De Paor (1996, 65) critiques these translations into non-sophisticated English as meeting the "cultural expectations of an audience which has been persuaded that funny and peculiarly bad English is a true representation of the unfamiliar strangeness of Irish." This bolsters the mistaken view that the world of the Irish-speaker "is the 'backward' 'primitive' world of a pre-modern peasant culture with its 'archaic' rituals of folk customs and belief and that the modern urban industrial world remains firmly within the Pale beyond its reach" (De Paor 1996, 65). Given the dynamics of the power relationship between the two languages, this primitive scenario is regrettable.

MAPPING AND LANDSCAPE

The translation of *An tOileánach* from Irish to English was not simply a change of language or a transition from oral to literary. It also involved a "transformation" of the original text by translators who framed the text with an introduction and, sometimes, maps, footnotes and glossaries. In the case of *An tOileánach*, in his original Irish edition of the memoir, An Seabhac had to a certain extent universalised the text with a title that anonymised the author. Instead of being Tomás's story, it had become the story of *The Islandman*, indicating a common experience with which everyone could identify.

Flower's introduction to the English translation framed key features of the island for the unfamiliar reader. There was a strong emphasis on the remoteness of the place. The English introduction emphasises not just the remoteness of the location but the mountains and divisions within that tiny area:

> It is a wild world of inter-tangled mountains, culminating in the great mass of Brandon, beyond Dingle. West of Mount Brandon again two hills, the pointed shape of Croaghmartin and the long body of Mount Eagle, divide the two parishes of Ventry and Dunquin, and beyond Dunquin, to the north, lies the parish of Ballyferriter. (Flower 1978 [1937], v)

Flower's reference to the difficulty for cattle and sheep in finding "scant pasturage" and the rabbits burrowing in "lofty cliffs" heightens the sense of poverty.

Although the Blasket Islanders were of comparatively recent origin, (people had inhabited the island from about 1700 AD onwards), Flower preferred to highlight the "ancient settlement, of which only fragments of beehive dwellings now remain" on the island (Flower 1978 [1937], vi). Moreover, he predicted the extinction of this Gaelic place with reference to a lighthouse on the "high pinnacle of rock" that is "the last light that Irish emigrants see on their voyage to America" (Flower 1978 [1937], vii).

Flower took the opportunity in his introduction to emphasise the wildness of the location and the outward emigration of the islanders, but also the "pre-modern" state of the islanders. This was a community "practically untouched by modern influences" (Flower 1978 [1937], vii). Like Native Americans (see Chap. 5), their implied inability to grapple with the modern world would result in their extinction. The book was describing a "vanishing mode of life" and was penned "by one who has known no other." A reader could easily get the impression that the islanders had failed to progress with modernity. They were still living in a time-warp. They had not made any progress since the time of Homer. Thomson (1988, 56) made a comparison between the circumstances in which the minstrels wrote the epic tales and that of the literature that emerged from the Blasket islands.

The harsh physical landscape in part hastened the extinction of the local population, this "small population of fishermen of comparatively recent mainland origin, who support themselves precariously by fishing and on the produce of their fields and flocks" (Flower 1978 [1937], vii). Life on the island was not easy, "and their faculties are the keener for that" (Flower 1978 [1937], viii). Bannister and Sowby in their introduction also focus on the poverty of the people. They note, "it was only the odd shipwreck or the arrival of a shoal of porpoises that saved them from starvation and gave them a reasonably comfortable life" (Bannister and Sowby 2012, xvii).

### Place-Names

Not only are the people and their landscape in danger, the colonial era had led to the displacement of original Irish place-names. In both English translations, the Blasket place-names are given in English. The Flower edition begins with a map of the Blasket Islands, which has all the place-names such as Ballyferriter, Ventry or Dunquin, in English. These would have been known to locals as Baile an Fheirtéaraigh, Ceanntrá or Dún Chaoin. There is no map in the second English edition, but Bannister and Sowby do refer to the challenge of place-names. They note that, with a few exceptions, they have given the English for place-names and for people. They have also done this for some of the local place-names that have ceased to exist on modern maps (2012, xxii).

Mapping in a postcolonial context is a complex issue. As Hannerz (2016, 49) notes: "Worlds can be made in texts, and worlds are also made on maps." There is a strong attachment to land in Ireland, which is probably a consequence of the colonial era, when many Irish were dispossessed of their land (see Wulff 2017). The Anglicisation of Irish place-names is a cultural practice that was carried out by the British soldiers in the nineteenth century when an ordnance survey was conducted in the island of Ireland, aimed to produce new (six inches to the mile) maps of the island for the British Crown (Nic Craith 2002). Re-naming of places in the language of the coloniser occurred in many colonised countries worldwide. Spivak cites the example of a nineteenth-century British soldier travelling across India. On his journey, he surveys the land, which is now under British imperial rule. The process involves more than the translation of words and names. The British soldier is actually consolidating British rule by obliging the native inhabitants to disconnect from the local place-name. It is now the British place-name that describes their home ground. "He [the soldier] is worlding their own world, which is far from mere uninscribed earth, anew, by obliging them to domesticate the alien as Master" (Spivak 1984, 253).

The Anglicisation of places has consequences that go beyond the name of the place. It often ruptures the reservoir of local folklore that is associated with a particular name by a local community. This theme was captured in Brian Friel's play *Translations*, which was first performed in 1980 in the Guild Hall at Derry/Londonderry (Friel 1984, see Nic Craith 2002). This play is set in the Northwest of Ireland at the beginning of the nineteenth century and explores the Ordnance Survey process. One of the strong implications of the play is that the Anglicisation of place-names has resulted in the severing of the connection between place and memory. This is evident in the character of Manus taunting his father with the question whether he would able to find his way—the implication being that "when the place-names have been changed from Irish to English, the landscape will take on different contours and life itself will change." The father must respond to this with "a new identity of man-in-the-landscape" (Pine 1999 [1990], 212).

It is ironic that the translation of *An tOileánach* may have been a key feature on its journey towards an international audience. The newly established Irish state focused its efforts on the expansion and consolidation of publications in the Irish language and what Anderson (1991 [1983]) has called a "print-community." The development of a truly Gaelic literature had been a priority for the newly established Irish state. An Seabhac urged his contemporary Irish-language writers to follow the examples of stories that: "Gaels created out of their own spirit when they had no knowledge of or contact with any storytelling but their own" (cited in O'Leary 1994, 36).

*An tOileánach* was a major contribution to the development of a modern Irish literary tradition. The book was of such importance that it was placed on the curriculum in schools and universities. However, the version Irish school-pupils read was sanitised since An Seabhac had deleted episodes as well as references to emblems such as royalty, which might be considered too Anglophone for Irish schoolchildren (Lucchitti 2009, 129–130). An Seabhac was convinced that the book would become an icon for Irish generations to come (Ó Siochfhradha 1937, 25). The volume would serve as a significant reference point for an Irish-language community and their lifestyle on the verge of extinction on the Western seaboard of Ireland. While the people might disappear, Tomás's memoir would give readers an accurate depiction of the lives of a group of ordinary people: their intellect, their great friendship, their faith, their talents, their faults—their whole way of life. We understand from Ó Coileáin (2002) that An Seabhac's prediction was accurate.

*An tOileánach* became an important dimension of the Irish language as well as of the history of the state. It was from this that generations of schoolchildren were nurtured and came to know a generation of people that had passed away. One question remains. Was it the original Irish-language edition or the English translation that brought this book to the attention of many generations of Irish people? While the Irish-language edition was on the school curriculum, it is likely that the English translation did much more to give visibility to the work of this peasant author among the wider reading public.

CHAPTER 5

# Native American and Indigenous Irish Narratives

Although some readers may be uncomfortable with the concept of Ireland as a colonised nation, Irish history provides ample evidence of the suppression of Irish language and culture and the Anglicisation of the indigenous Irish over a number of centuries, ostensibly to progress the country as a whole towards civilisation (Canny 1988; Nic Craith 1992; see also Chap. 4). Good relations between the indigenous Irish and Native Americans possibly stem from a shared colonised experience—a form of what Luke Gibbons calls "long-distance solidarity" (2008, 200).

Both American Indians and Irish-speaking Gaels attended a system of education which did not use their language and repressed their culture (Akenson 2012 [1970]; Coleman 2007). Native Americans and Irish-speaking peasants were perceived as living in the outpost far from civilised metropolitan areas. Those who subscribe to the diffusionist model of evolution assumed a linear path from the urban core to the rural periphery (see Chap. 1). At some point in the process of evolution, Native Americans and Irish peasants living on the periphery would mimic civilised manners and speech, although they would always be aware of their inability to become fully civilised and remain culturally inferior (Fanon 1967 [1952]). The Irish affiliation with the Native Americans has been expressed poetically. Paul Muldoon (an Irish poet) expressed his preoccupation with Native Americans and their heritage in poems such as "The Indians on Alcatraz" and "The Year of the Sloes" (Muldoon 1973). Ireland's Nobel prize-winning poet Seamus Heaney penned an elegy of Sitting Bull as a symbol of loss and origin, which had a distinct resonance among Irish-speakers in Ireland (Heaney 1990, 76; Cullingford 2001).

In Northern Ireland (a part of Ireland that still remains within the legislative framework of the United Kingdom), there is strong appeal from different parts of the divide to the image of the Native American. When signing his name, the Irish Republican Bobby Sands used to write "Geronimo" (a medicine man 1829–1909 from the Bedonkohe band of the Apache tribe and who was involved in resisting US and Mexican military campaigns against his people) (Geronimo 1996). In Long Kesh (the prison where Irish Republicans were held), there was a mural to Geronimo. This ongoing empathy between Native Americans and the Irish was symbolically captured in 2018 when the contribution of Choctaw people to the starving Irish in the mid-nineteenth century was saluted by the Irish prime minister Leo Varadkar. In 1847, the Choctaw people had sent the equivalent of €4000 to the starving Irish, although they themselves had been forced west of the Mississippi sixteen years earlier (Lynch 2018).

Although there was no direct contact between Blasket Islanders and Native Americans, comparisons have previously been made between memoirs from the Blaskets and those which have emerged from Native Americans. More than twenty years ago, Seán Ó Tuama (1995, 203) wrote: "From the Blasket Islands, in particular, has come a handful of autobiographies which by common European standards are *sui generis*.... The only vaguely comparable series of books known to me is that by Indian chiefs describing their ancestral life before the white man's conquest." This parallel has been further developed in a comparison between Tomás Ó Criomhthain's *An tOileánach* and a memoir entitled *Black Elk Speaks* narrated by an Oglala Lakota *wicasa wakan* or holy man and first published in 1932 (Eastlake 2008).

## BLACK ELK AND TOMÁS Ó CRIOMHTHAIN

There is a solid basis for a comparison between Black Elk and Tomás Ó Criomhthain. Both men grew up within the same time period. Black Elk was born in 1863 (or possibly 1866), while Tomás was born in 1855 (or possibly 1856). Black Elk died in 1950. Tomás passed away in 1937. Both had experiences of "island-ness" in different senses. While Tomás grew up on a physical island, Black Elk's later life was on a reservation—technically not an island but an isolated area with clear boundaries between the Native Americans and the Euro-American population. The Blasket Islanders were often isolated geographically from the mainland, living on an island in a region that was officially designated by the Irish Government as a *Gaeltacht* (see Chap. 4). In a similar manner, Native Americans were isolated physically from the larger society. Their culture was persecuted in the hostile environment. Although *Gaeltacht* and Indian reservations were specially designated areas, none of them had autonomy. Both were governed centrally from a distant metropolitan.

As a member of the Lakota, Black Elk's childhood seems to have been happy, but he had witnessed Lakota resistance against White invaders. While still a relatively young child, Black Elk experienced a vision, which he subsequently shared with John Neihardt. In 1881, Black Elk's status as a holy man was confirmed with the enactment of the Horse Dance ritual, which was the first part of his vision. Although native medicine was officially banned until the American Indian Religious Freedom Act (1978), it is likely that Black Elk practised it in private. However, as a source of income, the official banning of the practice would have impacted economically on the holy man.

In 1887, Black Elk joined Buffalo Bill's Wild West Show, which required that he become an Episcopalian. The show took him to many parts of Europe before he returned to the Pine Ridge Reservation in 1889, where he encountered (and possibly encouraged) the revival of Native American ritual and dance in the form of the Ghost Dance ritual. Black Elk subsequently engaged with efforts to promote Native American culture in a hostile environment. He was present at the 1890 massacre at Wounded Knee and was himself injured while encouraging his people to resist. Subsequently, Black Elk is supposed to have become Catholic (although his form of Catholicism is disputed).

In 1931 (two years after the publication of *An tOileánach*), Black Elk gave an account of his life to John Neihardt. Since the focus in that first memoir was on his life before Black Elk converted to Catholicism, Jesuits on the reservation were not happy with the published volume. When Black Elk was overrun by a wagon a year after the initial publication, he was denied last rites (a Catholic ritual) until a written recantation of the book was delivered. Having survived the accident, Black Elk worked for the Duhamel Sioux Indian Pageant, where he performed rituals for tourists, such as the offering of the pipe at the twice-daily shows. In 1944, Neihardt interviewed Black Elk again at Pine Ridge. In the intervening years, the focus had shifted, and the material covered in this latter collaboration looked at tribal history and memory. *When the Tree Flowered* was the publication that resulted from that collaboration (Neihardt 1991 [1951]). A subsequent book, *The Sacred Pipe*, focused on a Lakota ritual (Back Elk 1953).

Further comparisons can be made between the lives of Black Elk and Tomás. As already noted, both men grew up in societies that had experienced conquest. In the case of Ireland, the late twelfth-century Norman invasion marked the beginning of more than 800 years of direct English rule, which lasted until 1922 when Ireland was partitioned, and the South of Ireland became an independent state from Britain (Beckett 1966; Moody and Martin 1967). Porter (2008) suggests that the experience of English colonists in Ireland informed the Spanish subjugation of the Americas. Porter further proposes (2008, 64) that: "Cromwell's approach to Irish subjugation had clear links with Spanish practices and he sold many Irish people into West Indian slavery." This comparison is also endorsed by Nicholas Canny (1988) who argues that Ireland was an experiment for the colonisation of North America.

A common feature between Tomás and Black Elk is the denial of individuality to both authors. Instead, the documents produced by both Black Elk and Tomás were seen as representative of their communities (see Chap. 3). However, as Tom Farrington noted in an interview with me in November 2017: "Tribal politics are much more nuanced than any one person can describe." By implying that the memoirs were social documents—or even that their authors were representative of their respective communities (see Chap. 3)—critics were reducing diverse groups of people into homogeneous entities, with little or no divergence between generations, genders or roles in society. This lack of diversity enabled the "freezing" of a community at a particular moment in time, which facilitated their political usage in both circumstances.

In the case of Black Elk, Powers (1987) argues that the memoir cannot be representative of Native Americans, since it is a literary rather than an oral text. (The same argument could be made in relation to *An tOileánach*). Powers suggests: "that the act of raising one medicine man over another has been traditionally regarded as heretical among native Lakota" (1987, 1). It is also the case that Blasket Island was not a socially stratified society. Apart from the island king, there was little differentiation between the islanders materially, economically or socially. In a world where there was a strong emphasis on community, the production of a memoir, which highlighted the achievements of a particular individual, ran counter to the norm.

Eakin (1985, xvi–xvii) argues that the concept of autobiography is very much a product of European civilisation, with its emphasis on individuality and egocentricity. In the case of both the Lakota people and the Blasket Islanders, the emphasis on individuality that is required for the production of a memoir was contrary to the traditional emphasis on community. "Homologous with the bourgeois conceptualization of an opposition between the individual and society appears the corollary opposition between individual (private) and collective (public) production and composition. Individual composition means written composition, for only texts can have individual authors" (Krupat 1989, 10).

Technically, Tomás and Black Elk had emerged from cultures that were primarily oral—or at least they were portrayed as such. Their orality was regarded as evidence of their lack of progress towards civilisation. And yet, as noted in chapter 2, Jack Goody (2008, 27) queries the boundaries between oral and literate cultures. He asks: "At what point in the formalisation of pictographs or other graphic signs can we talk of "letters" or "literacy"? And what proportion of the society has to write and read before the culture as a whole can be described as literate?"

Moreover, the notion that these societies were entirely oral is not true. The Irish language had its Ogham alphabet, which may have been used as early as the first century AD (Carney 1975). Writing in Irish had declined during Ireland's period of colonisation. Although the Blasket Island is regarded as having been an oral society, the island had a primary school from 1864, which the islanders regularly attended and learned to read and write in English (Nic Craith 1995). It is also the case that some Native Americans had their own script. The Cherokee tribe had their own syllabary (created by Sequoyah) long before they learned to read and write in English (Carroll 2015).

Black Elk and Tomás are portrayed as rather passive creatures who were fortunately found by their mentors/collaborators. Just as Robin Flower and Brian Ó Ceallaigh were guided towards Tomás Ó Criomhthain, the poet and semi-anthropologist John G. Neihardt was directed towards Black Elk in August 1930. At the time, Neihardt was working on a narrative poem entitled, "The Song of the Messiah," which was to form the final religious poem in his Cycle of the West. Neihardt and his son Sigurd travelled to Pine Ridge Reservation in order to find a medicine man who had been active in the Messiah movement. Neihardt went to W.B. Courtright, the Field Agent-in-Charge at Pine Ridge Agency, who pointed him towards the old Sioux holy man (Black Elk) who lived in the hills some twenty miles east.

As with Robin Flower and Tomás, Neihardt spent time each day with Black Elk, but their time must have been very intense. They began soon after breakfast and often continued until late in the evening. Occasionally, when Black Elk became tired, he would halt the conversation, lie down and fall asleep. The book that was published as a result of these encounters was entitled *Black Elk Speaks 1* and was first published in 1932 by the University of Nebraska Press. Tomás's book *An tOileánach* had been published three years earlier in 1929.

Although the two authors found themselves in remarkably similar circumstances, there were also many differences between Tomás and Black Elk. The most notable is that Black Elk was illiterate, whereas Tomás had reading and writing skills in two languages (English and Irish). More significantly, Black Elk did not speak the language of his editor (i.e. English), whereas Tomás penned his story in his own native tongue. This was subsequently translated into English. Their knowledge of the wider world was also quite different. Although a regular visitor to the mainland, Tomás had never travelled beyond the local Dunquin community. In contrast, Black Elk had considerable first-hand experience of the wider world—having travelled in 1887–1888 to perform with the "Wild West" in London, Birmingham and Manchester. His performances with "Mexican Joe" took place in England, Paris, Belgium and Italy.

Both Tomás and Black Elk belonged to societies that were regarded as primitive or even backward by outsiders. It was this very "backwardness" that appealed to scholars and academics who encouraged Tomás and Black Elk to narrate their stories for a wider audience. While Black Elk's narrative was not an instant success, both life-stories gained the respect of notable academics and scholars on an international scale (Wilson Foster 1987). *An tOileánach* gained iconic status over time and is regarded as representing a truly Gaelic Ireland. *Black Elk Speaks* has been selected as one of the top ten spiritual books of the twentieth century. Both books have been translated into numerous languages. The authors could have anticipated neither the success of their stories nor indeed the influence of these narratives.

## TAPESTRY OF VOICES

The compilation of Black Elk's narrative was clearly a collaborative effort (Velie 2004). For the original encounter, Neihardt travelled with his son to Black Elk, taking an interpreter (Flying Hawk) with him. In the preface to the 1932 edition, Neihardt describes their initial encounter: "The first time I went out to talk to Black Elk about the Oglala Sioux, I found him sitting alone under a shelter of pine boughs near his log cabin that stands on a barren hill about two miles west of Manderson Post Office" (Black Elk 2000 [1932], xix).

It appears that the editor and author were comfortable with one another's company from the beginning. Black Elk noted at their initial encounter: "As I sit here, I can feel in this man beside me a strong desire to know the things of the Other World. He has been sent to learn what I know, and I will teach him" (Black Elk 2000 [1932], xxv). (Note the agency in Black Elk's voice). Of course, these words were spoken in Lakota and interpreted by Flying Hawk. From Neihardt's perspective, he had met a genuine, practising holy man. "He seemed even then to represent the consciousness of the Plains Indian more fully than any other I had ever known" (Black Elk 2000 [1932], xx). Black Elk's regard for Neihardt was such that he arranged for his adoption and that of Neihardt's two daughters into the Lakota tribe (Velie 2004).

Black Elk narrated his story in Lakota. This was then translated into English by his son Ben. Neihardt's daughter Enid (a stenographer) recorded the conversation and subsequently typed them up as transcripts. Neihardt reworked the transcriptions, edited the volume and put a preface and a postscript with the first publication that was issued in 1932. In a sense, most memoirs are a collaborative exercise involving an editor and an author, but in the case of *Black Elk Speaks*, the range of people involved in the process was considerable—as it became clear in the following excerpt from Neihardt's acknowledgements in the first edition:

> I am especially indebted to Benjamin, son of Black Elk, for his painstaking and efficient service as my interpreter through many days, and to my daughter, Enid, for the voluminous stenographic record of the conversations out of which this book has been wrought as a labor of love. Government officials were generous in helping me, and I have good reason to be grateful to Secretary of the Interior, Ray Lyman Wilbur; Malcolm McDowell, Secretary of the Board of Indian Commissioners; Flora Warren Seymour, a member of the Board; and to B. G. [W. B.] Courtright, Field Agent in Charge at Pine Ridge. (Black Elk 2000 [1932], xxii)

Over the following winter, Neihardt maintained communication with Black Elk. Arrangements were made for a return extended visit. In May 1931, Neihardt came back with his two daughters Enid and Hilda. The interpreter on this occasion was Black Elk's son Ben, who had some knowledge of English since he had attended Carlisle Indian school. Neihardt's mission was different now. In the preface to the 1961 edition, he notes: "I returned to Black Elk's home that he might relate his life-story to me in fulfilment of a duty that he felt incumbent upon him" (Black Elk 2000 [1932], xxv).

This collaborative process has been identified as commonplace in Native American autobiography (Krupat 1989, 30). Eastlake (2009b, 242–43) suggests that what characterises such autobiographies is the "process of production" rather than the end product. Three roles (which may involve numerous individuals) are usually involved in such narratives (Eastlake 2009a, 126). The core role is that of the "native"—that is, the individual who narrates his or her story. The editor (often also the instigator) collaborates with the narrator to structure the text. There is also a translator whose role may vary depending on the circumstances. S/he may mediate between the native and the editor or between the reader and the text. The translator may be engaged in translating the text from a "minority" to a globally read language. All roles are fluid and: "The interaction of these roles during the process of producing a collaborative text is what distinguishes native autobiography from other acts of self-representation" (Eastlake 2009a, 126).

There was a similar process of collaboration in the production of *An tOileánach*. Tomás Ó Criomhthain provided the core life-story in the form of a series of letters over a number of years. While Brian Ó Ceallaigh was initially involved in the role of editor, An Seabhac (the Hawk) completed the task for that first edition. Robin Flower did the initial translation into English—although unlike Black Elk's case, the translation occurred sequentially, after the initial publication of the original Irish language volume. Flower was a friend of Tomás's and had actively encouraged Tomás's literary skills in Irish. Flower's translation into English served as the basis for a number of further translations into other European languages (see Chap. 6). Since then, there have been further editions of *An tOileánach* in both Irish and English (see Chap. 2).

When it was first published, *Black Elk Speaks* did not receive a good reception from the general public and was soon "remaindered." No one could have anticipated the subsequent success of the book when, forty years later, it came to the attention of a number of German scholars, including Carl Jung, who were keenly interested in the visionary experiences described within the text and called for its translation into German. Before long, there was a new demand for the volume which was reissued (in English) in 1961 and immediately became a favourite among young people. A television interview with Dick Cavett in 1971 further popularised *Black Elk Speaks*, which was already being translated into a number of European languages. A new Bison edition with a foreword by Vine Deloria Jr. was issued in 1979.

The book has since had multiple incarnations including a new ("premier") edition *Black Elk Speaks* [II], issued by the State University of New York Press in 2008. That edition featured a preface by anthropologist Raymond DeMallie. *Black Elk Speaks* [III] was published by the University of Nebraska Press, while the "complete" edition (*Black Elk Speaks* IV) was published in 2014. As well as multiple paper editions, the book has also been adapted into a play, which was performed in the Folger Theatre in Washington, DC, in the 1970s and subsequently taken on national tour in 1978. A revised version of the play by Christopher Sergel was restaged in 1992 (Sergel 1996). Like *An tOileánach*, the book continues to sell today in many languages.

Although both memoirs emerged from a collaborative process, there are clear differences between the two. Black Elk narrated his story orally, whereas Tomás wrote his memoir with a pen. Black Elk's narrative was translated instantly, whereas Tomás's memoir was published firstly in his native tongue and subsequently translated into English. Black Elk was not in a position to read the publication, whereas presumably Tomás did. Despite these differences, there is some merit in exploring the process of production that occurred in both instances. "While the Blasket autobiographies might be read strictly in relation to the conventions of Western literary autobiography, a reading that is based on careful attention to the process of production offers greater insight into these texts" (Eastlake 2009a, 126). Eastlake used a model which he calls "native autobiography" as a framework for interpreting these texts. It is a framework which does not seek to reconstruct the original "*ur*-text" but instead takes an approach which acknowledges the variety of individuals in the co-production of the narrative (Eastlake 2009b, 242).

A particular feature of Indian autobiography (which may distinguish it from some other forms of native autobiography) is its bicultural dimension. (The process with Tomás was similar since Robin Flower was British). Paul John Eakin argues that given the co-operation between an Indian personality, a translator and a white editor, a defining feature of such books is their "original bicultural composite composition" (Eakin 1985, xvii). Given that the collaboration is between individuals from very different cultural perspectives, the partnership involves drawing from different cultural conventions (Brumble 1988). The Lakota people did not have a tradition of writing down their memoirs. It was only by combining with an individual from a written tradition, that the final memoir was achieved.

But there was a price to be paid for this engagement: "Only by submitting to the Euro-American form of autobiography could Black Hawk speak to the whites at all; only by accepting the graphematic supplement of the editor and the fall into writing and culture could Black Hawk achieve the book of his life, whose final form was not his to determine" (Krupat 1989, 52). In consequence, it is not always easy to discern whose voice we are hearing. Deloria (2000 [1979], xvi) says: "It is, admittedly, difficult to discover if we are talking with Black Elk or John Neihardt, whether the vision is to be interpreted differently, and whether or not the positive emphasis which the book projects is not the optimism of two poets lost in the modern world and transforming drabness into an idealized world."

The more voices involved in the collaboration, the more likely it is that the final product is at variance from the original words spoken. De Mallie (1984, 32) suggests that the first distortion occurred with Ben Black Elk's translation of his father's words. Then the shorthand notes were typed up into longhand by Neihardt's daughter, Enid. The text was then "polished" by Neihardt himself. Moreover, Neihardt demoted certain aspects of Black Elk's life (such as his conversion to Catholicism) in order to emphasise the authentic "Indian-ness" of his informant. Velie (2004) argues that Black Elk was betraying his ancestors by converting to Catholicism. From Neihardt's perspective, Black Elk already had a "perfectly good culture and perfectly good religion" (Velie 2004).

Both memoirs were pioneering efforts and the parallels with Tomás Ó Criomhthain are clear—although less drastic. Tomás was steeped in a rich oral culture that had no tradition of writing down life-stories. It was only when he came in contact with "outsiders"—people from the Irish mainland and further afield, that a written memoir was accomplished. What marked these memoirs as special was the voice of the insider. However, in the case of Tomás, it was assumed that the published text reflected his voice and there was no acknowledgement of the role of editor/translator in the shaping of that voice. Ó Tuama (1995, 203) notes:

> Books have frequently been written about isolated communities – generally, however, by people on the outside, or by members of the community who became writers and were not bound by the daily routine of life in their

communities. These Blasket books to which I am referring, however, have been written/dictated by serving members of this highly-cultured but non-literate community. Everything in this is reported from the inside, with very little reference to outside standards of living, of belief, or of writing.

In both instances, the meeting with the editors was presented as serendipitous rather than planned. Neihardt went to the Lakota people to further his research on the Messianic movement. He was specifically looking for Lakota individuals who had engaged with ghost dances in the 1880s after the "legal" suppression of expressions of Indian identity. Neihardt was directed towards Black Elk who was regarded as a holy man. Their encounter changed the nature of Neihardt's ambition. Both Robin Flower and Brian Ó Ceallaigh came to the Great Blasket Island to learn Irish for their own career advancement. While there, they were guided towards Tomás, a brother-in-law of the island king and an islander with literary skills (see Chap. 1). Prior to these encounters, neither Tomás nor Black Elk had any ambition to pen their life-stories. There was no particular reason that they should do so. Brandes (1982, 188–89) suggests that in many instances, the author of such autobiographies is just, "an ordinary member of his or her society, whose individual achievements are not noteworthy in and of themselves."

However, all of this raises questions regarding the authenticity of the final text. To what extent are such texts representative of particular worldviews or are they simply a concoction or a mishmash that has resulted from extensive collaborations? In the case of *Black Elk Speaks*, many scholars and Native Americans regard the text as truly representative of the Siouan worldview, while others see it as creative fiction that has resulted from the collaborative efforts of Black Elk, Neihardt and others (cf. Arnold 1999). The editorial interventions had many implications for the final narrative that emerged. As Farrington notes:

> When you've got that many people between the original voice and the printed version you have to take that into account – then it's almost inevitably been filtered through the perspectives of those people involved. It's almost impossible to maintain objectivity at each stage of the process as each individual had his own purpose, and how much they aligned with one another is interesting to critique and ask: Are there "spaces" between their objectives? How was that stretched from one purpose to another during the process? What was added along the way? (Farrington interview, November 2017)

Whatever, the pros and cons of the argument, it is clear that the case is complex and involves a number of voices which are "entangled." This is not necessarily a negative issue. Arnold (1999) argues that instead of concerning ourselves with this question of voice and who is speaking in the narratives, critics should really focus on how Black Elk grapples with textual narrative, given that he has emerged from a world that has been dominated by the oral tradition. Despite the complexity of the process, some statements/sentiments are clearly associated with particular authors. Tomás and Black Elk are no exceptions.

## The Vanishing Native Trope

Perhaps the most quoted phrase from Tomás Ó Criomhthain's memoir is *"mar ná beidh ár leithéidí arís ann"* (Ó Criomhthain 2002, 328) (our likes will never be here again) in O'Crohan (2012, 298). The phrase has become symbolic of a way of life that has disappeared, since the Blasket Islands were evacuated in 1953. This sentiment is also echoed in *Black Elk Speaks* at various points through the text. At the beginning of the volume we are told that: "The sun was near to setting when Black Elk said: 'There is so much to teach you. What I know was given to me for men and it is true, and it is beautiful. Soon I shall be under the grass and it will be lost. You were sent to save it, and you must come back so that I can teach you'."

Black Elk's text ends on a similar vein. Speaking about the massacre at Wounded Knee, he notes:

> And so it was all over.
> I did not know then how much was ended. When I look back now from this high hill of my old age, I can still see the butchered women and children lying heaped and scattered all along the crooked gulch as plain as when I saw them with eyes still young. And I can see that something else was buried in the blizzard. A people's dream died there. It was a beautiful dream. (Black Elk 2000 [1932], 207)

And it was not just the community's dream that had ended. There was also a personal sense of disappointment:

> And I, to whom so great a vision was given in my youth, – you see me now a pitiful old man who has done nothing, for the nation's hoop is broken and scattered. There is no centre any longer, and the sacred tree is dead. (Black Elk 2000 [1932], 207)

This message is hardly unique to Tomás Ó Criomhthain or Black Elk. Indeed, it features in a number of Native American memoirs. In his memoir, Crashing Thunder (1983 [1926], 203) says, "I thought I would write down and tell you all these things so that those who came after me would not be deceived." From these statements, readers might infer that the authors were aware of an impending ending. Wilson Foster (1987, 335–36) suggests: "both infused their recollections with a personal and cultural sense of an ending. Both were convinced that the past was superior to the present, a conviction that was more justified in the case of Black Elk whose people, the Oglala Sioux, faced not merely change but extinction. Although the Blasket Islanders too ceased to be."

This theme commonly referred to as the "vanishing native trope" had become commonplace by the mid-eighteenth century and had a focus on characters who were perceived to be the remnants or the last of their race (Stafford 1994). It was reinforced by the well-known photographer Edward Curtis with his famous picture of the Navajo people riding away from the camera. Curtis entitled this 1904 portrait "The Vanishing Race" (Curtis et al. 2000 [1976]). The trope appears uncomplicated in both Black Elk Speaks and An tOileánach, since these communities were well on the road to depredation. These men had few resources, but the production of a memoir allowed them to exploit one of the few resources they maintained control over—that is, their oral tradition and gain access to the wider world though the printing press.

However, in both instances, the issue is more complex than initially appears and the hint of a "vanishing race" may have had more to do with the editors of these books and the context in which they were initially published. At the time when Neihardt and Brown first met with Black Elk there was strong anticipation in Euro-American discourse that people such as the Native Americans and Indigenous Irish-speaking islanders were doomed to extinction. With the same perspective as the salvage anthropologists (see Chap. 1), Black Elk's editors sought to capture a vanishing lifestyle for the benefit of audiences that were primarily European and American.

There was also a political intention behind the vanishing race trope, which may not have been entirely explicit at the time. As noted in the first chapter, the vanishing race trope began with a desire to record a particular lifestyle for the benefit of humanity. However, as the process continued, it came to serve a particular political purpose. Farrington notes:

In the initial stages there were probably honourable purposes among people who were writing the Native American memoirs – but the promotion, dissemination and editing of this information very quickly becomes part of the erasure of native peoples from the colonial imagination. They needed to vanish, to be separate from modernity. They were the antithesis of modernity – to be placed in opposition to modernity in order to legitimise the land grab. The inevitability of erasure feeds into the narrative of manifest destiny which was not apparent in the Irish context. The Native American was being honoured at the same time that his land was being appropriated. (Interview with Farrington, November 2017)

Farrington emphasises the political perspective in the context of a settler-colonial mentality. He notes:

It's very clear why people were suddenly very interested in Native American literature – in talking to Native Americans and establishing that they were a vanishing race. There was a political point which established that which had gone before, and that which needed to be eradicated to make way for progress. This satisfied the settler-colonial mentality of the United States which was appropriating vast swathes of land from the Native Americans. It justified that land grab as the "race" no longer needed them. It had vanished. (Interview with Farrington, November 2017)

There is a sense in which the vanishing native trope was actually comforting for readers as it absolved them from making any efforts on behalf of the "native" who, more than likely, had already succumbed to his fate (Eastlake 2008, 283).

### Invention of Tradition

Although both books are most remembered for these final statements, it appears (controversially) that neither Black Elk nor Tomás had originally included these statements in their original narratives. Ó Criomhthain's memoir had originally concluded on a much more positive note. Tomás had linked this own survival with that of the Irish language, which was harnessing a new energy at that point in time. The Irish language had economic viability. Tomás wrote:

I've been involved with this language for twenty-seven years, and I suppose about twenty years writing it. And, as I've already mentioned, it's seventeen years since the Scandinavian came to visit me. .... I've heard many gasbags saying that you won't make money out of the native language, but I don't agree, because I'd be depending on handouts if it weren't for the language. (O'Crohan 2012, 294)

The new ending was written at the request of An Seabhac, who looked for something more conclusive. It was in response to this request that the new final paragraph "of doom" was written. It reads:

> I wrote in detail about a lot of all our goings-on so that there'd be some recollection somewhere about them, and I have tried to describe the character of the people who were around me so that there might be an account of them after we're gone, because our likes will never be here again. (O'Crohan 2012, 298)

Circumstances in the Black Elk volume were remarkably similar. In the original narrative, Black Elk concludes with his marriage. After the surrender of the Sioux tribe to the American Calvary, the Indians marched into Pine Ridge. Two years later, Black Elk was married. Most critics agree that the most quoted statement of "despair" from Black Elk was in fact never delivered by him. Instead, it appears that the infamous excerpt was composed by John Neihardt as a more suitable conclusion.

Velie (2004) suggests that Neihardt saw Black Elk as a symbol of defeat and the end of a race that was doomed to extinction. For this reason, he invented a speech that he felt might well have been uttered by Black Elk himself. Neihardt would not have regarded this as invention, since, Neihardt felt, it reflected Black Elk's perspective. Neihardt himself explains in the introduction to the 1972 edition that it was not the facts of the story that mattered to him. As an editor, he felt obliged to recreate the mood of the narration. This was often a difficult task. "Always I felt it a sacred obligation to be true to the old man's meaning and manner of expression" (Black Elk 2000 [1932]).

In the context in which Neihardt edited the volume, there was an appreciation that Western civilisation had impacted negatively on Native American culture, but there was also the view that this progression was inevitable. The laws of nature would ultimately determine the extinction of Native Americans. Neihardt possibly viewed the conflict in Homeric terms and had the utmost respect and sympathy for the Native Americans, who had a lot to teach modern society. "Life has been differently and admirably lived by great numbers of men and women who preceded us on this continent, and [...], in some very important respects their lives may have been saner, happier, nearer to the great realities than ours can be in the complex world that we have created with, perhaps somewhat more ingenuity than wisdom" (Neihardt 2002, 30). Neihardt's sense of alliance with the Native Americans was not that far removed from Robin Flower's relationship with Tomás in particular and the islanders more generally. Flower had the utmost respect for the way of life on the Gaelic island and would have wished it to continue unchanged.

## A Changed Context

However, the sense of doom perceived by both Neihardt and Flower has hardly been borne out by the subsequent publications of both books. By the time of the 1971 edition of *Black Elk Speaks*, American perspectives on Native Americans had begun to change. In a speech to Congress in March 1968, President Johnson sought legislation which would enable: "The Forgotten American" to pursue Indian self-determination. Native peoples themselves endeavoured to raise their own profile on a national front through the occupation of Alcatraz Island (1969), The Trail of Broken Treaties march to Washington (1972) and the armed standoff at the Wounded Knee (1973) (Stover 2000, 135).

This changed context inevitably impacted on the way the book was received, as it was becoming clear that the "vanishing native" was still alive and "Black Elk, formerly an obscure figure swiftly became European America's archetypal Indian" (Stover 2000, 137). Various critics responded to this retelling of Black Elk's narrative, calling the Holy Man "a new cultural hero" (Sayre 1971, 510) a "mystic" (McCluskey 1972, 234). A response from the Native American, Scott Momaday (1984, 36–7) focused on "the masterpiece of transformation of the oral tradition from one language and culture to another without the loss of the essential spirit of the original narrative."

Changes also occurred in the way the Tomás's memoir was received in Ireland. When the original edition of *An tOileánach* was published, Ireland was still part of the Commonwealth headed by the monarchy. The British Queen was head of state and the British navy had ships all around the island in the major and minor ports. The works of Arensberg and Kimball (see Chap. 1) had not yet been published. When the second edition of *An tOileánach* was published in 1973, there were many changes in Ireland which would have shaped a different response. The Irish state has its own president. Ireland had reasserted its status as a republic and had exited the Commonwealth. Ireland has suffered mass emigration in the 1940s and 1950s. The country had joined the European Union. Irish musicians such as the Dubliners and the Clancy Brothers have become an international phenomenon—thereby projecting an inter-generational Irish stereotype. The Irish language had acquired official status. Heinrich Böll had visited Ireland (see Chap. 6). One of the Blasket memoirs, *Peig*, was compulsory for Irish language learners at second level and most significantly, the Blasket Island had been evacuated—which to many minds would have confirmed Tomás's prediction. The parody of *An Béal Bocht* highlighted the idiosyncrasies associated with the original publication but also the high esteem in which the Irish language was held nationally and internationally (Nic Craith and Kockel 2018). Circumstances were different north of the Irish Border. It was the height of what was commonly known as "the Troubles" (Nic Craith 2002, 2003). There was direct rule from Westminster.

Within a decade, the perspective on Black Elk's narrative was changing. Stover (2000, 140) locates the third retelling of Black Elk in 1984 with the publication of De Mallie's edition of the *Sixth Grandfather*. This third retelling highlighted some elements that had been left out of *Black Elk Speaks* and elevated the status of the holy man to teacher or intellectual. De Mallie (1984) created, "an image of the Indian intellectual as a sort of teacher-archivist carrying around his trove of teachings that he is relieved to unload on Neihardt" (Stover 2000, 141).

A postcolonial reading of both texts suggests an active rather than a passive perspective. While previously it was assumed that both men were prophesying the end of their people. (Neihardt gives the title "the end of the dream" to the final chapter) perhaps it was the way of life at a particular point in time, rather than the people themselves that were doomed to extinction. Perhaps the communal spirit of living was extinguished as Western civilisation expanded. Tomás lamented the physical hardship of living on the Blasket Island that ultimately led to its evacuation. Although not living on a physical island, the Oglala Sioux were confined to virtual "little islands," which would inevitably destroy their cultural confidence and lead to a new lifestyle.

Both Tomás and Black Elk appropriated a "textual space" which would ensure the survival of their people—in memory if not in reality (Eastlake 2008, 284). As representatives of marginal peoples, both authors had made space for Lakota and Irish-speaking cultures in a global world. Both men were displaying a resilience that is sometimes "hidden" by the prophecy of doom. This is reminiscent of Lear's argument in *Radical Hope* (2006). Early in the volume, Lear introduces the reader to a Crow Chief named Plenty Coups. When speaking with Frank Linderman, Crow makes a comment that is similar in tone to those of Black Elk and Tomás Ó Criomhthain. He says: "But when the buffalo went away the hearts of my people fell to the ground, and they could not lift them up again. After this nothing happened" (Lear 2006, 2). Lear emphasises the phrase "After this nothing happened." Rather than interpreting this as an acceptance of defeat, however, Lear turns to Aristotle's five criteria for virtue and uses these as the basis for transforming the statement of doom into one of radical hope. Lear opens the possibility that the Native American was looking to the transformation rather than the destruction of the Indian way of life and was expressing a communal anxiety about the future of their traditions rather than a certainty of hopelessness.

With reference to a hero from Irish folklore, Eastlake (2008, 287) describes Black Elk and Tomás as Ossian-like figures. Their narrative strongly emanates from a sense of decline and loss—and yet the context in which they lived is still alive through the efforts of these authors. "So, while it appears that Black Elk makes no explicit demands of his reader, the text does argue that the Lakota are fully human, have a sophisticated culture, and deserve the reader's respect and/attention. In this sense, the text asks quite a lot of the reader, depending on their various perspective and assumptions" (Eastlake 2008, 284).

Tomás remarks that as the first author in a literary heritage chain that emerged from the Great Blasket Island, he had triumphed in conveying his culture to the rest of the world. He writes: "Since the first fire was lit on this Island, no one has written about their life here. I'm proud to be the one who did it. This book will tell how the Islanders got on in the old times" (O'Crohan 2012, 298–9). Despite the collaborative process, readers of either of these memoirs need to appreciate the agency of the authors in claiming a new textual space for their people. "The last of the race trope is not all decline and melancholy but is transformed into a triumph for the individual" (Eastlake 2008, 287).

The title of this chapter "Native Autobiography" refers to Eastlake's (2008) definition of the memoir in which the "native" is persuaded to speak. "This is in contrast with Robin Crusoe where Man Friday is never given voice" (Eastlake 2008, 34–5). Ironically, Black Elk's story is one in which that native has been persuaded to speak, but we are not sure whose voice we are hearing. The situation is clearer in the case of Tomás Ó Criomhthain, who penned his own story—and yet his voice has also been heavily edited. It is only in the final edition (O'Crohan 2012), that we get to hear Tomás's own voice—a voice that proved incredibly timely for a postcolonial state that was emerging from under the shadow of Britain.

CHAPTER 6

# A Continental Epic

When penning the original letters in which he described his life story to
Brian Ó Ceallaigh, Tomás could hardly have anticipated that his memoir
would be translated into several European languages. The range of translations illustrates a fascination with an island lifestyle with which many
continentals would empathise: "From Homer's *Odyssey* to Augustine's
*Confessions* to Shakespeare's *The Tempest*, from Defoe's *Robinson Crusoe*
to Golding's *The Lord of the Flies*, islands have served as archetypes of good
and evil, dream and nightmare, despair and fulfillment" (Lowenthal
2007, 202).

## THE EUROPEAN JOURNEY

The first continental translation of *An tOileánach* emerged in Sweden in
1949 (O'Crohan 1949). Retitled *Karg Kust* (Barren Coast), *An tOileánach* was translated by a professional Swedish Translator, Margot Margareta
Ångström (née Bergman-Olsson), who was born in 1899 and died in 1969.
*An tOileánach* was but one of many books translated by Ångström. In total
she translated almost 40 books, including volumes by Charles Dickens,
Daphne Du Maurier, William Thackerary and Anthony Trollope. Ångström
has no personal connections with Ireland, but her interest in *An tOileánach*
may have been inspired by a friendship with the author Harrie Hjorth
Wetterström. In 1947, Hjorth published the travel book *Irlandskust* (Irish
coasts), which contained a chapter on the Blaskets, which she had visited,



© The Author(s) 2020
M. Nic Craith, *The Vanishing World of* The Islandman,
Palgrave Studies in Literary Anthropology,
https://doi.org/10.1007/978-3-030-25775-0_6

and Crohan's book. Hjorth had previously received a grant to study Irish traditional folk life. Séamus Delargy had helped her organise her field trip to Ireland in 1946, and her mentor was the Swedish ethnologist/folklorist Albert Eskeröd, who wrote a foreword to the first edition of her book. Hjorth continued to publish books on islands from other corners of the world.

The French translation of *An tOileánach* was a collaborative venture between the Swiss-born Jean Buhler (1919–2017) and an Irish colleague, Úna Murphy (O'Crohan 1989). In the preface to the translation, Jean Buhler explains that he was inspired to undertake the translation in 1949 when working on an Icelandic trawler. Already familiar with island communities, he had brought *An tOileánach* (in English translation) with him on the fishing expedition. For him, the book was such an inspiring read, he felt that it should be translated into French. In the preface, he notes:

> I had boarded a small Icelandic trawler in Reykjavík and furnished myself with several works to read from my position between two loads of cod flung on board our fleet at the previous beach. From the very first lines, Tomás O'Crohan's story spoke to me in the same language that accompanied our work ploughing the depths of the ocean, suiting the camaraderie of this joint enterprise. My reading progressed as the holds of the Jón Thorlaksson filled up; when I saw my comrades falling asleep with tiredness, their noses in their bilberry stew, I heard the voice of old O'Crohan, promising a sort of revenge. (Translation from Buhler 1989, 7)

Buhler's translation was a collaborative effort with Úna Murphy, whom he met in Rome, and together they began what he describes as an "epic struggle" or "close combat" to translate *An tOileánach* into French.

Given his life-history, it is hardly surprising that Jean Buhler was fascinated with *An tOileánach*. A writer and journalist, Buhler had travelled widely around the world. His travels had inspired many publications, including *Sur les routes d'Europe* (On the Roads of Europe) as well *as Prends ma vie camarade* (Take My Life Comrade). Subsequent travels took him to Africa and South America. The Blasket Island off the west coast of Ireland would inevitably appeal to an avid explorer like Buhler. The first edition of *L'homme des Îles* was published by Favre in Lausanne. The book sold well, but the publishing house collapsed. The second and third editions (1994, 2003) were subsequently published by Payot &

Rivages, Paris. Since then, a number of further editions have been published.

When the German edition of *An tOileánach* was published, the title of the book was changed, and it now read *Die Boote fahren nicht mehr aus* (The Boats No Longer Set to Sea) (O'Crohan 1983). A subtitle reflecting the original title was added: *Bericht eines irischen Fischers* (An Irish fisherman's account). The translation was a collaborative effort between the renowned Heinrich Böll and his wife Anna-Marie. Indeed, it is more likely that the primary translation was completed by Anna-Marie and Heinrich's name was added to heighten the chance of sales (Holfter 2011, 148).

Given their interest in and long-standing association with Ireland, it is hardly surprising that the Bölls would undertake a translation of *An tOileánach*. Heinrich Böll had initially visited Ireland on his own in 1954. At that time, he was already well established as a writer but was becoming increasingly unhappy with the political scene in Germany. Ireland was a temporary haven from Adenauer's Germany. The appeal of the west coast of Ireland was such that the entire Böll family visited Achill Island the following year. This was the first of many return trips, and Achill Island became their "second home" (Holfter 2011, 149–50). "Ireland arguably became Böll's 'still point in the turning world', the centre of a revolving wheel, itself remaining in the same place but of crucial importance as the real source of movement" (Holfter 2011, 65). In 1958, the Bölls purchased a cottage on the north side of Achill Island. That year saw the publication of Heinrich's novel *Billard um halb zehn* (Billiards at Half-Past Nine). This was hot on the heels of their 1958 translation of Brendan Behan's play *Ein Gutshaus in Ireland* (The Big House), which had been broadcast in 1959 (Holfter 2011, 149–50). Their translation of O'Crohan's book was first published in 1983. Thereafter followed several editions of the German translation of *An tOileánach*.

Heinrich and Anna-Marie translated several other works of Irish literature (e.g. O'Brien 1966). Apart from their translation of Eilís Dillon's *The Island of Horses* (Dillon 1964), the Böll translation of *An tOileánach* was their most popular translation of Irish literature. It was republished in 1983 by Lamuv. Since then, the book has gone into its ninth edition. Heinrich also produced a film, *Irland und seine Kinder* (Children of Éire), which received great applause in Germany but attracted criticism in Ireland, where it was felt the country had been shown in an unfavourable light. In the 1970s, the focus of the Böll's translation work shifted somewhat and encompassed a range of non-Irish original material. However, the Bölls are generally regarded as leaders in the field of translations of material from Irish into German. "Assessing the overall volume of translations of twentieth-century Irish literature, the Bölls are probably second only to Elisabeth Schnack, the *grande dame* of translating Irish literature into German" (Holfter 2011, 152).

Given the long-standing connections between the folklore department in Lund and that at University College Dublin, it is hardly surprising that the first continental version of *An tOileánach* would be in Swedish. Carl Wilhelm von Sydow in Lund had originally initiated this connection, which encouraged Séamus Delargy to spend time in Lund and led to field trips from Lund to Ireland by von Sydow as well as his two younger colleagues, Åke Campbell and Albert Eskind, who were later to become leading folklorists in Sweden (Lysaght 1993). In fact, Campbell devoted considerable time and energy in the mid-1930s, collecting folklore and information on material culture from local crofters and farmers on the Kerry coast.

At this time, Nordic Europe had a fascination with outlying islands. Perhaps the accelerating road to modernity created an interest in the margins and in exoticised peripheries. There were a number of books on isolated islands published from 1935 onwards in Sweden. Ireland seemed of special interest to Swedes for many reasons—a small, neutral country but with a very different history and folk culture. An early example is the Swedish-Finnish author Olof Enckell with his 1937 book *De klagande vindarnas ö: romantisk resa till Irland* (The Island of the Complaining Winds. A Romantic Journey to Ireland), where he describes his travels along the West Coast and time spent on islands like Inishmore.

In 1996, a Danish version of *An tOileánach* was published (Ó Criomhthain 1996). The Danish translator was Ole Munch-Pedersen—a well-known academic and expert in the Irish language. Munch-Pedersen's initial interest in Ireland was sparked by his reading of a Danish translation of James Joyce's *Ulysses*, which inspired him to read an English edition of Joyce's life story. Given his limited skills in English at that time, the exercise proved quite challenging for Munch-Pedersen, but also motivated him to enrol on a Latin course in a quest to improve his language skills. While taking the course in Latin, Munch-Pedersen also took the opportunity to take a beginner's course in Irish with James Stewart. Munch-Pedersen felt that learning Irish would give him good insights into Ireland as well as the English language spoken there. He visited Ireland on a number of occasions during the 1970s and in 1972 enrolled on a formal academic Irish course at an institute in Dublin.

In 1972, Munch-Pedersen visited Corca Dhuibhne, where he met with folklorist Bö Almqvist, who introduced him to Mícheál Ó Guithín, the Blasket poet (more commonly known as *An File*). In an interview, Pedersen explains that he taped many stories from *an File* during his initial visit. On his return to Denmark, he played these tapes over and over again in order to improve his comprehension of the language. The following year, he recorded a further 16 stories from *an File*, and was awarded a *kandidatstipendiat* to work on and transcribe the tales. Munch-Pedersen was subsequently unemployed for two years, but in his free time nurtured his interest in the Irish-language taped stories.

A short-term university position led to the discovery of a hitherto unknown manuscript that contained some 500 pages of handwritten notes made on the Aran Islands by Danish linguist Holger Pedersen during a four-and-a-half-month visit in 1895. At that time, Holger Pedersen had hired the local storyteller Martin to narrate stories, which Pedersen then transcribed phonetically. Pedersen had added a dictionary to these recordings that included songs, poems, riddles, sayings, legends and fairy tales. A dispute with James Stewart over this unpublished manuscript led to Ole's dismissal from his university position, but did not diminish his interest in Irish. In 1992, Munch-Pedersen delivered a manuscript to Irish publishers based on Holger Pedersen's notes (Munch-Pedersen 1994).

Munch-Pedersen enjoyed the Aran Islands project so much that he began to think about translating a book from Irish into Danish. In his introduction to the translation, he says about himself: "The translator has known one of the King's daughters, several of his grandchildren, and Tomás's own daughter's son, who lives in Dublin" (translation from Munch-Pedersen 1996, 264). The translation was done outside of his regular employment as a substitute teacher in a school for special needs, and he had a little extra time on his hands. When his translation of *An tOileánach* was completed, Munch-Pedersen dispatched the manuscript to a major publisher in Denmark who declined the project.

In conversation, Munch-Pedersen explained that the subsequent publication of the Danish translation was serendipitous. Unexpectedly, Munch-Pedersen received a phone call from Husets forlag—a small publisher in Aarhus, requesting him to translate into Danish some poems by the renowned Irish language poet Nuala Ní Dhomhnaill for a forthcoming cultural festival in Aarhus on the theme of Ireland. When he informed the publisher of his personal translation of *An tOileánach*, the publisher agreed to review and subsequently accepted the manuscript. Two more translations of Irish language literature into Danish followed. Munch-Pedersen first translated *Deoraíocht* by Padraig Ó Conaire (Ó Conaire 1999) and subsequently Máirtín Ó Cadhain's novel *Cré na Cille* (Ó Cadhain 2000). There were no further Irish-Danish projects with this publisher.

In 1991, *L'Isolano*, the Italian translation of *An tOileánach*, was published (O'Crohan 2009). Originally from Geracu Siculo on the island of Sicily, the translator Antonio Fazio left his family as an adolescent and moved to Cefalù, where he first worked in the tourism sector and later dedicated himself to photography. At the same time, he also started to paint. Fazio then worked in Switzerland before moving to Dingle in 1991. There he established a business carving magnificent artworks in stone, inspired by Celtic design, Irish mythology and the Irish landscape in the Dingle Peninsula. The Italian translation was an individual effort, and personally funded and relied on Flower's English edition of the book. It was inspired by the empathy which Fazio felt with the lifestyle described in *An tOileánach*—an island lifestyle that reflected the values and traditions the translator had experienced on Sicily. In his preface to the volume, Fazio explains:

> After having lived for sixteen years on this peninsula and having visited since then various times the island of Tomás – which has since then become a touristic target – I decided to translate his book into Italian even before having finished to read it.
>
> While I translated it, I was deeply touched many times, I shed some tears of compassion but also because of joy. (Fazio 2009, 4 – in translation)

The most recent translation of *An tOileánach* is a Spanish edition of the first seven chapters, conducted as part of a dissertation on translation (Blebois 2007). Comparing and contrasting the French and German editions, which had already been done from the Irish and English translations respectively, the author herself translated a portion of the autobiography into Spanish to experience at first hand the challenges of translating *An tOileánach* into a continental language. She worked from both French and English editions.

## The Task of the Translator

In "The Task of the Translator," Walter Benjamin explores the link between an original literary piece and the life it takes on after translation. Translation can be interpreted as an act of homage that deems a literary piece worthy of being translated—but what is being translated is not simply the words. It includes: "the unfathomable, the mysterious, the 'poetic', something that a translator can reproduce only if he is also a poet" (Benjamin 1968 [1923], 4). Translation is an act that gives a work "an afterlife"—or "a stage of continued life" to an original work. In translation, it becomes something more than the original. Translation in that sense implies incompleteness, since the original is being translated because it has not yet reached its full potential. It is liberated and reconnected by the translator.

The task of translating *An tOileánach* was approached differently by various translators and during this research, it was fortunate that three of these translators, Munch-Pedersen (Danish), Buhler (French) and Fazio (Italian) were available for conversations. Given his fluency in Irish, Ole Munch-Pedersen relied on an Irish language edition rather than an English translation for his Danish translation. At the time of translating, he opted to use Ua Maoileoin's version. In the preface, he noted: "This edition is translated directly from the Gaelic second edition from 1973, but the translator has, however, occasionally glanced at the first edition from 1929 and in very few cases at Robin Flower's English translation from 1937" (Munch-Pedersen 1996, 264 in translation). Since then, however, he has changed his mind, and if Munch-Pedersen were to choose which version to translate today, he says that would opt for An Seabhac's original Irish-language edition.

The French language translators also relied on an Irish language edition, although not quite to the extent of the Danish translator. In the case of the French edition, the process was two-fold. Úna Murphy made the initial translation from Irish into French. Her text was then improved by Jean Buhler. Úna would suggest further "revisions," and together, they discussed the translation until they had teased out all the nuances to their satisfaction and arrived at a final version. In the preface to their translation, they justify the use of Ua Maoileoin's edition in the following terms:

> To present *An tOileánach* to French readers, is it necessary to be satisfied with the translation of a translation? Surely not, especially as Pádraig

(Patrick) Ua Maoileoin, Tomás's own grandson, the son of his surviving daughter, born in 1913 in Dunquin and himself a notable writer, brought out a revised and augmented edition of this major work devoted to the Great Blasket islands in 1973. This second version extends over a good 20 pages more than the 1929 edition and includes around 50 additions, some of which are very significant. It is this complete text, reworked by Pádraig Ua Maoileoin on the strength of some hand-written letters by his Grandfather, which is presented here for the French language reader. We are happy to see a piece represented here that is as important as the poem sung at Tomás Ó'Criomhthain's wedding. (Translation from Buhler 1989, 13)

In the above commentary, the translators note the process of indirect translation that occurred in other translations. Margot Ångström, the Swedish translator, had used Robin Flower's English edition as the basis for her translation. This was also the version used by Heinrich and Annemarie Böll. (Neither of the Bölls had a working knowledge of Irish). In translating the English rather than the Irish language edition, the German and Swedish translators engaged in an act of "double translation." In view of Walter Benjamin's assertion, in the "Task of the Translator," that translations are effectively untranslatable, "We must ask, however, what implications this act of double translation has for both the process and the product of translation" (O'Sullivan 2006, 381).

Some translators felt the need to revise the title of the original book. The French translators made some minimal changes and turned *An tOileánach* into *l'homme des îles* or the Man of the Islands. However, both the Swedish and German translators made more radical changes. In the case of the German edition, the translators did not opt for *Der Mann von der Insel*, which would have been the literal translation. Instead it became *Die Boote fahren nicht mehr aus* (The boats no longer set to sea). Holfter and Nic Bhloscaidh (2000, 43) critique the revised subtitle and conclude that: "By changing the title of the novel and relegating the eponymous Islandman to a subordinate position in the subtitle, the German edition removes the emphasis from the individual." There is a sense of doom implied in the main title, which is also apparent in the Swedish translation *Karg Kust* (Barren Coast), which placed the Blasket Islanders in a similar paradigm with Native Americans (see Chap. 5).

It is interesting to note how the translators approached the issue of expressions and oral traditions during the process of translation. Munch-Pedersen, the Danish translator who was working directly from the Irish language edition, was conscious of idioms that would not sound natural to Danish ears. And so, for example, when faced with an expression such as "like being on the piggy's back," Munch-Pedersen did not attempt to translate it literally. Instead, he opted for a Danish equivalent. In the preface, he writes: "I have followed a line that was all about representing the colloquial style of the author in corresponding Danish. This has meant that I have strived to find Danish expressions that in style and meaning correspond to the Gaelic, but that sometimes are not direct translations of them" (translation from Munch-Pedersen 1996, 265). Munch-Pedersen also made some stylistic changes. While the original Irish's language edition had many rhetorical questions, Munch-Pedersen translated these into ordinary statements. He also changed expressions such as "it was not long until" to the Danish, "shortly after."

Munch-Pedersen also addressed the issue of place-names from a cultural as well as a linguistic perspective. In the preface, he explains that Gaelic place-names give meaning to places, which had important implications for the way he translated them. He explains his methodology:

> Where the place-names are concerned, the situation is a bit different. Gaelic place-names are often immediately obvious, which means that if one understands the language one can immediately understand their meaning. Examples of this are a couple of local names from Blascaed: The White Strand and The Wives' Island. In many cases I chose to translate such names into Danish, especially concerning the local Blascaed names. In other cases I have kept the Gaelic form. (Translation from Munch-Pedersen 1996, 265)

Buhler and Murphy also discuss their approach to the cultural dimension of their translation. Songs were an integral part of Blasket Island culture. In the preface to the French edition, Buhler writes: "For the pleasure of readers, we have reproduced the text of songs we have been able to find in annex, but have let go of the jumble of notes and remarks in the margin so that the work retains its testimonial style. What it loses in scientific pretension it retains in moving frankness and dignity." (Translation from Buhler 1989, 13)

The Bölls also made changes when working on a German translation of *An tOileánach*. While Flower's translation of *An tOileánach* retained strong traces of an Irish oral tradition through the regular use of expressions such as "yerra" and "wisha," the German translators omitted many of these. In a critique of the translation, Holfter and Nic Bhloscaidh

(2000, 38–9) note further that they made other changes to the phrase "*Dar Muire*" which was translated by Flower as "Holy Mary" or "In God's name." In the German version, it is altered variously to "*bei der heiligen Jungfrau*" (Holy Mary), "*In Gottes Name*" (In God's name) and, in one instance, somewhat surprisingly, to "*Zum Teufel nochmal*" (By the devil), probably to avoid repetition.

Much more significant was the cultural shift in the Böll's translation, when the Irish mythological character Oscar becomes Hercules from Greek mythology, as in the following example: "*denn niemand hat mich je wieder für so etwas wie einen Herkules erklärt*" ("no one ever again declared me to be a Hercules"), instead of the English translation "that I was in any way an Oscar" (Holfter and Nic Bhloscaidh 2000, 39). One might assume that a reference to the mythical figure Oscar from the Irish Fenian (or Ossianic) Cycle would not have made sense to most German readers—which would, however, be a little surprising, given the widespread reception of MacPherson's Ossian on the continent decades earlier (Howard 2004).

## Continental Nostalgia

During the second half of the eighteenth century, James MacPherson published Scottish-Gaelic poems based initially on the Fingal epic and subsequently with Temora. MacPherson implied that the Ossian poems were translations of third-century Gaelic originals. These poems were enormously popular in Germany and enhanced the appeal of the "Celtic Soul" in Central Europe. O'Neill (2010, 81) argues that the Ossian contribution in Germany "was essentially to bring into prominence and strongly emphasize the mystery of the misty isle's *landscape*, readable now as a soulscape of melancholy grandeur peopled neither by saints and scholars nor by sexually uninhibited cannibals but by a noble race of shadowy giants combining majestic simplicity and a natural dignity worthy of Homer himself." Within two decades of the publication of the Ossian poems, five German travel books on Ireland were published.

It was more than a century later before it was concluded that the Ossianic poems were not genuine. The only Gaelic "original" was MacPherson's own translation into Scottish-Gaelic of his personally-composed English poems (Howard 2004). However, the discovery of this fraud did not dampen the enthusiasm for Celtic literature on the continent, and the allure of the Scottish Highlander as noble primitive had been consolidated. "The intellectual world of the larger society became interested in the primitive at a time when the Highlander was peculiarly suited for the role, in a way that neither, say, the Lothian peasantry, who were too close, nor the South Sea Islander, who was too far away, could approach" (Chapman 1992, 127).

The ancestry of the Gaelic Highlander was shared by all Celts. The French preface to *An tOileánach* noted of the Blasket Islanders that: "They were just like half of us Europeans who are Celtic without knowing it, enamoured of independence and of cultivating our differences despite the pressures of those who wish us to conform" (in translation from Buhler 1989, 11). And the Celtic appeal was not confined to Celtic peoples in Western Europe. Many Germans who read the Ossianic poems were convinced that they also belonged to a Celtic tribe. O'Neill (2010, 81) argues that it was commonly assumed that the Celts were forefathers not just of the Irish, Scots-Gaels, Welsh and Bretons—they were also the ancestors of the Germans. As the poet Klopstock wrote: "*Ossian war* deutschen *Stammes, weil er ein Kaledonier war*" (Ossian was of *German* stock in being a Caledonian; quoted in O'Neill 2010, 81).

### The Noble Savage

*An tOileánach* connects with the eighteenth-century European fascination with the "noble savage," a concept that is usually credited to Rousseau's *Discourse in Inequality* (1999 [1755]). Ashcroft et al. (2000, 192f.) link the popularity of that concept with a European nostalgia for a pre-industrial, rural society—a nostalgia that regarded modernisation as the loss of innocence and freedom of the human being in a natural environment. "The crucial fact about the construction is that it produces an ostensibly positive oversimplification of the 'savage' figure, rendering it in this particular form as an idealized rather than a debased stereotype" (Ashcroft et al. 2000, 173).

The primitive was no longer a "backward" creature to be despised. Instead, he had become an object of appeal. Attitudes towards the primitive were neither evolutionary nor condescending. Instead it represented an ideal—a stability, cohesion and moral uprightness that was being wiped out by industrialisation. From this perspective, Flower and the other folklorists on the Great Blasket were in the spirit of Mauss (2002 [1954]), who saw the benefits of archaic times for society. In concluding his volume on *The Gift*, Mauss proposed that we should endeavour to recapture the *zeitgeist* of former times when: "the clan, the tribe, and peoples have learnt how to oppose and to give to one another without sacrificing themselves to one another. This is what tomorrow, in our so-called civilized world, classes and nations and individuals also, must learn. This is one of the enduring secrets of their wisdom and solidarity" (Mauss 2002 [1954], 106).

The concept of the Noble Savage would have heightened the reception of an island memoir in which life was portrayed as simple and uninterrupted by modernity within the continent of Europe. However, this was a lifestyle on the margins of the continent, and which would eventually "give way" to modernity. Several translators took the opportunity to explain that, since the publication of the original memoir, the Blasket Island had become deserted. Buhler remarked that:

> The pathways where wild children ran in bare feet is now green again, in bloom, covered with short grass. Sheep, having returned to a wild state, wait for the shearers who round them up once a year to groom them and then leave, only returning the following summer. Three redundant donkeys have hooves like Charlie Chaplin's shoes and ski on the sodden grass. The levees which used to demarcate the island's fields are still well marked, as are the stone shepherds' shelters, the road which rose up to the peat bogs of the hill and the ruins of the tower constructed at the time of the war between England and France at the end of the 18th Century. (Translation from Buhler 1989, 8)

At the time of translation, the island was deserted and the "Noble Savage" had vanished from the continent of Europe:

> All that remains today of this small, unique and tenacious civilisation are crumbling stones, uncultivated fields, heathlands and an undefinable atmosphere created by hanging cliffs like the one at this Eastern point, above the pebble beach, where you stay in balance by pure power of concentration, watching the seagulls and storm-riding fulmars gliding underneath you. One level below are the black-headed sheep tangled up in the torn crinolines of their ragged fleeces and at the very bottom, the ocean crashes against the mouths of caves from which unforgettable voices seem to rise up. (Translation from Buhler 1989, 9)

The "noble peasants" on the Great Blasket Island had bequeathed a literary legacy in the form of a series of memoirs with broad European appeal. O'Toole (2002, 10) remarks that the island memoirs were "both profoundly modern and deeply European." They had emerged under the influence of British and European scholars such as Flower and Marstrander (see Chap. 2). Moreover, the standardised Irish language in which they were written had fascinated German scholars such as Kuno Meyer, Ernst Windisch and Heinrich Zimmer, and French scholars like Henri Gaidoz and d'Arbois de Jubainville.

### European Literary Gems

In the prefaces to their translations, some scholars had ranked *An tOileán-ach* among other European literary gems. A Danish reviewer noted that the book was "just as exciting and informative as Albert Dam's *Jomfruen og soldaten*" (Lundbye 1996, 8). *Jomfruen og Soldaten* (The Virgin/Maid and the Soldier) is a novel that was published in 1989. It is a story set in the early 1900s about a young girl from the city of Copenhagen who marries a soldier and becomes a peasant's wife in Jutland.

In the French preface to *An tOileánach*, Jean Buhler ranked An *tOileán-ach* highly indeed:

> It is not for me, as a humble intermediary, to tell you how highly you should rank this piece of work among those truthful works you have on your shelves – the truest of the true as our grandmothers would say, that truth to which art, at its very best, lends itself, like a feather in its cap. I imagine that you will slide it between *The Notebooks of Captain Coignet*, *My Childhood* by Gorki, *Hunger* by Knut Hamsun, *Aimless Journeys* by stoker Harry Martinson, *Memoirs (Vieux Souvenirs) of the Prince de Joinville* and other books by discoverers, explorers or poets, those reporters of a reality that reality hides from us. (Translation from Buhler 1989, 14)

The magical qualities of the island of Ireland had been reinforced in the popular imagination by the 1826 German translation of Thomas Crofton Croker's *Fairy Legends and Traditions of the South of Ireland* by the renowned Grimm brothers. "The *Irische Elfenmärchen* finally domesticated the myth of the Island of Marvels to the scale of the drawing room, and coalesced with Ossianic mists and the wistful half-lights of Lady Morgan and Thomas Moore to form a nineteenth-century Romantic image of Ireland that persists essentially unchanged in Germany down to the present day" (O'Neill 2010, 83).

Interest in the German translation of Tomás's memoir had been further helped by the publication in 1957 of Heinrich Böll's *Irisches Tagebuch* (An Irish Diary) (Böll 1988 [1957]). Böll's diary was initially published as short pieces on German radio or in German newspapers. As well as dealing with life on Achill Island, the journal also deals thematically with topics such as "Irish time" and "Irish rain." Böll's book contained eighteen impressions based on his Irish experiences and achieved cult status in Germany. It "brought Ireland to German popular consciousness as an irresistible place to visit, initiating the love affair that so many Germans have had and continue to have with Ireland" (Martin Elsasser quoted in Fattori 2010, 101).

In twentieth-century France, readers were already interested in peasant and working-class life histories, and *An tOileánach* was compared on many occasions with *Le Cheval d'Orgueil* (The Horse of Pride), which has been described in the foreword to the English translation as "an epic of peasant life in Brittany during the first half of this century…an ethnographic description of a culture that has all but disappeared…a case study in the quarrel over ethnicity…an account of a childhood" (Wylie 1978, xi). The author of that foreword was Laurence Wylie, an anthropologist who had conducted an anthropological study of Provence that was subsequently published as *Village in the Vaucluse*, 1957 (see Reed-Danahay 1997a, 126).

*Le Cheval d'Orgueil* had been written originally by Pierre-Jakez Hélias, himself of peasant origin, who was an academic and specialist in Breton folklore at the University of Rennes. He spent over fifteen years writing the book, which was intended to be scientific as well as ethnographic. The publishing company planned the volume as part of Jean Malaurie's collection "Human World." The memoir focuses on a child growing up in rural Brittany. The "horse of pride" in the title is a metaphor for the sense of pride in their Breton cultural heritage and traditions among a rural community in the Bigouden region of France—a sense of pride that was being diluted by the promise of better economic prospects through the more dominant French culture. The author Hélias was living "a double life"—one with Breton language and box beds, the other with French language and education.

*The Horse of Pride* had unprecedented success in France. Initially the book had a small print run of 3000 copies. By the time the author died, it had sold 2,000,000 copies. As with *An tOileánach*, *Le Cheval d'Orgueil* portrayed "a vanishing race." Its author was pessimistic regarding the future of Breton culture, although he also recognised the inevitability of progress. In a comment reminiscent of Tomás's "*Ní bheidh ár leithéidí arís ann*" (our likes will never be here again) (Ó Criomhthain 2002, 329; O'Crohan 2012, 298), Hélias struck a note that was not entirely pessimistic:

> As for me, I was convinced that the accelerated mutation of the world would shortly lead to the demise of the milieu in which that language and that civilization – in other words, traditional peasant life – had flourished. But I also knew that a civilization never dies altogether and that a language, even one no longer used (and that is far from true in the case of Breton) is a concern to scholars, who are trying to unravel and clarify the characteristic features of the world of today. (Hélias 1978, 343)

Urbanisation, Hélias argued, diluted and denegraded regional identity. For those who did not know Brittany, *Le Cheval d'Orgueil* introduced readers to Bigouden culture, with its deeply-rooted traditions. The author had restored pride in an endangered peasant culture, not unlike that on the Great Blasket Island.

The appeal of *An tOileánach* was wider than any national interest. Many Europeans could identify with the simplicity of the lifestyle described. The French translation noted:

> O'Crohan is the spokesperson of a culture that was indeed nearly erased by the misery of history. Rough and tender, naive and full of humour, he presents us with family and neighbours in unforgettable traits. We sing with him, we drink with him, we row, we tussle, we suffer, we pardon, we fish lobster, we chase hare, seal, walfish, shark, we discover the charm of a civilisation bathed in froth, whiskey, stout and music. And we laugh. A lot. *L'homme des îles* praises liberty, the dignity of work, the humility and the greatness of the human condition. (Back cover of O'Crohan 1989, in translation)

In the postscript to the Danish translation, Munch-Pedersen felt that his readers could easily empathise with the lifestyle described in the book. He compared land distribution and the lifestyle more generally in Ireland and Denmark:

> Probably very few modern readers would have imagined that a community as primitive as described in *Manden på Øen* existed in western Europe right into the twentieth century. The local community on the Blasket Island was an

almost pre-literary community with roots in Europe's Middle Ages. For example, the land was distributed in the same way as it had been in Denmark until the agricultural reforms at the end of the 1700s, the inhabitants were largely self-sufficient, and an actual monetary economy seems hardly to have existed. The bit of money they earned by selling their catch outside of the island was first and foremost spent on paying taxes and rent, and the local economy was a pure barter economy. (Translation from Munch-Pedersen 1996, 262)

Although the island was evacuated, the translators were convinced of the "universal appeal" of the tale. The book describes a place that was everywhere and nowhere. Fazio, the Italian translator, noted:

When I moved from my homeland Sicily to Ireland in 1991, "The Island Man" ("L'Isolano") was the first book of local writers that I started to read. Nearly immediately I felt really touched. I knew this miserable way of life – dependent on the environmental conditions – of Tomás and his people well enough. This is what he writes about in this book. (Fazio 2009, 3 in translation)

Translations of *An tOileánach* into continental languages continue, and the turn of the millennium has not dampened enthusiasm for the project. The most recent edition of *L'homme des Île* appeared in 2003, while the most recent *Die Boote fahren nicht mehr aus* was issued in 2004. *L'Isolano* was published in 2009, while the most recent English language edition, *The Islander*, was published in 2012 (O'Crohan 2012). There can be no one explanation for the appeal of the book on the continent without at least setting the memoir more generally in the more widespread nostalgia for times past.

The translators of the French edition noted the universality of the human condition in the book. "It comes from the most Irish part of Ireland, certainly, but also from a corner of the world where, with strength and simplicity, people knew how to give an account of their fate with a universal emphasis" (translation from Buhler 1989, 7). Perhaps like Böll, readers of *An tOileánach* are indulging in escapism—to a place and time that no longer exists—to an Utopia that is both eu-topia (a "good" place) and ou-topia (a "non"-place that does not exist). It describes a way of life that has vanished from Europe in the face of progress, but has not been forgotten.

CHAPTER 7

# Museum and Memoir

Although there is considerable international interest in the Great Blasket Island, many visitors who come to the peninsula for a morning or afternoon may not be prepared to take the time and effort to actually visit the island. Instead, they are perfectly happy to spend two hours or so in the interpretative centre before purchasing a number of books about the island in the centre's bookshop—only then to scramble on the tour bus towards the next tourist attraction. This chapter aims to explore the representation of Tomás and his literary journey in the centre. It also explores the relationship between the literary portrayal of island life in the book and the visual portrayal of that life in the museum.

## THE INTERPRETATIVE CENTRE

The Blasket Centre is an interpretative centre rather than a museum. Such institutions are often located in or near heritage sites with the aim of interpreting a specific heritage for visitors and are often linked with cultural tourism. "The aim of heritage interpretation is to raise public awareness and provide guidance which will enable visitors to see, explore, situate, observe, analyse, understand, feel and truly 'experience' the site" (Izquierdo Tugas et al. 2005, 16). In interpretative centres, the tourist experiences the site without actually visiting it. From this perspective, one might argue that the interpretative centre is a simulacrum—a term which Baudrillard (1983) uses for an image or representation of something. It is

© The Author(s) 2020
M. Nic Craith, *The Vanishing World of* The Islandman,
Palgrave Studies in Literary Anthropology,
https://doi.org/10.1007/978-3-030-25775-0_7

not the same as an actual visit to the island, which involves several modes of transport and considerable physical effort.

Guy Beiner (2005, 66) suggests that interpretative centres are akin to Plato's cave—a replica which pretends to be the original, although it is not. In the case of the Blasket Island, my own experiences of the boat journey to the island are that it is both physically and mentally demanding—and requires a minimum of four hours for the actual visit. It is also dependent on favourable weather conditions. In contrast, a tour of the interpretative centre is not weather-dependent and guarantees a certain minimum level of understanding of the island context without undue waste of time. "Similarly, day trippers to the Boyne Valley, who are pressed for time when visiting the World Heritage site at Newgrange, need not queue up to enter the megalithic tomb. Instead they can experience a substitute recreation of the ancient burial chamber in the adjacent visitor's centre, where year-round the rays of an artificial solstice are guaranteed to shine" (Beiner 2005, 66). Sites such as these generally represent something that is no longer there. As Barbara Kirshenblatt-Gimblett discusses in relation to the Abbey Church of St. Peter and St. Paul in Cluny in France: "The museum openly imagines the site into being – in the very spot where it should be still standing but is no more" (Kirshenblatt-Gimblett 1998, 377).

### Architecture

The initial venture was a collaboration between the Office of Public Works (OPW) in Ireland and the Blasket Foundation. "Nestling in the Dunquin landscape which overlooks the Blaskets, the centre has been developed as a tribute to the Blasket Islanders, their heritage and traditions, and as a monument to the Irish language" (Hogan 1994, 2). The OPW is an official government agency established in 1831, which manages and regulates many heritage sites across Ireland including Kilkenny Castle and Dublin Castle. The Blasket Foundation is a much younger organisation. It was established in 1985 in reaction to an initiative to sell the Great Blasket in the US. The Foundation succeeded in raising £400,000 and petitioned the Irish Government to transform the Great Blasket into a national park. In 1989, considerable funding became available under the EU funded Operational Programme for Tourism which (among other things) facilitated the establishment of an interpretative centre in Dunquin. *Ionad an Bhlascaoid Mhóir* (the Great Blasket Interpretative Centre). The centre was opened in 1994, and the local community was involved from the beginning.

The centre is located within sight of the Great Blasket Island and involves a considerable journey on fairly minor roads from the city of Cork. The nearest town is Dingle, some fourteen miles from the centre, along minor curly roads, which in the summer are crowded with large tourist buses. The journey to the centre itself is almost a pilgrimage into the wild and the route features as part of Ireland's latest tourism promotion of the Wild Atlantic Way. "Looked at in the larger frame of history and present policy, Ireland has always been represented to the tourist in terms of the sublime. Like the Highlands of Scotland, like Brittany and the Alps and other regions, Ireland (especially in western coast) has stood for the primitive, the unspoilt, the wild and the natural" (Brett 1996, 127).

The building concept is linked with the ecology of the place. Considerable thought was given to its architectural shape, which was designed by Ciarán O'Connor, currently the Principal Architect of the OPW. A crucial element was that the building would be close to the Great Blasket Island—and, as one journeys through the centre, one is constantly confronted with a view of the island itself. Moreover, an "architectural grammar" was created which took account of the natural environment as well as the local soundscape. Practical issues such as the flow of visitors as well as car-parking were considered. The local community was consulted throughout.

The centre is an unusually large building for the area. Its shape is quite unusual with a long central passage or spine entitled *slí an Bhlascaoid*, or the Blasket way. Essentially, this is a corridor which runs the length of the building and the route drops downward as one progresses through the building. There are many windows on the west side of the corridor which give significant natural light to the walk but also keep the Great Blasket Island within constant view of the tourist. Brenda Ní Shúilleabháin (2014) suggests that the building itself is a piece of artwork. Until he or she goes inside, the visitor does not understand the impact of light, coming in a westerly direction from the island and through the huge windows onto the multicoloured glass walls. This space goes to the middle of the centre and you can see the flow rising and falling under your feet in the same way as a wave rises and falls on the sea (Illustration 7.1).

The long narrow passage has been described as an "architectural metaphor" which provides "an equivalent of the field stone wall pattern or *Slí*, following the contours of the land" (Stanley 1998, 133). Moreover, it can

**Illustration 7.1**   Corridor of Blasket Interpretative Centre. (© Máiréad Nic Craith)

serve as a reminder that the Blasket Islanders always walked in single file—a custom that probably derived from the narrow paths on the island—but a style of walking which they maintained even within the town of Dingle. More significantly, there are "side-spaces" or "off-shoots" strung off the corridor to left and right. These cut the straight lines of the corridor at angles and resemble the shape of ancient Ogham Irish writing (Stanley 1998, 133). It is somewhat ironic that the shape of the building, which represents the transition from a primarily oral tradition to a written culture, is itself designed in a native script which was in use in Ireland long before the arrival of the monks who brought the Latin script with them in the fifth century AD (Nic Einrí 1971).

At the beginning of the *slí* is a stained glass artwork by Róisín de Buitléir (in collaboration with Sala Kawala). This huge artwork contains over three hundred pieces of window glass. Three tons of steel and three and a half tons of glass were used in this artwork, which took almost a year to make. A panel explains that this piece has been inspired by the daily lives of the Blasket Islanders and the frequent journeys they made in and out of each other's houses, to and from the fields and out to sea beyond the island itself.

### *Curator*

Part of the challenge facing Pat Cooke, the curator of the exhibition, was the strategy one should adopt when tasked with representing a distinct way of life. This is particularly acute when the heritage being represented is still living. Although the island was deserted in the 1950s, the history that the interpretative centre draws on is recent and people connected with it still have memories. (Until lately, elderly islanders were still alive.) Representing living heritage brings challenges of reconciling different, even sometimes contradictory opinions: "To create a heritage centre within a living community is to invite a debate about the nature of the record and the society that is documented" (Stanley 1998, 130).

Cooke was aware of the creative potential at the interface between the art world and the heritage sector. While the individual artist's and his/her self-reflectivity is central to the creative practice, heritage is a collective process which values commonality as well as distinction. The relationship between the two involves compromise on both sides. Cooke (2014) argues that artists are required to negotiate with issues of history and memory in their own terms in the heritage space. However, the heritage dimension also needs to give ground. Enthused by this conceptual framework, the curator opted for an open exhibition that would allow for multiple interpretations.

In conversation with Pat Cooke, he was clear that his exhibition strategy was one that offered a range of possibilities for visitors, thereby giving them the chance to construct their own narrative about the Blaskets. This would be achieved by a variety of techniques, including artwork.

> I felt that art is amazingly helpful and liberating in its power to basically suggest a non-prescriptive and deeply ambivalent sense of history. I carried that

philosophy into my curatorial approach in the centre. You don't want to tell people what to think about history. The great advantage of visual mediation is that it works through visual cues or symbols that require an effort of personal interpretation on the part of the visitor or viewer. I am not a fan of text-heavy didacticism in exhibitions. (Interview with Cooke, August 2019)

Aware of the many different types of audiences that would potentially visit the centre, Cooke rejected a didactic approach in the centre, in favour of one that would offer the visitors a series of impressions. His curatorial vision was of negotiation and potential. Set as it was on the "edge of Europe," it was that very "edge-ness" that inspired him to work with a series of artists and collaborators to transform the experience of the building and its contents into a multiplicity of narratives. Cooke writes:

On the edge of things our vision can become distorted, even surreal. On the edge of things, the horizon is always in view, like a seam between the dream-world and the real world. A horizon can be viewed from different perspectives. The dreams and realities of natives and emigrants can become interwoven or confused. It is this perspective that gives the photographs their edge: people speaking the same language but different body languages. (Cooke 1996, n.d.)

The initial collection contained a range of elements from photographs to objects, dioramas and maps along with some elements of interactivity—although one should bear in mind that in 1994, interactive technologies were clunkier and far less developed than they are today. As part of the process of curation, Cooke familiarised himself with *An tOileánach* and the other Blasket memoirs. In conversation with me, he notes:

I read all the main Blasket texts and studied them closely. I determined that the main voice of the exhibition would be the voices of the island people as expressed through those classic texts: *The Islandman and Twenty Years a-Growing*, complemented by some of the contemporary commentaries by those such as Flower and Thomson, which bore witness to the uniqueness of their lifestyle and culture. When I selected texts from these sources, I choose them for their power of voice. (Interview with Cooke, August 2019)

Cooke's reading led him to focus on two themes in particular—namely the literary heritage of the Great Blasket Island and the Irish language in which the memoirs were written. As well as gathering copies of printed books, manuscripts and so on, he wanted a strong photographic dimension—to capture a sense of the environment that moulded island culture and a sense of the contemporary Gaeltacht community, many of whom were the sons and daughters of islanders and members of a generation on whom the nurturing of a culture lived through the Irish language now depended. Anthony Haughey was commissioned to develop the visual dimension.

### Photographer

Excited by the commission, Haughey familiarised himself with the significant number of photographs already taken of the island and its inhabitants over the previous century. "In response to the Othering gaze of visiting anthropologists, the Islanders themselves produced a significant collection of Irish-language anthropologies, thus asserting their agency as authors" (Haughey 2017, 56–7). Many of these photographs are captured in De Mórdha and De Mórdha (2013). The earliest known photograph of the Great Blasket was taken by the Alma Curtin, wife of the Harvard folklorist, Jeremiah Curtin, who visited the Island in 1892. John Millington Synge, Carl W. Sydow, George Thomson and many other visiting scholars (see Chap. 2) wished to photograph the "vanishing native" (see De Mórdha and De Mórdha 2013).

In Haughey's case, he decided to become an "insider" rather than an "outsider." He spent a year living in Dunquin, photographing the local Irish-speaking community. Pat Cooke describes his technique as follows: "Haughey had an extraordinary ability to create subtle intimacies with community, and just to be there and be a fly on the wall. It's a unique talent he had, and still has" (interview with Cooke, August 2019). Haughey subsequently visited relatives in America (Haughey 1996) and his photographs appeared throughout the opening exhibition in 1994.

Haughey was an appropriate choice to work with Cooke, since his philosophy also advocated an open, flexible approach. Guided by the work of Mitchell and others (see Mitchell 2002 [1994]) who propose that landscape is a process and not an object, Haughey (2017, 58) did not set out to photograph the landscape as a static "object to be read." Instead, he wanted to capture the landscape as process—as a series of "human interventions, intersubjective relations, and ideology that determines our understanding of the landscape" (from Mitchell 2002 [1994], 58–59). Haughey didn't regard his photographs as "truthful" records of an event.

Instead they were designed to "question and draw our attention to the ways in which notions of the real are discursively produced" (Green and Lowry 2003, 58).

As well as a strong visual dimension, the museum contains a number of ethnographic objects, which Barbara Kirshenblatt-Gimblett (1998, 17) explains, "are artefacts created by ethnographers." It is the process of detachment from the original environment and their re-definition by ethnographers that turn them into ethnographic objects. "They are ethnographic, not because they were found in a Hungarian peasant household, Kwakiutl village, or Rajasthani market rather than in Buckingham Palace or Michelangelo's studio, but by virtue of the manner in which they have been detached, for disciplines make their objects and in the process make themselves" (Kirshenblatt-Gimblett 1998, 18).

The challenge for any curator such as Cooke is the management of such objects. How does one represent the multiple meanings of these objects? How does one incorporate such objects into a museum without oversimplification? How does one portray these meanings without becoming didactic? (Karp and Kratz 2014, 56). Although Cooke opted for a flexible approach in the museum, there is undoubtedly a dominant narrative there—one which emphasises the significance of the literary heritage which emerged from the island and the Irish language in which the texts were written. In a sense this approach has been almost unavoidable—since the expectation of tourists is that the Blasket writers, and Tomás in particular, will feature strongly.

## REPRESENTING *THE ISLANDMAN*

Inevitably, tourists are drawn to the interpretative centre by its magnificent literary heritage. Urry and Larsen (2011 [1990], 2) define the tourist gaze as being "conditioned by personal experiences and memories and framed by rules and styles, as well as by circulating images and texts of this and other places." In this instance, the tourist gaze is largely focused on the writers from the Great Blasket, Tomás, Muiris Ó Súilleabháin and Peig Sayers. In a chat with representatives of the museum, they explained that people from all around the world come to visit the interpretative centre, since they have read *An tOileánach*. Yet not all islanders were writers. They had other occupations as well and there are obvious tensions between the impulse to focus on the literary heritage of the island, without neglecting the farming, fishing and child-rearing dimensions of the island lifestyle.

Given the significance of Tomás in Blasket literary heritage, it is hardly surprising that he features right at the beginning of one's visit. Outside the main entrance, is a beautiful piece of brass set into the ground about the size of a pothole cover. The piece is quite simple and foregrounds in Irish a significant moment in Tomás's literary career. "1993 *Dúirt sé gur mhór an truagh me a bheith diomhaoin, ar nós an fhile Seán Ó Duinnshléibhe fadó, agus gur cheart dom cúpla leabhar do sgríobh, an fhaid do bheinn beó, chun go mbeinn beó agus me marbh.*" (He told me that it would be a great pity for me to remain idle like the poet Seán Ó Duinnshléibhe and that I should write a couple of books while I am alive so that I would be alive after my death) (Ó Criomhthain 1928, iv). Interestingly, the quote is written in circular rather than in linear form and one is required to walk around it to read it. This literary quote sets the tone for the interpretative centre as a whole.

Once one has entered the museum and admired the glasswork piece, one begins the journey through the *slí*. Two quotes on hanging brass plaques at either side of the corridor set the tone for the journey. The quote from *An tOileánach* reads: "do thugas iarracht ar mheor na ndaoine do bhí im thimpeall do chur síos chuin go mbeadh a dtuairisc 'ár ndiaidh, mar ná beidh ár leithéidí arís ann" (Ó Criomhthain 2002, 327–8). (I have tried to describe the character of the people who were around me so that there might be an account of them after we're gone, because our likes will never be here again) (O'Crohan 2012, 298). In the museum, this excerpt is not translated—possibly because it is so often used, it is felt there is no need to translate it—which does not take account of the range of visitors that come to the centre.

On the other side is a quote from George Thomson's *The Prehistoric Aegean* (1949)—which unfamiliar visitors may inadvertently assume is a translation of Tomás's quote on the other side. It reads:

> Then I went to Ireland. The conversation of those ragged peasants, as soon as I learnt to follow it, electrified me. It was as though Homer had come alive. Its vitality was inexhaustible, yet it was rhythmical, alliterative, formal, artificial, always on the point of bursting into poetry.

This quotation tends to frame the island's distinct culture within the somewhat artificial analogy of classical literature. It might be considered unfortunate to have this quotation at the entrance to the museum as it gives the impression of a group of islanders in a time-warp, unable to cope with modernity. Alternatively, one might regard this quotation as a compliment to the islanders since it had ranked them among the Greeks at the peak of European civilisation.

The dominance of Tomás in the museum narrative is evident throughout, but it could hardly be considered overpowering. Instead he is part of a package of what one might call "the trinity of the Great Blasket island," namely Tomás, Muiris Ó Súilleabháin and Peig Sayers. The trajectory is clearly focused on literature and language and visitors are initially given the opportunity to view a documentary that has been compiled by staff at the interpretative centre and which gives an overview of island life.

At the beginning of *slí*, Tomás features as a visual backdrop in the film. Later his literary journey features more strongly and there is emphasis on his status as the pioneer writer on the island whose work has been translated into many European languages. As one journeys through the *slí*, the island's remarkable literary heritage becomes more evident. The Blasket museum uses what Kirshenblatt-Gimblett (1998, 21) calls an "in-context" approach throughout much of the visitor journey. She defines this as the attempt to "establish a theoretical frame of reference for the viewer, offer explanations, provide historical background, make comparisons, pose questions, and sometimes even extend to the circumstances of excavation, collection, and conservation of the objects on display." This is achieved through a series of panels. The left-hand side features a series of panels of writers from the island. Each panel contains a photograph of the writer and a short biography in Irish and in English. Inevitably Tomás is the first panel encountered.

### Visual Panels

Interestingly, the first panel on Tomás begins with the word "perhaps"—noting that "perhaps [Tomás] was the greatest of the Island writers." Strong emphasis is placed on the locality of the writer who "lived all his life on the Island." Before noting his literary skills, the panel frames Tomás as "a farmer and a fisherman" and informs the viewer that Tomás only acquired his literary skills in Irish in his middle-age (which may possibly be untrue). The panel acknowledges the impact of learned men such as Carl Marstrander, Robin Flower, Brian Ó Ceallaigh and Pádraig Ó Siochfhradha on the islanders. Highlighting the significance of the literary body of work that emerged from a primarily oral society, the panel concludes with the statement:

As works of high literary merit coming out of an oral culture, they [the islanders] wrote triumphs of determination to master the written word – to leave a record, as he wrote in the closing lines of *An tOileánach*, "of what life was like in my time and the neighbours that lived with me."

Several other biographies feature on subsequent panels and sometimes links are made between them. Muiris Ó Súilleabháin's panel acknowledges the pioneering role that Tomás played in island writing with the statement that: "It was the success of Tomás Ó Criomhthain's autobiographical book *The Islandman*, combined with the encouragement of his friend George Thomson, that promoted Muiris to undertake his own account of his formative years on the Blasket." This presentation does not hint at any rivalry between the older and younger man—although clearly the fact that Muiris's memoir was translated into English before Tomás's must have jarred (see Chap. 2). Tomás's youngest son, Seán, has a panel dedicated to him and there is a separate panel for Eibhlís Ní Shúilleabháin, Seán's wife and Tomás's daughter-in-law. The panel on Eibhlís notes the care this couple gave Tomás in his final years.

Pádraig Ua Maoileoin's panel and that of Seán Sheáin Uí Chearnaigh each acknowledge the familial relationship with Tomás. On an island this size, many of the writers were inevitably related to one another—although this was not always the case. As one moves along the corridor, the panels feature writers who lived and died on the island as well as those who continued to write after the evacuation of the island in 1953. Of these later writers, Pádraig Ua Maoileoin has written: "they are all draining the last drop with melancholic longing for the past, while the Island where they were born and reared is now home to one-night strangers and stragglers – gulls and ravens – who merely pick bones" (1996, unpaginated).

### Sense of Place

One of the more interesting sections of the museum is entitled *Radharcanna* (Perspectives). This section geographically profiles all the Blasket Islands collectively and individually, historically and in contemporary times. One panel is particularly striking on the relationship between the islanders and the island they called home (and is reminiscent of the Scottish Nan Shepherd (2011 [1977]), who writes about going into rather than onto the mountain).The panel reads: "The Blasket Islanders talk about going **in** to the Island and **out** to the mainland. For them the

Great Blasket was home, a familiar place to go **in** to. And they went **out** into the wider, unfamiliar, uncertain world of the mainland" (bold original on the panel). This is very different from a mainlander's perspective.

> As we mainland dwellers look out at the Island, what strikes us is its small-ness set against the immensity of the ocean. But the Islanders spent most of their lives with their backs to the ocean, facing the mainland. It is a perspec-tive that called up feelings both of closeness and separation.

Unlike mainlanders who cannot clearly define or conceptualise their homeland, islanders can clearly delineate it. The panel continues:

> To be able to climb to a high place above where we were born and raised and say of a town or village or a sketch of countryside, "That is my place, where I was born," is a powerfully self-defining gesture. But towns blur into suburbs, suburbs fade off into countryside, and in the countryside the lines that divide one town land from another are invisible.

Inspired by Tuan's *Topophilia* (1990 [1974]), this quotation clearly reso-nates with a reflection by Barbara Cassin (2016) on the nature and speci-ficity of island places. She writes: "An island is real in a way that is very precise. Its edges can be seen from a boat or a place."

Another sense of place features in artwork by Cathy Carman, a member of *Aosdána* (Arts Council of Ireland), who is widely acclaimed for her work in bronze, ceramic, stone and wood. Carman's magnificent, impres-sionistic piece entitled "women at the well" portrays tall, slender women dancing with glee along with their children. Pat Cooke describes his reac-tion to this artwork in the following terms:

> There is that wonderful description in Tomás's book of the women at the well. That was where they did the washing. It was their place – a place where they could chat. If you were a man and you went near the women when they were having their chat, you would be told to leave straightaway. I just love that. I love the idea that the women had space for themselves. We needed to capture that sense of space, that sense of their independence of mind. (Interview with Cooke, August 2019)

Accompanying the artwork is a quote from Tomás's *Allagar na hInise*, which contextualises the "privacy" of island women in an open space. The well is a place for women and children. The menfolk know better than to invade. The quote from *Allagar na hInise* reads (in translation):

> I see above me at the Holy Well as many women, you would imagine, as would fill the town of Killarney. Some have buckets, bowls and kettles to fetch water; others have two-handled tubs of clothes for washing, with soap and a beetle on top of each. Those of them that weren't smoking a pipe had steam coming out of their mouths. I can't think of another spot in Ireland to beat it for such spirited talk. They drowned out the voice of the King and the sound of the sea. And although I was nearby, and they were speaking in Irish, it might as well have been French for all I could make of it. (Ó Criomhthain 1977 [1929], 170; O'Crohan 1986, 69)

This is an interesting quote for many reasons—not least of which are the references to Killarney and the French language—both of which indicate an awareness of cultural and linguistic diversity beyond the island.

### Visitors

Inevitably, Tomás's literary journey features prominently in the museum and a section called *Scríbhneoirí agus Oileánaigh* (Writers and Islanders) gives an account of the many different visitors to the island. The panels emphasise the "strong voice" of the individual authors, which had derived from an ancient and poetic oral tradition. Moreover the panels infer that: "The affection and mutual respect that grew up between these genteel scholars and semi-hardened Islanders is a remarkable example of the positive meeting of trained and disciplined minds with the keen intelligence of men and women with little or no formal education."

Strong emphasis is placed in these panels on the "cultural capital" (Bourdieu 1986) the visitors conferred on the island's cultural heritage. Terms such as "respect" and "confidence" feature. In the case of the panel on Marstrander, the blurb notes that "Marstrander was the first visitor to arouse in the Islanders, and particularly in Tomás Ó Criomhthain, a sense of the value and uniqueness of their language and culture." The panel on Brian Ó Ceallaigh remarks that when he left the island on New Year's Eve, he: "made a gesture that showed his respect for Tomás as a writer: he gave him his Waterman fountain pen." The original pen is on display among the artefacts—as well as a signed copy of an original edition of *An tOileánach*, which Tomás sent to his son in Hungry Hill, Massachusetts.

There is a strong visual emphasis throughout the museum. A section entitled *Albam Oileáin* (Island Album) notes the coincidence of the island's golden age with a period of salvage ethnography (see Chap. 1) when many visiting folklorists/ethnologists used the camera as a research tool. Moreover, the prominence of the visual is "explained" with reference to a quote from Tomás which says: "We are a poor simple people, living from hand to mouth." The panel continues with the suggestion that clothes, furniture and other implements on the island were used until they were worn out.

This might be taken as an apology for prevalence of visual over material culture in the interpretative centre. But the curator explained to me that he was also drawing on his previous experience as director of Kilmainham Gaol, where there was very little material evidence for the lives of the ordinary Dublin men, women and children who had been imprisoned there. As Cooke noted, "there is a class dimension to the keepsakes and souvenirs that generally comprise the holdings of museums—these are largely the detritus of a middle-class lifestyle." However, artefacts are not entirely absent.

### An Island Cottage

A section entitled *Áitreamh an Bhlascaoid* (The Blasket dwellings) contains a partial reconstruction of a Blasket house. Inside the house is an array of furniture and objects that might typically be expected in any house on the island. It is important to note that this presentation, largely inspired by Edna Ní Chinnéide (local school-teacher, cultural activist and poet), displaced the initial installation in that space, which was called *Áit an Uaignis* (the lonely place). The original artwork was inspired by a visit to the island by the curator in the company of Sean Pheats Taim in the early 1990s, in which he solemnly alluded to this spot just above the island harbour, where the bodies of the dead would rest for last prayers before removal to the mainland for burial. The original piece was quite impressionistic. A stage-designer with the Abbey Theatre, Deirdre Lavery, created it. The artwork showed a body laid out with the ribs in the form of the framework of a naomhóg. A musical installation with the sound of the sea accompanied it.

The subsequent dwelling scene adopts a more sentimental folk approach. The scenario is quite nostalgic, as the house has an "almost" lived-in feel. Karp and Kratz (2014, 56–7) note that, "objects are prominent resources for invoking a world that seems to have been lost, for nostalgia, which could be related to identities, playfully enacted (as colonial nostalgia often is), or called upon in defense of an existing order. In other words, there is another set of meanings and relationships through which things can be expository." Visitors can look in but not enter this house, which highlights the sense of otherness. The fact that the house is dimly lit also emphasises its place in the dim and dark past.

The link with *An tOileánach* is quite strong in this section. One panel features a quotation in which Tomás describes the house he grew up in:

> I was cradled in one of the medium-sized houses. It was a cramped little house, but what there was of it was kept neat, for my father was a very handy man, and my mother never knew what it was to be idle. She had a spinning-wheel for wool and another for flax, and combs for carding, and she used to have the job of spinning threads ready for the tailor with the distaff from her own wheel. Often enough she would spin it for the other clumsy women who couldn't put themselves in shape to do it, and were too lazy, anyhow, even if they knew the trick. (O'Crohan 1951 [1937], 29)

This section also features a quotation from *An tOileánach*, where Tomás describes building his own house. He says:

> After ten years of marriage I built a new house. Nobody handed so much as a stone or a lump of mortar to me all the time I was at work on it, and I roofed it myself. It isn't a large house, but, all the same, if King George were to spend a month's holiday in it, it isn't from the ugliness of the house that he would take his death. (O'Crohan 1951 [1937], 29)

I find this quotation (which also features in the introductory film) intriguing. Is it likely that no one on the island offered to help Tomás with building the house? If this is the case, was this a normal or an unusual scenario on the island? When I questioned an OPW worker about this, his personal view was that it was highly unlikely that Tomás built the house entirely by himself. Why then would Tomás paint this pen-picture? Perhaps he wished to indicate that he was a man apart from the other islanders—or perhaps he was an unpopular character on the island! (Tomás's house on the island has recently been restored by the OPW under the direction of architect Paul Arnold) (Illustration 7.2).

**Illustration 7.2**    Restored House of Tomás Ó Criomhthain. (© Máiréad Nic Craith)

## AT THE INTERFACE

### *Tradition and Modernity*

Outside of the museum (on the side of the Great Blasket Island) one sees a life-size sculpture of Tomás. The piece was commissioned by the OPW and created by the Cork sculptor Michael Quane, in 1992. Upon receiving the commission, Michael Quane read *An tOileánach* and other memoirs that had come from the island. These texts and the history of the island were to strongly influence his creation. In conversation with the sculptor, he told me that this was his first major commission and that he had "put a lot of himself" into it. The sculpture of Tomás is very dynamic, representing a writer battling with the elements. Tomás's body is twisted against the wind—his jacket is stretched out behind him, and his heavy trousers are pressing against his thighs. He has a firm grip on his hat. If one looks closely, one can see that Tomás holds a copy of *An tOileánach* under his jacket—protecting the memoir from the onslaught of the elements.

The sculpture is quite typical of Quane's work, which is rarely at ease and his sculpture of Tomás is at once both powerful and vulnerable. Gerry McCarthy from the *Sunday Times* traces Quane's depiction of that interface between power and vulnerability to a moment in his childhood when Quane was staying with his grandmother in Co. Offaly and witnessed a donkey drowning in a bog-hole. This experience may explain an artistic style where people and animals are writhing or battling with contorted limbs. McCarthy describes Quane's work in formal terms as belonging "to a stone-carving tradition that reaches back to the ancient world; yet his sensibility is acutely modern, mixing science and personal memory in a meditation on the place of humanity in the natural world" (McCarthy 2009).

McCarthy (2009) notes that the living creatures that emerge from Quane's stonework "are sinewy and muscular, yet they seem to be at odds with their own existence." The result, in this instance, is a representation of the writer that is dramatically different, for example, from Henry Kernoff's painting of Tomás in the museum. In Kernoff's artwork, Tomás is portrayed as a content old man at peace with himself. As Brenda Ní Shúilleabháin (2014) explains, Quane's sculpture is not the gentle Tomás that we see in photographs, but the man of the earth and sea that spent his life battling against the elements—the harsh weather and the strength of wind. Moreover, the sculpture of Tomás is battling against the tide of English, of mass-media and a demand for a life more comfortable that could be lived on the island.

The location of the sculpture outside of the museum facing towards other islands is interesting. Initially there was some disagreement about where the sculpture would be placed. While the OPW wanted the sculpture to face the museum, Quane told me that he was keen that Tomás would face the prevailing south-west wind. The OPW were possibly concerned that visitors would exit the museum to see a frontal view of the statue—which is precisely what happens! 

The form and location of the sculpture reminds me of Walter Benjamin's "angel of history." In his *Concept of History*, Benjamin (1974) refers to a painting by Klee called "Angelus Novus." In this piece of art, the Angel's face is turned towards the past, but the wind and the storm drive him irresistibly towards the future. While the angel would like to pause and ponder the past, "progress" determines that he is pushed towards a future which is catastrophic. While not looking at any island in particular, the sculpture of Tomás is facing westward rather than towards the mainland. At the same time, he is being blown by a wind back onto a mainland and a future which sees the evacuation of the island and a destruction of an island way of life. As Pat Cooke remarked to me: "The future, of course, contains the very visitor centre into which Tomás backs!"

The sculpture is a powerful representation of the interface, which is represented in both book and museum alike. Throughout the museum trajectory, visitors are reminded that the Blasket "library" emerged from a purely oral culture. One museum panel notes: "it is not possible to appreciate the extraordinary nature of the literary achievement of the Great Blasket writers without understanding that their books came out of a primarily oral culture." This is set in the context of a colonial era in Ireland when the Irish language was neglected and suppressed by the British Government who routed the native aristocracy who had maintained a written tradition. In consequence, the panel notes that "by the end of the nineteenth century, it existed largely as an oral medium among people living in the more remote parts of Ireland."

### Text and Visual

The museum also reflects a period of transition from literary text to a visual form of representation that involves photographs, artwork and some artefacts. Stanley (1998, 135) notes that the "photographic record completes the cycle of representation. If the Blasket authors achieved the heroic task of moving from verbal to written, then the written becomes extended into a new dimension creating a sense of immediate recognition which then feeds the reading of the texts afresh." There is strong emphasis on the visual in this museum. As we read texts from the memoir and from other Blasket books, we see images of Tomás and other islanders through the "camera eye" of the many ethnographers that visited the island. Moreover, "Haughey's contemporary photographs demonstrate not only how the past persists in the present, but how it too has an historical, an archival aspect even as it is created" (Stanley 1998, 135).

Walter Benjamin makes a connection between words and artefacts when he notes how:

> "traces of the storyteller cling to the story in the way the handprints of the potter cling to the clay vessel" (Benjamin 2006 [1936], 367). In compiling a yarn, a storyteller such as Tomás engages with that "slow piling one on top

of the other of thin, transparent layers which constitutes the most appropriate picture of the way in which the perfect narrative is revealed through the layers of a variety of retellings." Michael Ames (1992) draws on the image of a palimpsest to portray the different layers of text and thought that go into the making of a story. Just as Tomás has built up his life story into a complete memoir, the museum is also telling his story with a focus on particular moments or snapshots of points in time which may deepen our understanding of the story as a whole. (Cruikshank 2000)

Both book and museum offer an "afterlife" to a way of life that has technically disappeared. In writing his memoir, Tomás ensured that the memory of his people would not be forgotten. Indeed, the multiple editions and translations of his memoir have ensured that the memory of his fellow islanders and their way of life has been disseminated to a far wider audience than was originally anticipated. "Tomás's memoir and the other Blasket books have become artefacts in their own right – artefacts that are 'composed of congealed memories'" (Stanley 1998, 128).

In the museum Tomás's memoir sits alongside a range of artefacts. Like the artefacts in the museum, the memoir act as mnemonic device, which is capable of carrying the past into the present and giving an afterlife to the author who wrote it (Macdonald 2013, 152). But very few such objects are present—only one room in the museum has a series of artefacts that represent the traditional activities on the island. The bulk of representation comes from the panels set along the long corridor, confirming Stanley's interpretation that: "The linkage to the past is generated through a form of anthropology, albeit a highly distinctive one that privileges language and literature through visual representation" (Stanley 1998, 117–8).

### Home and Away

And yet describing this as "an afterlife" is not, strictly speaking, correct. As the emigration and American sections of the museum remind us, the Blasket Islanders did not die out. Instead, they emigrated to the mainland or further afield to Holyoke and Springfield, Massachusetts (see Chap. 8), Stanley (1998, 119–20) suggests that the museum (like the book) could be regarded as anti-romantic and (almost) postmodern. Like the Black Pit miner's museum in Wales, the Blasket Interpretative Centre offers "a form of 'historic revenge' in that it offers unexpected vistas on contemporary life. The Blasket Centre surprises the visitor by documenting photographically how the community has survived by the very activity it defied, emigration" (Stanley 1998, 119–120). Images in the final section of the centre do not display the poor "ragged peasants" so powerfully captured in George Thomson's pen-picture at the beginning of the *slí*. Instead we witness a community that is thriving in its adopted country.

The narrative in the emigration section is focused on integration into American society rather than the departure from the island and in this way offers an alternative image of the Blasket migrant as entrepreneur rather than pauper. Pat Cooke observes:

> You can have this image of the Blasket people as being doomed to extinction, or you can have the image of these islanders just moving on and continuing life in America and on the mainland. You are confronted with that choice in the migration section at the end of the exhibition. (Interview with Cooke, August 2019)

Throughout the migration section, the focus is on narrative rather than on objects such as suitcases or travel tickets. One of the more memorable images in the first section of the exhibition is the image of the New York skyline off the Blaskets, which the curator explains draws directly from Muiris Ó Súilleabháin vision of the gold-paved streets of New York, which he describes as follows:

> I looked west at the edge of the sky where America should be lying, and I slipped back on the paths of thought. It seemed to me now that the New Island was before me with its fine streets and great high houses, some of them so tall that they scratched the sky; gold and silver out on the ditches and nothing to do but gather it. (O'Sullivan 1983, 235–6)

While the reality was hardly that simple, the museum narrative tells stories of successful emigrants. We read, for example, the narrative of Maurice Thomas Kearney, who was born on the Great Blasket Island in 1891 and emigrated to the US at the age of 22. In 1919, at the age of 27, he became a US citizen. He spent his entire life employed with Moore Drop Forging Co.

We are informed that America as the land of spectacular success and failure was no different for the islanders than anyone else. "Many adapted well to their new surroundings, while others could never quite adjust to the pace and impersonality of the melting pot culture." Particular profile is given to Mike Carney, who was born on the Great Blasket in 1920 and emigrated to the US in 1948. He never forgot his link with the island and was conferred with an honorary doctorate from the National University of Ireland, Maynooth in 2009. This section in the museum abounds with photographs of a well-dressed and an apparently comfortable diaspora who have never forgotten their homeland, but who are prospering in America.

Both museum and memoir are biographical objects. "And although the museum is a public space, it acts as a biographical object as a witness to the unity of its 'owners' and as a making of their everyday experience 'into an experience', 'into a thing'" (Hoskins 1998, 8). In the case of the Blasket Interpretative Centre, the local community has not lost the link with the island. Both book and museum serve as links in a chain that bridges from the time the island was a hive of activity to the present day. In the words of David Brett (1996, 158), heritage "offers the possibility (not entirely illusory) of maintaining contact with a vanished 'habitus' and keeping some sense of social continuity and valued difference consciously alive."

Today, the interpretative centre attracts at least 50,000 visitors a year. Through its exhibitions, the museum posits the Blasket in a wider discourse about Irishness and the major immigration wave towards America of the twentieth century. Since it opened in 1994, the emphasis has shifted somewhat. In the initial stages, strong emphasis was placed on local literary heritage. The original museum brochure included many quotations in Irish and in translation from *An tOileánach* and the other Blasket books. A number of temporary exhibits softened the focus on the writers and drew attention to other dimensions of island life. A more recent booklet by Pádraig Ua Maoileoin (1996) was subsequently informally used as a tourist brochure, and featured topics such as the weather, occupations, food and musical traditions. Writers from the island were showcased at the end rather than the core of that booklet.

In my latest visit to the heritage centre, it seemed to me that Tomás and the other writers were again moving centre stage in the interpretative centre. A number of factors such as the publication of new Irish and English editions of *An tOileánach* (Ó Criomhthain 2002; O'Crohan 2012) as well as the inclusion of the memoir in the *Ireland in 100 objects* volume may have precipitated this shift (O'Toole 2013). Tomás's book is an act of defiance—an action that went against the rising tide of Anglicisation, of modernisation and marginalisation and makes a proud statement of his identity—one that does not shrink from portraying the hardships endured

by himself or his fellow islanders. On reading the book, we mentally re-
visit that community. The museum experience gives us a more embodied
experience of that community—allowing us—albeit temporarily to locate
ourselves in a particular time and island space that helps us understand this
island community. It allows us to indulge in a form of nostalgia for a
slower rhythm of life. Indeed, we can also participate in this act of rebellion "against the modern idea of time, the time of history and of progress"
(Boym 2001, xv).

# CHAPTER 8

# Irish-American Networks

Given the remoteness of Great Blasket Island, it is often assumed that Tomás and the other islanders were blissfully unaware of other locations—except perhaps for Dingle town and the surrounding hinterland. While isolation is a lived reality for people living on islands both in the past and in contemporary times, "islands are also very much spaces that link and map into relational activity and events around them" (Danson and Burnett 2014, 154). From this perspective the peripherality of island life is a social construction, but one that is well established and well rehearsed.

This chapter challenges the image of local insularity that is often associated with Tomás Ó Criomhthain as well as the opposition that is uncritically assumed between America as centre and the Blasket Island as peripheral in the early twentieth century. America has been presumed to be the metropolitan centre and the site of modernity for the Blasket Islanders. "On this reading it is the tie to America that brings the west coast of Kerry into the cultural space of the modern world system, not its position on the Atlantic seaboard of Ireland" (Gibbons 2008, 202). From this perspective, the west of Ireland became modern through its absorption of trends from the US. The Blasket Islanders "embraced" modernity only when they emigrated to America (Radhakrishnan 2003, 111).

© The Author(s) 2020
M. Nic Craith, *The Vanishing World of* The Islandman,
Palgrave Studies in Literary Anthropology,
https://doi.org/10.1007/978-3-030-25775-0_8

## COSMOPOLITAN CONNECTIONS

The Great Blasket has often been described as located "on the edge of Europe"—a phrase which projects its marginality and peripherality. Yet, the reality was different, and America was very central to the "imagined community" (Anderson 1991 [1983]) of the islanders until the evacuation of the island in 1953. Such networks are in line with Doreen Massey's observation that remoteness does not necessarily imply isolation. In such places "the security of the boundaries of the place one called home must have dissolved long ago, and the coherence of one's local culture must long ago have been under threat" (Massey 2013, 165–66).

The link between the islanders and Springfield/Boston was long-term. De Mórdha (2015, 350) notes that emigration to the US had begun some time before the middle of the nineteenth century. At that time "there was more talk about Springfield, Massachusetts and Hartford, Connecticut than there was about Limerick, Cork or Galway" (de Mórdha 2015, 350). In conversation with me, the author Gerald Hayes describes the movement of people from the Great Blasket to the US:

> Our ancestors somehow conjured up the courage to get on a boat and travel 3,000 miles across the Atlantic Ocean with very little in their pockets. They put down roots and, for the most part, they did pretty well for themselves and their families. They were extraordinary people. They were motivated to take a great leap into the unknown by the pain and suffering that they were experiencing in Ireland. And, of course, they were also driven by the stories about great opportunity in America. So, they put the two ideas together and said: "let's give it a go." (Hayes interview, June 2016)

When the islanders arrived in Massachusetts, they were prepared to work hard:

> When they came to America, most of them had the ability to speak English. They took the lowest paying jobs – the jobs that other people didn't want. When they came to the Springfield area, for example, they worked in mills, dug canals and laid pipes for the gas company. They took lousy jobs got paid poorly for it. But, they spoke English. which gave them an advantage over other ethnic groups immigrating to the United States. (Hayes interview, June 2016)

At the beginning, the islanders settled in clusters in particular areas but, as they prospered, they dispersed:

> Initially, the Irish lived in cheap housing near the city center. As they accumulated money over time, they literally moved up the hill. Later, many moved out to the suburbs. When they arrived in America, the Irish said to themselves: "my kids aren't going to go through this kind of hardship." And so, they emphasised education so that their children could move up the social and economic ladders. (Hayes interview, June 2016)

The Blasket community in Springfield has thrived for decades, even centuries, and is sometimes referred to as a diaspora—a term that was originally used to refer to the Jewish community which is now dispersed globally. Cohen (1997) defines diasporas as communities of people living together in one place who still fantasise about "the old country" and have an emotional attachment to it. The Blasket diaspora in Springfield looks across space and time to this tiny island off the west coast of Ireland and their relationship with it has continued long after the death of Tomás in 1937 and the evacuation of the island in 1953. The diasporic legacy continues today between those living on the mainland in Kerry and the descendants of islanders that emigrated to Springfield. The affective link applies even to those who were not born on the island.

## THE ISLANDMAN AND THE US

Just like any other islander, Tomás's connections with America were strong (Nic Craith 2019). Solnit (1997) remarks that emigration may be the mark of an Irish person. She says if the emphasis is on origins then the real Irishman is "some crusty old Gaelic-speaking fisherman on the Aran Islands." If the emphasis is on destination, however, then "to be Irish is to be destined to emigrate" (Solnit 1997, 114). The link with Boston is introduced on the very first page of *An tOileánach*. Tomás tells the reader that two members of his family are living in the US. This was quite common since many islanders emigrated to Springfield, Massachusetts. From the perspective of the islanders, the sea was a point of contact with the mainland and with the US. The island community was internationally connected, and the cultural dispositions of the people were much more layered and nuanced than previously recognised by visitors (see Chap. 1). While folklorists and other academics visiting the island regarded the island as a "closed, territorially bounded community," emigration to America was not unusual, and in some instances, the emigrants eventually returned to the island (Hill and Nic Craith 2016).

The US connection was an integral part of island life. Tomás's sister Máire emigrated to the states when her husband died leaving herself and her son penniless. Máire travelled to the states to earn the funds to sue her husband's family back in Ireland. While in the states, she took the opportunity to pay the fare for her sisters Nóra and Eibhlín to come and join her. Máire, herself, eventually came home and successfully won a court case against her husband's family. Her son, Pádraig, would eventually migrate to the US as a young man.

When the daughter of the lady next door returned from America with considerable savings in her purse, Tomás feared that a marriage would be arranged between himself and the newly-returned migrant. In the following excerpt, he tells of her return:

> She was wearing an ornate hat with a couple of feathers sticking out of it, and an ostentatious gold chain hung from her neck. She carried a parasol, and spoke with an accent, both in Irish and in English.
>
> She had a couple of large trunks, full of all sorts of things. Best of all, though, she'd brought a purse of gold from the States: she'd been over there seven years and she'd become very astute at amassing money. (O'Crohan 2012, 89)

Even her savings would not convince Tomás to marry his neighbour's daughter. Subsequently, Tomás hoped to marry a girl on the neighbouring island in Inishvickillane (see Chap. 2). However, his sister prevented that marriage and Tomás married a close neighbour. The young woman he had intended to marry emigrated herself to the US but returned home some years later in poor health. Tomás tells the reader:

> A while after this, the daughter of Mr Daly Senior, the caretaker of Inishvickillane, came home from America. This was the girl the rake Dermot, my uncle, had in mind for me in my early youth. She spent a few years over there, but her health failed, as happened to many others like her. She didn't get better when she came back but fell sick again, even though she came to the healthiest island in Ireland. (O'Crohan 2012, 227–8)

It is interesting that Tomás appears never to have considered emigrating himself and had a rather negative view of America. He gives great attention to his brother Páidí, who did not prosper abroad. Páidí had left the island unexpectedly and his subsequent return was also without warning. Unlike many other migrants, Páidí had not saved money and had nothing to his name apart from the clothes he was wearing. Páidí did not stay on the island. When his two sons invited him back to the States, he migrated again but fared equally badly on this second round. Ten years later, he returned to the Great Blasket. His sisters paid for his fare home as he hadn't the price of the boat trip.

Páidí coped well after his second return to the island and was keen to emphasise the benefits of work on the island compared with that abroad. When Páidí realises that two fresh lobsters earn a shilling each for the fisherman, he remarks on the difficulty of earning a similar amount in America. He exclaims: "'Oh good Lord! you'd have to sweat blood and tears in America to earn yourself two shillings, and all you need to do here is to lift a pot through twelve feet of water and toss it into a boat!' said he" (O'Crohan 2012, 216). Tomás was inclined to agree with him (Nic Craith 2019).

Tomás and his wife had twelve children, but only three of these lived until their thirties. While two of these, Cáit and Seán remained locally, the third (his namesake Tomás) emigrated at the age of 23. (Two other islanders Mícheál Ó Conchubhair and Mícheál Ó Guithín were with young Tomás on this journey). Eight years later, Tomás married Cáit Ní Mhainnín, a girl from Ventry. After the First World War, the couple and their two children paid an extended eight-month visit back to the Great Blasket. This visit is mentioned in *An tOileánach*. However, as funds were running out, they did not stay beyond the eight months. *The Islandman* writes:

> There was no fishing or anything being done when they came over, and they were spending whatever small amount of money they brought over with them. He said that if things were to carry on like this much longer, the money he had brought with him would be spent, and then he'd be in a queer fix. I didn't contradict him, but said that perhaps he might be right. (O'Crohan 2012, 293)

The sea did not hinder correspondence between them. In one letter, Tomás explains the importance of American dollars for people in Ireland. Tomás's son died in America on 4 July 1954. He was sixty-nine years of age (Hayes 2018, 266). By this time, the Great Blasket Island had already been evacuated.

When Tomás wrote the famous lines: "*mar ná beidh ár leitheidí arís ann*" (because our likes will never be here again) (Ó Criomhthain 2002, 328; O'Crohan 2012, 298), he is sometimes represented as correctly anticipating the eventual evacuation of the island in 1953. His son Seán is not actually convinced that this is the case, saying that Tomás was merely noting that times were changing. Seán says: "I suppose he had some inkling that because the generation that went before him wasn't like himself in any way" (Tyers 1998, 117). Whether or not Tomás had anticipated the actual evacuation from the island, there were many factors influencing a steady emigration of a small population to the "promised land." Tomás's memoir already gives insights into the harsh economic conditions that prevailed on the island. In his *Allagar na hInise* (written before *An tOileánach*), Tomás "recounted" a conversation between a mother and daughter. Although the islanders had been out on their naomhógs for three nights in a row, they had failed to catch any mackerel or herring, When the daughter asked her mother whether the lack of fish was due to the big fish eating the little ones, the mother explained that there were not even big fish to be caught now (O'Crohan 1986, 204).

Three years before the publication of Tomás's life story, the census recorded 143 people living on the Great Blasket Island. It appears that women were more likely to go to the US than men as their employment prospects were considerably poorer. While the men (in principle at least) could earn a living from fishing, women had no such opportunities except to go into service or get married. Once one member of the family emigrated, they were expected to earn the fare for the next member to join them. This phenomenon of "chain migration" (Miller 1985, 397; Nic Craith 1992, 10) had been well established throughout Ireland at least since the time of the Great Famine. Sometimes two members of the family would emigrate together. Only one or two children remained at home in the end to take care of the older folks.

The "straw on the camel's back" for the Blasket Islanders occurred within twenty years of Tomás's death in 1946. A young *islandman*, Seánín Ó Cearnaigh, was struck by meningitis, but weather conditions prevented the islanders from getting a doctor to attend him. His consequential, untimely death shook the island community and wiped out any regret they might have felt in leaving the island. The body could not be buried on the island graveyard, since it has not been blessed and there was no coffin on the island (Carney and Hayes 2013). The journey to bring a coffin to the island encountered many difficulties. Due to bad weather conditions, only those that had rowed the boat attended the funeral. Despite several appeals to the Irish government and a trip to the island by Éamon de Valera, the Irish Taoiseach at the time, help was not forthcoming. It took a further six years before the final islander was evacuated. The words of Tomás Ó Criomhthain had come to fruition. While he himself had not contemplated leaving the island, it was clear even by the time that he wrote *An tOileánach* that times were changing and the island lifestyle was not sustainable into the future.

## The Literary Legacy

When Tomás penned *An tOileánach*, he could hardly have anticipated the number of books that would subsequently flow from the island. Given the difficulty of finding partners on the island, it was inevitable that many of the Blasket authors were relatives of Tomás, himself. Seán Ó Criomhthain (1989–1975) was Tomás's youngest child. Having grown up on the island, he married Éibhlís Ní Shúilleabháin in 1933. (Her grandfather was married to Tomás's sister). They had two daughters but the lack of facilities for children on the island meant the family moved to mainland after Tomás's death. Seán died in a "hit-and-run" accident in 1975. His memoir *Lá dár Saol* (*A Day in the Life*) reflects on the evacuation from the island (Ó Criomhthain 1969; O'Crohan 1992). This is an important account of the islanders' relationship with the Great Blasket as they settled down in the mainland.

Pádraig Ua Maoileoin (1913–2002) (Tomás's grandson) also took pen to paper and was the editor of the second Irish language edition of *An tOileánach* (see Chap. 2). Pádraig was born in Coimínéol, on the Kerry. His mother Cáit Ní Chriomhthain died within ten years of his birth and his father married again. His parents had intended that Pádraig would enter the religious life, but the young man had other ambitions and won a scholarship to University College, Cork. After a year in Cork, he opted to join the Irish police force and served as a guard for thirty years. *Na hAird Ó Thuaidh*, his first memoir, describes his youth in Corca Dhuibhne and the local literary "disease" of writing memoirs (Ua Maoileoin 1960). This was followed by *De Réir Uimhreacha* (Ua Maoileoin 1969) which describes the next stage in Pádraig's life story as a trainee policeman.

Although Tomás's memoir was the first to be written on the island, another life story written by a much younger man was the first to be translated into English. *Fiche Blian ag Fás* (Twenty Years a-Growing) was written by Muiris Ó Súilleabháin, who had been born on the island in 1904. Muiris had been placed in an institution in Dingle at six months following the early death of his mother. He was brought to the Blasket Island as an eight-year old child to live with his father, his grandfather and his siblings. He knew no Irish at that time. Although Muiris considered emigrating to America, he was ultimately persuaded to stay in Ireland and left the island at twenty years of age to enter the *Garda Síochána* (the Irish police force), where he served in the *Gaeltacht* region of Galway. Seven years later, he left the guards and subsequently drowned while swimming in 1950. Muiris's memoir describes his childhood and teenage years on the island. The original Irish language edition as well as the English Translation (*Twenty Years a-Growing*) were published in 1933 (Ó Súilleabháin 1933; O'Sullivan 1933). This meant that Ó Súilleabháin's memoir was the first Blasket life story to appear in English translation (see Chap. 2). Subsequently, it was translated into French (O'Sullivan 1936), German (O'Sullivan 1956) and Polish (O'Sullivan 1986).

Memoirs from women on the Great Blasket were rarer than men and the best known of these is the Blasket book written by Peig Sayers, which was first published in Irish (Sayers 1936). Her life story was subsequently published in English (Sayers 1962, 1972), German (1996) and French (1999). Peig had been born on the mainland. At twelve years of age, she went into service in Dingle but had to return home due to illness. As a teenager, Peig fully intended to go to America, but when her friend Cáit had an accident and could not send her the fare, Peig married an islander, Páidí Ó Guithín and moved onto the Great Blasket. Peig remained on the island until 1942. She only left it in her old age when her health failed and was brought to an old folk's home in Dingle, where she died in 1958. Peig narrated rather than penned her life story. In this she was encouraged by folklorists Máire Ní Chinnéide and Léan Ní Chonalláin from the Irish Folklore Commission (Nic Craith 2019).

Another female memoir was written by Máire Ní Ghaoithín (1909–1998). A daughter of the island king, Máire grew up in a household where there were regular academic visitors in search of the primitive island lifestyle. Her mother had been described by Synge as:

> A young married woman of about twenty, who manages the house, shook hands with me also and then, without asking if we were hungry, began making us tea in a metal teapot and frying rashers of bacon. She is a small, beautifully formed woman, with brown hair and eyes – instead of the black hair

and blue eyes that are usually found with this type in Ireland – and delicate feet and hands that are not common in these parts, where the woman's work is so hard. (Synge 1912, 39)

Having grown up on the island, Máire moved to Dublin to work in a college of education for Protestant children. (Girls from the *Gaeltacht* were regularly employed there). She subsequently returned to Kerry, where she married and had two children. Her first book *An tOileán a Bhí* (The Island that was) was more an objective description of life on the island rather than a life story.

In 1940 Nóra Ní Shéaghdha published *Thar Bealach Isteach* (Across the Sound). Nóra (1907–1975) was born in Muiríoch, on the Dingle hinterland. Educated as a primary school teacher, she took up a position in the island school in 1927 and spent seven years teaching on the island. Her memoir was written at the promptings of the local clergy and presented an account of her years as a school teacher on the island—a place that was previously as foreign to her as the continent of Africa.

The literary outpourings continued even after the evacuation of the island in 1953. That year saw the publication of *Is Truagh ná Fanann an Óige (A Pity Youth does not last)* from Mícheál Ó Gaoithín (1904–1974), more commonly known as An File (the poet), (Ó Gaoithín 1953; O'Guiheen 1982). He was Peig Sayer's son. In the English language translation, the memoir is subtitled "Reminiscences of the Last of the Great Blasket Island's Poets and Storytellers." Although born and bred on the island, Mícheál did venture to the US, but only stayed a few months. When he returned home, it was clear to him that the island community was on the verge of extinction. He describes the island as follows:

> The long years have vanished and all I can see today are the old ruined houses where people used to live. I remember strong and brave men and women to be living in the houses, that are, my sorrow, ruined now. Twelve houses have gone to rack, to my memory that were at their height in my young days. Cliff grass and nettles are growing round them today. (O'Guiheen 1982, 82)

A few years after his return to the Great Blasket, Mícheál and his mother Peig moved to the mainland.

Seán Sheáin Í Chearnaigh's (1912–1997) volume *An tOileán a Tréigeadh* (the Deserted Island) was published in 1974 (Í Chearnaigh

1974). This was followed four years later by his *Iarbhlascaodach ina Dheoraí* (A Former Islander in Exile) (Í Chearnaigh 1978). Seán's grandmother Máire was Tomás's sister. Seán attended school on the island and then began earning his living as a fisherman. He subsequently moved to the mainland and spent time with a married sister in Galway as well as with Muiris Ó Súilleabháin in Conamara. Subsequently he was employed in a sorting office in Dublin. He then returned as postmaster to the Great Blasket until it was evacuated in 1953. After the evacuation, he went to live with his mother in Muiríoch. In the 1950s he went to live in Dingle and died in a hospital there in 1997.

There were numerous further publications from the Great Blasket which ranged from folklore to novel, including Tomás's own *Dinnshenchus ón mBlascaod* (Placelore from the Island) which was published posthumously in Irish but never translated into English (Ó Criomhthain 1935). Along with these first-hand accounts of life on the island, a number of academics conducted several analyses of this literary legacy in the form of books and journal essays (e.g. Céitinn 1992; Nic Craith 1988; Ó Coileáin 1979, 1998; Ó Conaire 1992).

Apart from the publication of these memoirs, one should also note the parody of Tomás's original memoir in the form of *An Béal Bocht (the Poor Mouth)* by Flann O'Brien (Na gCopaleen 1941; O'Brien 1973) (see Chap. 6). The principal character in the plot is Bonaparte O'Coonassa, who is born into a stinking cabin in a village called Corkadoragha. While that place-name is fictitious, it is remarkably similar to the name Corca Dhuibhne, a Gaeltacht in the south-west of Ireland. Although this fictional place is beautiful, it is also horridly poor. People eat potatoes on a daily basis (an Irish stereotype) and typically share their accommodation with their pigs and sheep (yet another stereotype). Bonaparte's mother and an old man also live in the house. His father is absent since he is in jail (implying a link between Irish-speakers and crime). The novel describes the life of Bonaparte, which culminates in a twenty-nine year prison sentence for murder. As readers, we are unclear as to whether Bonaparte is actually guilty of any crime. Since the trial is conducted in English, the main character understands nothing of the proceedings and cannot defend himself. On entering the prison, he meets a man whom he assumes to be his father, implying that the son is continuing a family tradition of criminality.

The title of the book, *An Béal Bocht (The Poor Mouth)*, is an expression used to describe "exaggerated distress, concocted for the express purpose of extorting something from the audiences." Kennelly (1977, 86) calls it "the slave's weapon." The title infers a self-pitying whinge and reflects a sense of complaint and injustice for the condition of the Irish-speaker in Ireland even after the country had gained independence from the UK. It also reflects a long tradition of complaining in Irish language literature, and the image of poverty associated with the Irish-speaking peasant. The subtitle of the book, *An Milleánach*, literally means the "fault-finder" and rhymes with *An tOileánach*. The subtitle has been translated in the English language version as "A Bad Story about a Hard Life"—reinforcing the moaning element implied in Tomás's life story (Nic Craith and Kockel 2018).

## Reflective Nostalgia and Loss

Despite the loss of their island home, the islanders who went to America gained a new perspective on their traditional Gaelic culture. Far from the suspicion that they encountered on the mainland, in America the string of books that had been pioneered by Tomás and *An tOileánach* were known and respected. Daithí de Mórdha explains:

> I think perhaps that when emigrants from the island went to America and found that the island books were known and valued internationally they became even more proud of their roots here. Because there was certainly discrimination here in Ireland against the islanders at one time, and not just in Dingle where they might have been seen as wild or a bit uncouth. There were times when they were treated as outsiders in rural communities here on the mainland – there are stories of them being treated that way at weddings and gatherings here. So, in a way, who they were and where they came from was validated in America and elsewhere by the island books. (de Mórdha 2017, 95)

There are numerous accounts of the islanders in Springfield and Holyoke (the Republican 2012; Hayes 2018). At the time that Tomás wrote his memoir, there was already a close-knit community from the Dingle Peninsula in the US. While they adapted well to their new environment (anglicising their names, finding work, etc.), they also retained a sense of their island home and its culture. Some of these sought membership in the John Boyle O'Reilly Club, which has been in existence since 1880.

In recent years, a number of volumes have been penned in America, highlighting the ongoing cultural connections between Blasket Islands and Springfield, Massachusetts. Not all of these are from former islanders. In 2012, for example, Robert Kanigel (a retired Professor from MIT) published his "love letter" to a vanished way of life. The blurb on the cover of *On an Irish Island* highlights the remote nature of the place and promotes the book as: "the remarkable story of a remote outpost nearly untouched by time in the first half of the twentieth century, and of the adventurous men and women who visited and were inspired by it." The author had no family connections with the island. A chance trip on his honeymoon to the Blasket Centre (see Chap. 7) sparked the author's interest in the island community, its disappearing way of life and the complex relations at home and abroad.

A narrative of loss permeates this text and prompts the question of whether one can be nostalgic for a place one has never lived. Svetlana Boym is convinced that this can be the case. She notes that while "nostalgia is a longing for a place, but actually it is a yearning for a different time – the time of our childhood, the slower rhythms of our dreams. In a broader sense, nostalgia is a rebellion against the modern idea of time, the time of history and progress" (Boym 2001, xv).

Another volume written by an "outsider" was Cole Moreton's *Hungry for Home* (2000). As with Kanigel, Moreton has no Irish connections. Born in East London, Moreton is a journalist, and formerly wrote for the newspaper, *The Independent on Sunday*, and for various magazines. As the title suggests, Moreton's volume specifically focuses on the emigrant narrative, which is told from the perspective of the Kearney/Carney family—and the geographic and cultural connections across the Atlantic between those who remained "at home" on the mainland in Co Kerry and those who set up a new life for themselves in America.

Moreton's book is divided into three parts. Part one entitled "The End of the World" describes life on the island at the time of the unfortunate death of the young islander from meningitis. The emigrant narrative features strongly in this section and so, for example, we meet Cáit Ní Chearnaigh, the sister of this deceased islander, who remained at home to look after her ageing father. Moreton writes:

> There were very few women like herself among the fifty or so people left on the island, and hardly enough young men to crew more than a couple of canoes. So many of her friends left for America before the war and now that

is over there is talk of the remaining ones being allowed to follow. Whenever the weather allows the island postman to cross to the mainland for mail he always brings back parcels from her cousins, who write that life is wonderful. Cáit knows more people in America that are left on this island. Most of those that remain are growing old like her father. The boys may go. No doubt they will. Perhaps they will send money home because she cannot leave him. (Moreton 2000, 7)

The second part of the book focuses on the island story from 1653 to the time of writing. Part 3 is entitled "The Land of Youth" and begins with the arrival of a letter with the fare to America for a young man on the island. Neither the young islander nor his father doubt that the journey is necessary (Moreton 2000, 149).

At the beginning of the book, Moreton seems taken aback at the type of nostalgia displayed by Mike Carney (originally from the island and then living in Springfield). Moreton describes their encounter as follows:

His [Mike Carney's] account of it all was so nostalgic that I was surprised when he said he would never go back and live on the Great Blasket, even if it were possible to do so. "Everything went against us on the island. The weather was against us. The living was tough. When somebody got sick you had to go through hell, just like my brother's death. It's beautiful to look at, but scenery doesn't fill the stomach." (Moreton 2000, 231)

The title implies an unsatisfied appetite—a hunger for a home that no longer exists in reality but still persists in the imagination.

Much more significant from the perspective of this book is the memoir subsequently produced by Michael Carney himself. The memoir was written in conjunction with his son-in-law Gerald Hayes who explained to me how it all began:

Over the course of the thirty or so years since I met him, Mike would tell me stories and more stories about the Great Blasket. As I moved towards my retirement, I realised that these stories had real value. So, I started a series of Saturday morning conversations where he would talk about his life growing up on the island and eventually emigrating to Springfield. I tape recorded these chats and eventually transcribed them. Finally, I weaved them all together into a book that comprises Mike's memoirs. (Hayes interview, June 2016)

In this writing partnership, Hayes had a strong sense of obligation to facts, whereas Mike was more interested in communicating the story to his audience. Hayes explains:

> One of the challenges that I had in collaborating with Mike is distinguishing between his stories and the absolute truth. I sometimes found that there was some "Blarney" involved in his version of events. That's a frightening thing for an author, because you have a certain obligation for accuracy. But to a storyteller, there is no issue here, because his objective is to communicate a story. It's not unlike the parables in the Bible. Parables are intended to communicate an underlying truth, but not to be true in and of themselves. That's what Mike was all about. (Hayes interview, June 2016)

The memoir that emerged from this process, *From the Great Blasket to America,* was linked directly with *An tOileánach.* The blurb on Carney and Hayes's cover makes a direct connection with Tomás's memoir and also refers to the issue of individual versus collective voice (see Chap. 3). It reads:

> Written when Mike approached the age of ninety-three, with his son-in-law Gerald Hayes, his memoir is probably the last in a long line of books written by Blasket Islanders, including Tomás Ó Criomhthain, Muiris Ó Súilleabháin and Peig Sayers. Recounting one man's life but relating the experience of many, it chronicles a lifetime devoted to family, community and legacy. All the while, he seems haunted by the immortal words of Ó Criomhthain: the like of us will never be again. (Carney and Hayes 2013, blurb)

Michael had been born on the Great Blasket Island in 1920, when Tomás was still alive. In his memoir, he "remembers" Tomás as an old man who once gave him a pinch of sugar when he expected something more as a handout on St. Stephen's Day. "For the most part, he [Tomás] was quiet and kept to himself." Carney suggests that "It was just his old age and the hard life he lived" (Carney and Hayes 2013, 72). At seventeen years of age, Michael left for Dublin but ended up in America ten years later. While in Dublin, he played an active role in pursuing the welfare of those he had left behind on the island and continually lobbied the government for their evacuation to the mainland. As one might anticipate, his memoir is highly nostalgic and his first chapter calls the island: "The most beautiful place on earth." Even though he had spent decades in the US, Michael still regarded the island as his homeland He tells us:

This island is my homeland. Even at almost ninety-three years of age, I dream about it almost every night.

The first thing I see in my dreams is the white sandy beach (an tráigh bhán) on the coast of the island facing the mainland. When we were children, we used to roll up our trousers and run in the surf or play Gaelic football and other sports on the beach that we called "the strand". This is the only flat land on the whole island. To the right and left of the beach is a coastline of black jagged rock running north and south with cliffs averaging about 30 feet high. (Carney and Hayes 2013, 1)

Carney's nostalgia is not the sentimental kind which portrays the island as a utopia. Instead, it is more in line with what Svetlana Boym calls reflective nostalgia, which she explains as one that "does not pretend to rebuild the mythical place called home" (Boym 2001, 50). This type of nostalgia recognises that gap between what was in the past and what is in the present. In this situation, nostalgias are at a distance in both time and space from "home" which had often degenerated into ruins or have become gentrified into something quite different. Boym notes, "reflective nostalgia has elements of both mourning and melancholy.... Reflective nostalgia is a form of deep mourning that performs a labor of grief through pondering pain and through play that points to its future" (Boym 2001, 55).

Recognising the difficulties that were associated with the former "home," this type of nostalgia does not attempt to rebuild a "lost cause." In Carney's memoir, the ex-islander notes the hardship of island life:

While the scenery was beautiful, island life involved quite a lot of hardship. It was a tough existence because of the bad weather, the rough ocean and the isolation. Weather was very important because the people made their living fishing out on the ocean. When high winds and rain kicked up, you couldn't go fishing out on the ocean, or go get the mail in Dunquin, or go to mass on a Sunday at St Gobnet's Church over on the mainland. Weather was a big problem. In fact, I think the word "Blasket" came from the word "blasted", referring to the weather. (Carney and Hayes 2013, 9)

Given the untimely and possibly unnecessary death of his brother, Carney has no illusions about the lack of services on the island and the implications of that for the community who lived on the island. He writes:

The island was a "bare-knuckle" place. There was no police department, no courthouse, no post office, no general shop, no doctor, no electricity, no running water, no church and no pub. The islanders had to make do with what they had, which was not much. I maintain that the island people were saintly, but didn't know it. We lived quietly among ourselves. We were hard-working. We got along well together. We were very understanding and accepting of our situation. (Carney and Hayes 2013, 10)

This acknowledgement of hardship connects *An tOileánach*, the first memoir from the island, with Carney's volume—effectively, the last memoir to be written by someone who was actually born on the island. Carney's reflections on the difficulty of island life mirror those of *The Islandman* himself who wrote:

We are a poor and simple people, barely getting by, day by day, one following the other. I think it's just as well that we weren't greedy people. We were skilled and we were satisfied with the way of life that the Blessed Master had ordained for us – to do everything without shirking; to plough the waves, often without hope of making headway, but our hope was always in God, We had differences of opinion with one another. We had our own virtues and our own small faults. I never shied away from writing about the worthy traits or the small failings we had; neither did I hide the hardship that befell us, and which we faced, because we had no alternative but to endure them. (O'Crohan 2012, 296)

Unlike Tomás Ó Criomhthain, Carney has emigrated from the island and allows himself to indulge in some reflective nostalgia:

In my dreams, I remember the island as a happy place. Maybe we didn't know any better, I still get nostalgic over it. After all these many, many years, I still miss it dearly.
To me, the island today looks lonely all by itself in comparison to when I was growing up there. It was so lively then. It is my belief that the island doesn't deserve to be lonely like that. I would like to see it to go back to the way it was, a lively community of friendly people. Well, I suppose I can always dream. (Carney and Hayes 2013, 11)

However, Carney appreciates the literary inheritance that was sparked by Tomás—a quality he attributes to their both being in an island place:

I think the sea has some kind of quality to it that makes you able to see things more clearly. There are fewer distractions. Someone once said, "if you want to become a good writer, go live on an island". Maybe that's why the island was home to such a large number of famous storytellers and authors for the small size of the population. (Carney and Hayes 2013, 69–70)

Carney's memoir is effectively the last compiled by someone born on the island. Nevertheless, the flow of books about the islanders remains unabated. Inspired by his father-in-law's biography, Carney's son-in-law was responsible for the publication of a biography of Pádraig Ó Catháin, the last island king. Hayes explains how he became interested in the character of the king:

> It was very interesting for me. You have a certain preconceived notion of a king – royalty, crowns, robes and castles etc. But this was an island with 176 inhabitants at maximum and yet, they had a king. It was, in fact, an exceedingly modest kingdom. So, I became intrigued. I sat with Mike and he explained that the king was a kind of unelected mayor. I started doing some research and the result was *The Last Blasket King*. The king was a pivotal character in the history of the island, their most prominent civic leader in the early part of the twentieth century. (Hayes interview, June 2016)

This book, entitled *The Last Blasket King*, was a collaborative venture between Hayes and Eliza Kane, a great-great-granddaughter of the last king himself (Hayes and Kane 2015). Eliza had been exploring her own Blasket heritage, and when her brother decided to shoot a documentary film about the family's Blasket heritage, she became involved in the project. While filming in Dingle, Eliza and Gerald met and decided to collaborate on the king's biography. Eliza delved into relevant archives and located a very illuminating interview of her grandfather (the king's grandson) by her father.

The character of Tomás features quite strongly in the king's biography, with the authors noting that although Tomás and the king were "giants" in the community, there was no rivalry between them. Instead they were lifelong friends leading mutually beneficial lives. The authors propose that this friendship was nurtured by the different roles each played in the island. While the king's role was political, Tomás's was literary. However, the king and Tomás held very different political perspectives. While the former was partisan towards Redmond, an Irish nationalist member of the British parliament, Tomás's sympathies lay with Sinn Féin (a nationalist party) who refused to cooperate with the British parliament.

Matson (1996) speculates that for all their friendship, there was some rivalry between them. Tomás used to call the king "*fear na coronach*" (the man of the crown) which may have been somewhat ironic. However, any such irony might be outweighed by the positive pen-pictures Tomás portrays of his lifelong friend. In an early reference to the island king, Tomás explains how his former schoolmate earned the title:

> The King used to be beside me on the bench, and he was a fine placid hunk of a chap, and has been ever since. We were the same age. He often pointed his finger at another boy who was being bold, someone screeching, another pair punching each other, a big yellow snot running down from the nose of other hunks here and there. The King didn't like these sights and he was always pointing them out to me. Look at the nature that is innate in a person from early youth and which always remains with him. It was the same with the King, who didn't like to see ugly, dirty sights in school when he was young, sights that others didn't notice at all. It was no wonder, therefore, that when the authorities came round wanting to name a King for the Blasket they concluded that he would be the best person to bear the title. (O'Crohan 2012, 16–17)

The final American volume of relevance is the recent biography of Tomás Ó Criomhthain by Gerald Hayes. Published in 2018, *The Blasket Islandman: the Life and Legacy of Tomás Ó Criomhthain* is a detailed account of *The Islandman*'s lifestyle and his literary legacy. The biographer's stated intention is "to describe the circumstances and forces that influenced his [Tomás's] writing and to delineate his literary and cultural impact" (Hayes 2018, xiv). It is clearly intended to be a biography of Tomás rather than an analysis of his writings from a literary perspective. One could hardly suggest that a sense of nostalgia emanates from this book which contains considerable detail on the emigration of islander after islander to Springfield, Massachusetts. The volume pays particular attention to *The Islandman*'s descendants both at home in Kerry and in the US.

The author critiques Tomás's legacy in terms of six major achievements. In the first instance, Tomás gave voice to the common man. "He was a simple fisherman and farmer who wrote brilliantly in his native tongue" (Hayes 2018, 320). Second, Tomás furthered the transition from oral to literary in rural Ireland. When (third) Tomás perceived the fading away of life on the island, he wrote down the community's life story in order to ensure that it would not be forgotten. "His works facilitated the spread of the story of the Great Blasket worldwide" (Hayes 2018, 321–2). Fourth,

Tomás documented the folklore of the island. Fifthly, he advanced the cause of the Irish language and culture. Finally (and crucially), he inspired a vast literary heritage. "His example led to at least eleven other native islanders publishing books in Irish – a rare feat indeed for such a small and isolated community" (Hayes 2018, 322).

Although hardly nostalgic, the book does portray a narrative of loss that is inherent in all the Blasket volumes. Hayes (2018, 324) notes "by devoting himself to his writing, Tomás provided us with a lively portrayal of a vanishing community, so that he and he and his community would live on after they had passed away." Although the island was evacuated in 1953, the island community and its heritage are not forgotten. It lives on in Tomás's *An Oileánach* and its literary legacy.

The physical movement of islanders from Kerry to the US did not rupture the Blasket literary heritage. Instead, the emergence of Blasket diasporic writing opened up a new horizon of Blasket literary space and the concept of the island home has transferred not just across time but also across geographical space. Although the island community experienced disruption, dislocation and displacement, it has also reclaimed those roots in postcolonial life. As de Mórdha (2015, 555) notes:

> The Blasket Island community is scattered in all directions but it can be said that the island did not die. Tomás Ó Criomhthain wanted to make an account of his life available "so that I would still be alive when I am dead." Certainly, in Ó Criomhthain's words, the island is still alive while it is dead because there is more mention of it now that there ever was.

While the migration of the Blasket islanders struck a death knell for the community actually living on the island, the new sense of pride in their culture that emerged in former islanders was empowering. The Blasket story had become a global narrative and their likes will never be forgotten.

# Bibliography

## Archival Material

Dingle Library Collection entitled *Cnuasach Cuimhne Thomáis Uí Chriomhthain* (Memories of Tomás Ó Criomhthain), Dingle Library, Kerry. In this collection one finds (i) the new final chapter of *An tOileánach*, (ii) a letter/essay that Tomás wrote about Brian Ó Ceallaigh, (iii) letters that Tomás wrote to An Seabhac as well as two letters that he dictated to his son Seán for An Seabhac, and (iv) Tomás Ó Criomhthain, Brian Ó Ceallaigh agus mé féin written by An Seabhac. This was broadcast on Raidio Éireann.

Ms 15,785, National Library, Dublin, ten letters from Tomás Ó Criomhthain to Brian Ó Ceallaigh.

Ms 11,000 (22), R. I. Best papers. Letters from Robin Flower to Richard Irvine Best, National Library, Dublin.

Ms Oslo. Catalogue of terms that Tomás Ó Criomhthain sent to Carl Marstrander. University of Oslo.

Ms *Seanchas ón Oileán Tiar*. National Folklore Collection, University College, Dublin.

## Editions of the Memoir

Ó Criomhthain, Tomás. *An tOileánach*, An Seabhac a chuir in eagar. Baile Átha Cliath: Clólucht an Talbóidigh, 1929.

Ó Criomhthain, Tomás. *An tOileánach*, Pádraig Ua Maoileoin a chuir in eagar. Baile Átha Cliath: Cló Talbóid, 1973.

© The Author(s) 2020
M. Nic Craith, *The Vanishing World of* The Islandman,
Palgrave Studies in Literary Anthropology,
https://doi.org/10.1007/978-3-030-25775-0

Ó Criomhthain, Tomás, *An tOileánach*. Seán Ó Coileáin a chuir in eagar. Baile Átha Cliath: Cló Talbóid, 2002.

TRANSLATIONS OF THE MEMOIR

Ó Criomhthain, Tomás. *Manden på Øen*, translated by Ole Munch-Pedersen. Århus: Husets, Forlag, 1996.
O'Crohan, Tomás. *The Islandman*, translated by Robin Flower. Dublin, and Chatto and Windus, London: The Talbot Press, 1951 [1937].
O'Crohan, Tomás. *Karg Kust*, translated by M. Angström. Stockholm: Bokförlag K F: S, 1949.
O'Crohan, Tomás. *Die Boote Fahren Nicht Mehr Aus*, translated by Annemarie Böll and Heinrich Böll, Göttingen: Lamuv, 1983.
O'Crohan, Tomás. *L'homme des îles*, translated by Jean Buhler and Úna Murphy. Lausanne: Éditions Favre S.A., 1989.
O'Crohan, Tomás. *L'Isolano (The Island Man)*, translated by Antonio Fazio. Italy: Arianna, 1991.
O'Crohan, Tomás. *The Islander: A Translation of an tOileánach* by Garry Bannister and David Sowby. Dublin: Gill & Macmillan, 2012.

TEXTS

Akenson, Donald. *The Irish Education Experiment: The National System of Education in the Nineteenth Century*, New York: Routledge 2012 [1970].
Ames, Michael. *Cannibal Tours and Glass Boxes: The Anthropology of Museums*. Vancouver: University of British Columbia Press, 1992.
Anderson, Benedict. *Imagined Communities: Reflections on the Origin and Spread of Nationalism*. London, New York: Verso, 1991 [1983].
Anderson, John D. The *Navigatio Brendani*: A Medieval Best Seller, *The Classical Journal*, 83(4), (1988): 315–22.
An Fear Eagair. Tagra. In: Tomás Ó Criomhthain, *An tOileánach*, Baile Átha Cliath, lgh, 1929, 5–6.
Anon. The Missing Link, *Punch*, XLII/1862, October, p. 165.
Appadurai, Arjun. Introduction: Commodities and the Politics of Value. In: Arjun Appadurai ed. *The Social Life of things: Commodities in Cultural Perspective*. Cambridge: University Press, 1969, 3–63.
Arensberg, Conrad M. and Kimball, Solon T. *Family and Community in Ireland*. Cambridge, MA: Harvard University Press, 1940.
Arensberg, Conrad M. Preface to *Family and Community in Ireland*, 2nd edition by Conrad M. Arensberg and Solon T. Kimball. Cambridge, MA: Harvard University Press, 1968.

Arensberg, Conrad M. *The Irish Countryman: An Anthropological Study.* Long Grove: Waveland Press, 1988 [1937].

Arnold, Matthew. *Culture and Anarchy: An Essay in Political and Social Criticism.* London: Smith Elder and Co. 1869.

Arnold, Philip P. Black Elk and Book Culture, *Journal of the American Academy of Religion*, 67(1), (1999): 85–111.

Asad Talal ed. *Anthropology and the Colonial Encounter.* London: Ithaca Press, 1973.

Ashcroft, Bill, Griffiths, Gareth and Tiffin, Helen. *PostColonial Studies. The Key Concepts.* London and New York: Routledge, 2000.

Bakhtin, M.M. *Problems of Dostoevsky's Poetics.* Ed. and trans. Caryl Emerson. Minneapolis: University of Minnesota Press, 1984.

Bannister, Garry and Sowby, David. Introduction. In: Tomás O'Crohan, *The Islander: A Translation of an tOileánach* by Garry Bannister and David Sowby, Dublin: Gill and Macmillan, 2012, pp. xvi–xxii.

Barton, David, and Papen, Uta. *Anthropology of Writing: Understanding Textually Mediated Worlds.* London: Continuum, 2010.

Baudrillard, Jean. *Simulations.* Translated by P. Foss, P. Patton and P Beitchman. New Oak: Semiotext (e), 1983.

Beckett, J. C. *The Making of Modern Ireland 1603–1923.* London, Boston: Faber and Faber, 1966.

Behan, Brendan. *Die Geisel* (The Hostage). Translated by Annemarie Böll and Heinrich Böll. Cologne: Gustav Kiepenheuer, 1958.

Behar, Ruth and Gordon, Deborah, eds. *Women Writing Culture.* California, London: University of California Press, 1995.

Beiner, Guy. Commemorative Heritage and the Dialectics of Memory. In: Mark McCarthy ed., *Ireland's Heritages: Critical Perspectives on Memory and Identity.* Aldershot and Burlington: Ashgate, (2005), pp. 55–69.

Benjamin, Walter. On the Concept of History. Suhrkamp Verlag. Frankfurt am Main, 1974. https://folk.uib.no/hlils/TBLR-B/Benjamin-History.pdf (accessed 11 August 2018).

Benjamin, Walter. The Storyteller: Reflections on the Works of Nicolai Leskov. In: Dorothy Hale ed. *The Novel: an Anthology of Criticism and Theory 1900–2000*, Malden MA Blackwell 2006 [1936], pp. 361–78.

Benjamin, Walter. The Task of the Translator. In: Hannah Arendt ed. *Illuminations*, translated by Harry Zohn. New York: Harcourt, Brace and the World, 1968 [1923], pp. 69–82.

Berliner, David. Are Anthropologists Nostalgist? In: Olivia Angé and David Berliner eds. *Anthropology and Nostalgia.* New York, Oxford: Berghahn Books, 2015, pp. 17–35.

Binchy, Daniel A. Two Blasket Autobiographies, *Studies* 23(92), (1934): 545–60.

Black Elk, Nicholas and Neihardt, John G. *Black Elk Speaks: Being the Life Story of a Holy Man of the Oglala Sioux.* Lincoln and London: University of Nebraska, 2000 [1932].

Black Elk, Nicholas and Neihardt, John G. *Black Elk Speaks: The Complete Edition.* With a new introduction by Philip J. Deloria and annotations by Raymond J. DeMallie. Lincoln and London: University of Nebraska Press, 2014.

Black Elk. *The Sacred Pipe: Black Elk's Account of the Seven Rites of the Oglala Sioux.* Edited by Joseph Epes Brown. Oklahoma: University of Oklahoma Press, 1953.

Blesbois, Hélène. *An tOileánach, de Tomás Ó Crohan: El enriquecimiento del proceso traductológico mediante la retraducción.* Master Thesis, Escuela de Literatura y Ciencias Del Lenguaje Maestría Profesional en Traducció, 2007.

Boas, Franz, ed. 2002. *Handbook of American Indian languages.* Bristol, UK: Thoemmes.

Boas, Franz. *The Mind of Primitive Man.* New York: The Macmillan Company, 1938 [1911].

Boas, Franz. *Tsimshian Mythology. Reports.* Washington D.C. Bureau of American Ethnology, (1916), pp. 29–1037.

Böll, Heinrich. *Billard Um Halb Zehn.* Köln: Kiepenheuer & Witsch, 1990.

Böll, Heinrich. *Irisches Tagebuch.* Cologne: Kiwi, 1988 [1957].

Bourdieu, Pierre. The Forms of Capital. In: J. Richardson ed. *Handbook of Theory and Research for the Sociology of Education.* Westport CT: Greenwood (1986), pp. 241–58.

Boym, Svetlana. *The Future of Nostalgia.* New York: Basic Books, 2001.

Brandes, Stanley. Ethnographic Autobiographies in American Anthropology. In: E. Adamson Hoebel, Richard Currier and Susan Kaiser eds *Crisis in Anthropology: View from Spring Hill 1980.* New York: Garland Press, 1982, pp. 187–202.

Brett, David. *The Construction of Heritage.* Cork: University Press, 1996.

Brody, Hugh. *Inishkillane: Change and Decline in the West of Ireland.* London: Allen Lane, 1973.

Brumble, David H. *American Indian Autobiography.* Berkeley, CA: California University Press, 1988.

Buhler, Jean. Préface. In: O'Crohan, Tomás. *L'homme des îles,* translated by Jean Buhler and Úna Murphy. Lausanne: Éditions Favre S.A., (1989), pp. 7–16.

Buhler, Jean. *Prends ma vie, camarade* Roman. Avec un propos liminaire de Henri Guillemin. Porrentruy, Éditions des Portes de France, 1944.

Buhler, Jean. *Sur les routes d'Europe: Souvenirs d'un vagabond.* Lausanne, Payot, 1942.

Burgess, Glyn. *The Voyage of St Brendan.* Exeter: University of Exeter Press, 2002.

Byrne, Anne, Edmondson, Ricca, and Varley, Tony. Arensberg and Kimball and Anthropological Research in Ireland: Introduction to the Third Edition,

*Conrad Arensberg and Solon Kimball, Family and Community in Ireland.* Ennis, County Clare: CLASP Press, 2001.

Cahillane, S., Moore, P., Fitzgerald, B., Warwick, D., Carney Hayes, M., Carney Jnr, M. Growing Up with Blasket Immigrants in Springfield, MA. In: Mícheál de Mórdha eag. *Ceiliúradh an Bhlascaoid 13.* Baile Átha Cliath: Coiscéim (2011), lgh. 99–124.

Cambon Jules. Loti Pierre. In: Loti Pierre *An Iceland Fisherman,* translated by Jules Cambon, USA: CreateSpace Independent Publishing Platform, 2014, pp. 6–12.

Canny, Nicholas, *Kingdom and Colony: Ireland in the Atlantic World, 1560–1800.* Johns Hopkins University Press, 1988.

Caputo, John D. *Truth: the Search for Wisdom in the Postmodern Age.* Milton Keynes: Penguin, 2013.

Carney, James. The Invention of the Ogham Cipher. *Ériu,* 26, 1975, 53–65.

Carney, Michael and Hayes, Gerald. *From the Great Blasket to America – The Last Memoir by an Islander.* Cork: Collins Press, 2013.

Carroll, Clint. *Roots of Our Renewal: Ethnobotany and Cherokee Environmental Governance.* Minneapolis: University of Minnesota Press, 2015.

Cashman, Ray. Critical Nostalgia and Material Culture in Northern Ireland, *Journal of American Folklore* 119 (472), (2006): 137–160.

Cassin, Barbara. *When are We Ever at Home?* Translated by Pascale-Anne Brault. New York: Fordham University Press, 2016.

Castro, Placido. *A Galician in Ireland.* Galicia: Placido Castro Foundation, 2013 [1932].

Céitinn, Seosamh. *Tomás, Oileánach.* Baile Átha Cliath: An Clóchomhar Teo, 1992.

Chapman, Malcolm. *The Celts: the Construction of a Myth.* UK: Palgrave Macmillan, 1992.

Clifford, James and Marcus, George eds. *Writing Culture: The Poetics and Politics of Ethnography.* Berkeley: University of California Press, 1986.

Clifford, James. Introduction: Partial Truths. In: James Clifford and George E. Marcus eds, *Writing Culture: The Poetics and Politics of Ethnography.* Berkeley, CA: University of California Press, (1986), pp. 1–26.

Clifford, James. The Others: Beyond the "Salvage" Paradigm. In: Rasheed Araeen, Sean Cubitt, Ziauddin Sardar eds, *Third Text Reader on Art, Culture and Theory.* London: Continuum, 2002 [1986], 160–65.

Cohen, Robin. *Global Diasporas: An Introduction.* London: UCL Press, 1997.

Coleman, Michael. *American Indians, the Irish, and Government Schooling: A Comparative Study.* University of Nebraska Press, 1 Jun. 2007.

Cook-Lynn, Elizabeth. Some Thoughts about Biography, *Wicazo Sa Review,* 10(1), (1994): 73–74.

Cooke, Pat. Art and Kilmainham Gaol: Negotiating Art's Critical Intervention for the Heritage Site. In: I. A. Russell and A. Cochran's eds. *Art and Archaeology, One World Archaeology*. New York: Springer (2014), pp. 83–96.

Cooke, Pat. Preface. In: Anthony Aughey ed. *The Edge of Europe: Imeall na hEorpa*. Dublin: Dept of Arts, Culture and the Gaeltacht, (1996).

Crashing Thunder. *Crashing Thunder: The Autobiography of an American Indian*. Edited by Paul Radin. Lincoln: University of Nebraska Press, 1983 [1926].

Cross, Eric. *The Tailor and Ansty*. Cork: Mercier, 1942.

Cruikshank, Julie. *The Social Life of Stories: Narrative and Knowledge in the Yukon Territory*. Lincoln and Lincoln: University of Nebraska Press, 2000.

Cullingford, Elizabeth Butler. *Ireland's Others: Ethnicity and Gender in Irish Literature and Popular Culture*. Cork: University Press, 2001.

Curtin, Jeremiah. *Memoirs of Jeremiah Curtin*. State Historical Society of Wisconsin, 1940.

Curtis, Edward S., Curtis Graybill, Florence and Boesen, Victor. *Edward Sheriff Curtis: Visions of a Vanishing Race*. Albuquerque: University of New Mexico Press, 2000 [1976].

Custer, George Armstrong. *My Life on the Plains or Personal Experiences with Indians*. Carliste: Applewood Books, 2009 [1874].

Dam, Albert. *Jomfruen og soldaten*. Denmark: Lindhardt og Ringhof Forlag, 1989.

Danson, Mike and Burnett, Kathryn. Enterprise and Entrepreneurship on Island. In: Colette Henry, Gerard McElwee eds, *Exploring Rural Enterprise: New Perspectives on Research, Policy and Practice*. Bingley: Emerald Group, (2014), pp. 151–74.

Darwin, Charles. *The Descent of Man, and Selection in Relation to Sex*. 1. London: John Murray, 1871.

Deloria, Vine Jr. *Custer Died for Your Sins: An Indian Manifesto*. New York: Macmillan, 1969.

Deloria, Vine Jr. Foreword. In: *Black Elk Speaks as through John G. Neihardt*. Lincoln and London: University of Nebraska Press, 2000 [1979], xiii–xvii.

De Mallie, Raymond J. ed. *The Sixth Grandfather: Black Elk's Teachings given to John G. Neihardt*. Lincoln: University of Nebraska Press, 1984.

De Mórdha, Dáithí and De Mórdha, Mícheál. *The Great Blasket, a Photographic Record: An Blascaod Mór, Portráid Pictiúr*. Cork: Collins Press, 2013.

De Mórdha, Daithí. The Blasket Centre. In: Felicity Hayes-McCoy and Wilf Judd eds. *Dingle and Its Hinterland: People, Places and Heritage*. Cork: Collins Press, 2017, pp. 83–100.

De Mórdha, Mícheál. *An Island Community: The Ebb and Flow of the Great Blasket Island*. Dublin: Liberties Press, 2015.

De Paor, Louis. Disappearing Language: Translations from the Irish, *The Poetry Ireland Review*, 51, (1996): 61–68.

De Saussure, Ferdinand. *Course in General Linguistics*. Translated and annotated by Roy Harris. Chicago: Open Court, 2003 [1983].

Dillon Eilís, *Die Insel der Pferde* (The Island of Horses). Translated by Anne-Marie Böll and Heinrich Böll. Freiburg: Hertner, 1964.

Doan, James E. Revisiting the Blasket Island Memoirs, *Irish Studies Review* 9(1) (2001): 81–86.

Donnan, Hastings. Re-Placing Ireland in Irish Anthropology. In: Diarmuid Ó Giolláin ed. *Irish Ethnologies*. Notre Dame: University of Notre Dame Press, 2017, 19–35.

Drew, F. Next Parish to Boston: The Blasket Islands and Their Literature, *Éire/Ireland* 3(1),(1968): 6–22.

Dunleavy, Janet and Dunleavy, Gareth. *Douglas Hyde – A Maker of Modern Ireland*. Berkeley: University of California Press, 1991.

Eakin, Paul John. "Foreword." In: Arnold Krupat ed. *For Those Who Come After: A Study of Native American Autobiography*. Berkeley, CA: University of California Press, 1985, vi–xvi.

Eastlake, John. *Native American and Irish Native Autobiography: A Comparative Study*. Unpublished PhD Dissertation, National University of Ireland, Galway, 2008.

Eastlake, John. Orality and Agency: Reading an Irish Autobiography from the Great Blasket Island. *Oral Tradition*, 24(1), (2009a): 125–141.

Eastlake, John. The (Original) Islandman? Examining the Origin in Blasket Autobiography. In: John Eastlake, Seán Crosson, and Nessa Cronin eds, *Anáil an bhéil bheo: Orality and Modern Irish Culture*. Newcastle upon Tyne: Cambridge Scholars, 2009b, pp. 241–58.

Eller, Jack. *Cultural Anthropology: Global Forces, Local Lives*. London: Routledge, 2016.

Enckell, Olof. *De klagande vindarnas ö: romantisk resa till Irland*. Stockholm: Bokförlaget Natur och kultur, 1937.

Enright, Tim. George Thomson: A Memoir. In: George D. Thomson ed. *Island Home: The Blasket Heritage*. Dingle: Brandon Book Publishers, (1988), pp. 119–150.

Eriksen, Thomas Hylland. In What Sense do Cultural Islands Exist? *Social Anthropology*, 1(18), (1993): 133–47.

Fabian, Johannes. *Time and the Other: How Anthropology Makes Its Object*. New York: Columbia University Press, 1983.

Fanon, Frantz. *Black Skin, White Masks*. Translated by Charles Lam Markmann. New York: Grove Press, 1967 [1952].

Fattori, Anna. Ireland as a "Better Elsewhere". In: Gisela Holfter ed, *Heinrich Böll's 'Irisches Tagebuch'"*, Trier: WVT, (2010), pp. 99–114.

Fazio, Antonio. *Inspiration in Stone*. West Kerry: Antonio Fazio, 2007.

Fazio, Antonio. Prefazione alla traduzione Italiana. In: O'Crohan, Tomás. *L'Isolano* (The Islandman), translated by Antonio Fazio, 2009, pp. 3–4.

Flower, Robin. Foreword. In: O'Crohan Tomás, *The Islandman.* Oxford: Oxford University Press. 1978 [1934], pp. v–xi.

Flower, Robin. *The Western Island.* Oxford: Clarendon Press, 1944.

Flower, Robin. *The Irish Tradition.* Oxford: Clarendon Press, 1947.

Foster, John Wilson. *Fictions of the Irish Literary Revival: A Changeling Art.* Syracuse: University Press, 1987.

Friel, Brian. *Selected Plays.* London, Boston: Faber and Faber, 1984.

Geertz, Clifford. *The Interpretation of Cultures: Selected Essays.* New York: Basic, 1973.

Geertz Clifford. *Works and Lives: The Anthropologist as Author.* Stanford: Stanford University Press, 1988.

Geronimo. *Geronimo: His Own Story,* S. Barrett ed. New York: Penguin, 1996.

Gibbon, Peter. Arensberg and Kimball Revisited. *Economy and Society* 2(4), (1973): 479–98.

Gibbons, Luke. Peripheral Modernities: National and Global in a Post-Colonial Frame. In: Keith Hanley and Greg Kucich eds, *Nineteenth-Century Worlds: Global Formations Past and Present,* Abingdon, Oxon: Routledge, 2008, pp. 199–210.

Gillis, John. Places Remote and Islanded, *Michigan Quarterly Review,* 40 (2001): 39–58.

Goody, Jack. *Literacy in Traditional Societies.* Cambridge: University Press, 2008.

Gorky, Maxim. *In the World.* Translated by Gertrude M. Foakes. London: T. Werner Laurie, 1917.

Gorky, Maxim. *My Childhood.* Translated and introduced by Ronald Wilks. London: Penguin Books, 1966.

Gorky, Maxim. *My Childhood.* Translated from the Russian by Gertrude M. Foakes, London: T. Werner Laurie, 1915.

Gourfinkel, Nina. *Gorky.* Translated by Ann Feshbach. Connecticut: Greenwood Press, 1975 [1960].

Green, David and Lowry, Joanna. From Presence to the Performative: Rethinking Photographic Indexicality. In: David Green ed. *Where is the Photograph?* Brighton Photo works/Photoforum, 2003.

Habermann, Gerhard E. *Maxim Gorki.* New York: Ungar Pub Co., 1971.

Hamsun, Knut. *Growth of the Soil.* London: Picador edition, 1980 [1917].

Handler, Richard and Segal, David. *Jane Austen and the Fiction of Culture: An Essay on the Narration of Social Realities.* Washington, DC, Rowman & Littlefield, 1999.

Hanks, William F. and Severi, Carlo. Translating Worlds: the Epistemological Space of Translation, *HAU: Journal of Anthropological Theory,* 4(2), (2014): 1–16.

Hannerz, Ulf. Other Transnationals: Perspectives Gained from Studying Sideways, *Paideuma* 44 (1998): 109–123.

Hannerz, Ulf. *Writing Future Worlds: an Anthropologist Explores Global Scenarios.* Switzerland: Palgrave/Macmillan, 2016.

Hare, Richard. *Maxim Gorky: Romantic Realist and Conservative Revolutionary.* Connecticut: Greenwood Press, 1978 [1962].

Harris, John. Orality and Literacy in Tomás Ó Criomhthain's Narrative Style. *The Canadian Journal of Irish Studies* 19(2), (1993): 20–30.

Harrison, Alan. Review Article: Blasket Literature, *Irish Studies Review*, 31(2), (2001): 488–94.

Haughey, Anthony. *The Edge of the World: Imeall na hEorpa.* Dublin: Roinn Ealaíon, Cultúir agus Gaeltachta, 1996.

Haughey, Anthony. A Landscape of Crisis: Photographing Post-Celtic Tiger Ghost Estates, *The Canadian Journal of Irish Studies*, 40, (2017): 53–71.

Hayes, Gerald and Kane, Eliza. *The Last Blasket King: Pádraig Ó Catháin, an Rí.* Cork: Collins Press, 2015.

Hayes, Gerald. *The Blasket Islandman: The Life and Legacy of Tomás Ó Criomhthain,* Cork: Collins Press, 2018.

Heaney, Seamus. *New Selected Poetry 1966–1987.* London, Boston: Faber and Faber, 1990.

Hélias, Pierre-Jakez. *The Horse of Pride: Life in a Breton Village.* Yale: Yale University, 1978, pp. xi–xvii.

Hill, Emma and Nic Craith, Máiréad. Medium and Narrative Change: The Effects of Multiple Media on the "Glasgow Girls" Story and Their Real-Life Campaign. *Narrative Culture*, 3(1), (2016), 87–109.

Hingley, Ronald. *Russian Writers and Society 1825–1904.* London: Weidenfeld & Nicolson, 1967.

Hjorth, Harriet. *Irlandskust.* Stockholm: H. Geber, 1947.

Hogan, Dick. £4m Great Blasket Centre expected to attract thousands, *The Irish Times,* April 7, 1994, p. 2.

Holfter, Gisela and Nóilín Nic Bhloscaidh. From Tomás Ó Criomhthain's *An tOileánach* to the Bölls' *Die Boote fahren nicht mehr aus.* In: Christopher Shorley and Maeve McCusker, eds, *Reading across the Lines.* Dublin: Royal Irish Academy, 2000, pp. 35–46.

Holfter, Gisela. *Heinrich Böll and Ireland.* Newcastle Upon Tyne: Cambridge Scholars Publishing, 2011.

Hooton, Earnest, Dupertuis, Albert, Wesley, Clarence, and Dawson, Helen. *The Physical Anthropology of Ireland,* Volume 1. Cambridge, MA: The Museum, 1955.

Hoskins, J. *Biographical Objects: How Things Tell the Stories of People's Lives.* New York and London: Routledge, 1998.

Howard, Gaskill (ed.). *The Reception of Ossian in Europe*. London: Continuum, 2004.

Hyde, Douglas. *The Necessity for De-Anglicising Ireland*. Delivered before the Irish National Literary Society in Dublin, 25 November 1892. Accessed June 12, 2018 http://www.gaeilge.org/deanglicising.html

Hyde, Douglas. Canon Peter O'Leary and Dr. Kuno Meyer, *Studies*, 9, (1920): 297–301.

Í Chearnaigh, Seán Sheáin. *An tOileán a Tréigeadh*. Baile Átha Cliath: Sáirséal Agus Dill, 1974.

Í Chearnaigh, Seán Sheáin. *Iarbhlascaodach ina Dheorai*. Baile Átha Cliath: Sáirséal agus Dill, 1978.

Ingold, Tim. In Defence of Handwriting. https://www.dur.ac.uk/writingacross-boundaries/writingonwriting/timingold/. n.d. (accessed 2nd October 2018).

Izquierdo Tugas, Pere Jordi, Juan-Tresserras, Matamala Mellin, Juan Carlos, eds. *Heritage Interpretation Centres, The Hicira Handbook*. Barcelona: Diputació de Barcelona. 2005.

Jackson, Michael. *The Politics of Storytelling – Variations on a Theme by Hannah Arendt*. Copenhagen: Museum Tusculanum Press, 2013.

Jacquin, Danielle. *Les Autobiographies Gaeliques: Voix Personnelle, Voix Collective, Voix Mythique*, *Études Irlandaises* 23(1), (1998): 13–25.

Jaffe, Alexander. Narrating the "I" Versus Narrating the "Isle". In: Deborah Reed-Danahay ed. *Auto/Ethnography: Rewriting the Self and the Social*, Oxford and New York: Berg, (1997), pp. 145–66.

James, Alison, Hockey, Jennifer, Dawson, Andrew, eds. *After Writing Culture: Epistemology and Praxis in Contemporary Anthropology*. London: Routledge, 1997.

Kanigel, Robert. *On an Irish Island*. New York: Alfred A. Knopf, 2012.

Karp, Ivan and Kratz, Corinne. Collecting, Exhibiting, and Interpreting: Museums as Mediators and Midwives of Meaning, *Museum Anthropology*, 37(1), (2014): 51–65.

Kavanagh, Patrick. Epic. In: John Montague ed. *The Faber Book of Irish Verse*. London: Faber and Faber, 1974, p. 286.

Kennelly, Brendan: "An Béal Bocht" by Myles na gCopaleen (1911–1966). In: John Jordan ed. *The Pleasures of Gaelic Literature*. Dublin: Mercier Press in collaboration with Raidió Teilifís Éireann, (1977), pp. 85–96.

Kiberd, Declan. *Irish Classics*. London: Granta Books, 2000.

Kierkegaard, S. *Concluding Unscientific Postscript to the Philosophical Fragments*, Transl. W. Lowrie & D. Swenson. Princeton, NJ: Princeton University Press, (1992 [1845]).

Kirshenblatt-Gimblett, Barbara. *Destination Culture: Tourism, Museums, and Heritage*. Berkeley and Los Angeles: University of California Press, 1998.

Kockel, Ullrich. Putting the Folk in Their Place: Tradition, Ecology, and the Public Role of Ethnology, *Anthropological Journal of European Cultures*, 17(1), (2008): 5–23.

Krupat, Arnold. *For Those Who Came After: A Study of Native American Autobiography*. Berkeley and Los Angeles: University of California Press, 1989.

Larsen, Lars Frode. *Knut Hamsun: The Author and His Times*. Oslo: Font Forlag, 2012.

Lear, Jonathan. *Radical Hope: Ethics in Face of Cultural Devastation*. Cambridge, MA: Harvard University Press, 2006.

Leerssen, Joop. The Western Mirage: On the Celtic Chronotope in the European Imagination. In: Timothy Collins ed. *Decoding the Landscape*. Galway: Centre for Landscape Studies, NUI Galway (1994), pp 1–11.

Levin, Dan. *Stormy Petrel: the Life and Work of Maxim Gorky*. London: Frederick Muller, 1967.

Lindberg, Christer. The Noble and Ignoble Savage. *EthnoScripts*, 15(1), (2013): 16–32. Universität Hamburg. Accessed September 29, 2017. https://www.ethnologie.uni-hamburg.de/forschung/publikationen/ethnoscripts/es-15-1/es-15-1-lindberg.pdf

Loti, Pierre. *An Iceland Fisherman*, translated from the French by Helen Dole. New York: Thomas Y. Crowell & Company, 1896.

Lowenthal, David. Islands, Lovers, and Others, *The Geographical Review* 97(2), (2007): 202–29.

Lucchitti, Irene. *The Islandman: The Hidden Life of Tomás O'Crohan*. Bern: Peter Lang, 2009.

Luce, John V. Homeric Qualities in the Life and Literature of the Great Blasket Island, *Greece and Rome*, 15 (1969): 151–68.

Lundbye, Vagn. *Sande skrøner fra verdens begyndelse* 1996, 8.

Lynch, Susanne. Choctaw Generosity to Famine Ireland saluted by Varadkar, *Irish Times*, March 13th, 2018.

Lynd, Robert and Lynd, Helen. *Middletown in Transition: A Study in Cultural Conflicts*. New York: Harcourt Brace, 1943.

Lyngstad, Sverre. *Knut Hamsun Novelist: A Critical Assessment*. New York: Peter Lang, 2005.

Lysaght, Patricia. Swedish Ethnological Surveys in Ireland 1934–5 and their Aftermath. In: Hugh Cheape ed. *Tools and Traditions: Studies in European Ethnology presented to Alexander Fenton*. Edinburgh: National Museums of Scotland, (1993), pp. 22–31.

MacClúin, An tAthair Seoirse. *Réilthíní Óir*. Baile Átha Cliath: Comhlucht Oideachais na hÉireann, 1922.

Mac Conghail, Muiris. *The Blaskets: A Kerry Island Library*. Dublin: Country House, 1987a.

Mac Conghail, Muiris. Tomás Ó Criomhthain: Islandman, *Études Irlandaises*, 12(2), (1987b): 156–64.

MacCana, Proinsias. *Literature in Irish*. Dublin: Department of Foreign Affairs, 1980.

Macdonald, Sharon. *Memorylands: Heritage and Identity in Europe Today*. London: Routledge, 2013.

MacFayden, John. *An t-Eileanach: Original Gaelic Songs, Poems and Readings*. Glasgow: Maclaren, 1921 [1890].

Maher, Eamon. Island Culture: The Role of the Blasket Autobiographies in the Preservation of a Traditional Way of Life, *Studies: An Irish Quarterly Review*, 97, (387), (2008): 263–74.

Malinowski, Bronislaw. *Argonauts of the Western Pacific: An Account of Native Enterprise and Adventure in the Archipelagoes of Melanesian New Guinea*. London: Routledge and Kegan Paul, 1922.

Marshall, Catherine. "Carry me to the Cornfield:" The Landscape Art of Maria Simonds-Gooding. 2004 http://www.simonds-gooding.com/assets/PDFs/CMarshall-Confield2004.pdf (accessed 10 October 2018)

Massey, Doreen. *Space, Place and Gender*. Cambridge: Polity Press, 2013.

Marstrander, Carl. Deux Contes Irlandais. In: Osborn Bergin and Carl Marstrander eds. *Miscellany Presented to Kuno Meyer*. Halle a.S.: M. Niemeyer, (1912), pp. 371–486.

Matson, Leslie M. *Méiní: the Blasket Nurse*. Cork: Mercier Press, 1996.

Mauss, Marcel. *The Gift: The Form and Reason for Exchange in Archaic Societies*. Abingdon: Routledge. 2002 [1954].

McAuliffe, John, "Epic" Patrick Kavanagh, *Irish University Review*, 39(2), (2009): 195–201.

McCarthy, Gerry. An Exhibition at the Glucksman Gallery Reflects Half a Century of Irish Art, but it Reveals as Much about Humanity as it does History, *Sunday Times* (London) September 13, 2009.

McCluskey, Sally. Black Elk Speaks and so does John Neihardt, *Western American Literature*, 6, (1972): 231–42.

McGahern, John. *An tOileánach*/The Islandman, *The Canadian Journal of Irish Studies* 13(1), (1987): 7–15.

Merriman, Brian. *The Midnight Court*. In: Frack O'Connor, ed. Kings, Lords and Commons. London: Penguin, 1961 [1780].

Messenger, John C. *Inis Beag: Isle of Ireland*. New York: Holt, Rinehart and Winston, 1969.

Miller, Kerby A. *Emigrants and Exiles: Ireland and the Irish Exodus to North America*. Oxford: Oxford University Press, 1985.

Mitchell, W. J. T. *Landscape and Power*. Chicago: University of Chicago Press, 2002 [1994].

Momaday, N. Scott. To Save a Great Vision. In Vine Deloria Jr. ed, *A Sender of Words: Essays in Memory of John G. Neihardt*. Salt Lake City: Howe Brothers, 1984, pp. 30–38.

Moody, T.W. and Martin, F.X. eds. *The Course of Irish History*. Dublin: Raidió Teilifís Éireann, 1967.

Moreton, Cole. *Hungry for Home – Leaving the Blaskets – A Journal from the Edge of Ireland*. London: Viking, 2000.

Muchnic, Helen. *From Gorky to Pasternak: Six Modern Russian Writers*. London: Methuen, 1963.

Muldoon, Paul. *New Weather*, London: Faber and Faber, 1973.

Munch-Pedersen, Ole (ed.), *Scéalta Mháirtín Neile: Bailiúchán Scéalta ó Árainn*, Baile Átha Cliath, Comhairle Bhéaloideas Éireann, 1994.

Munch-Pedersen, Ole. Oversætterens efterskrift. In: Ó Criomhthain, Tomás. *Manden på Øen*, translated by Ole Munch-Pedersen. Århus: Husets, Forlag, 1996, pp. 261–67.

Na gCopaleen, Myles. *An Béal Bocht*. Baile Átha Cliath: An Press Náisiúnta, 1941.

Na gCopaleen, Myles. Review, *Irish Times*, 3 January 1957, p. 6.

Narayan, Kirin and Kenneth, George. Personal and Folk Narrative as Cultural Representation. In: James A. Holstein and Jaber F. Gubrium eds, *Inside Interviewing: New Lenses, New Concerns*. California: Sage, (2003), pp. 449–69.

Neihardt, John G. *When the Tree Flowered: the Story of Eagle Voice, a Sioux Indian*, Lincoln and London: University of Nebraska Press, 1991 [1951].

Neihardt, John G. *Knowledge and Opinion: Essays and Literary Criticism of John G. Neihardt*, edited by Lori Holm Utecht. Lincoln: University of Nebraska Press, 2002.

Neihardt John, G. Preface. In: *Black Elk Speaks: The Complete Edition*, by Black Elk, Nicholas and Neihardt, John G, xxi–xxv. Lincoln and London: University of Nebraska Press, 2014, xix–xxii.

Nic Craith, Máiréad. *An tOileánach Léannta*. Baile Átha Cliath: An Clóchomhar, 1988.

Nic Craith, Máiréad. *Malartú Teanga: An Ghaeilge i gCorcaigh sa Naoú hAois Déag*, Bremen: European Society for Irish Studies, 1992.

Nic Craith, Máiréad. Primary Education on the Great Blasket Island 1864–1940, *Journal of the Kerry Historical and Archaeological Society*, 1995, 77–137.

Nic Craith Máiréad. *Plural Identities, Singular Narratives: The Case of Northern Ireland*. New York: Berghahn, 2002.

Nic Craith, Máiréad. *Culture and Identity Politics in Northern Ireland*. Basingstoke: Palgrave, 2003.

Nic Craith, Máiréad. *Narratives of Place, Belonging and Language: An Intercultural Perspective*. Basingstoke: Palgrave, 2012.

Nic Craith, Máiréad. A Sense of Place in Irish-Language Memoirs: the West Kerry Gaeltacht, 1929–1939. In: Maurice Bric ed. *Kerry, History and Society*, Dublin: Geography Publications, 2019.

Nic Craith, Máiréad and Leyland, Janet. The Irish language in Britain: A Case Study of North West England, *Language, Culture and Curriculum*, 10(3), (1997): 171–85.

Nic Craith, Máiréad and Kockel, Ullrich. Blurring the Boundaries between Literature and Anthropology. A British Perspective, *Ethnologie Française* 44(4), (2014): 689–97.

Nic Craith, Máiréad and Kockel, Ullrich. Homo Hibernians Rusticus Revisited: Flann O'Brien's Parody of National Myth Making. In: Regina Bendix and Dorothy Noyes eds. *Terra Riddens*, Dortmund: Betraige zur Kulturgeshichte des Islamischen Orients, 2018, pp. 220–242.

Nic Einrí, Úna. *Stair na Teanga Gaeilge*. Baile Átha Cliath: Folens, 1971.

Nic Eoin, Máirín. Twentieth-Century Gaelic Autobiography: From *lieux de mémoire* to Narratives of Self-invention. In: Liam Harte ed. *Modern Irish Autobiography: Self, Nation and Society*. London: Palgrave Macmillan UK, 2007, pp. 132–155.

Ní Ghaoithín, Máire. *An tOileán a Bhí*. Baile Átha Cliath: An ClÓchomhar, 1978.

Ní Shéaghdha, Nóra. *Thar Bealach Isteach: Leabhar eile ón mBlascaod Mór*. Baile Átha Cliath: Oifig an tSoláthair, 1940.

Ní Shúilleabháin, Brenda. Na Blascaodaí sna hAmharcealaíona. In: Mícheál de Mórdha eag. *Na Blascaodaí agus na hEalaíona* (Ceiliúradh an Bhlascaoid 16). Baile Átha Cliath: Coiscéim, 2014, lgh. 49–62.

Ní Shúilleabháin, Eibhlís. *Letters from the Great Blasket*. Edited by Seán Ó Coileáin. Cork: Mercier Press, 1978.

Oakdale, Suzanne and Course, Magnus, eds. *Fluent Selves: Autobiography, Person, and History in Lowland South America*. Lincoln: University of Nebraska Press, 2014.

O'Brien, Edna. *The Country Girls*. Great Britain: Hutchinson, 1960.

O'Brien, Flann. *Das Harte Leben* (The Poor Mouth). Translated by Annemarie Böll and Heinrich Böll, Hamburg: Nannen, 1966.

O'Brien, Flann. *The Poor Mouth*. Translated by P. C. Power. London: Hart Davis, Mac Gibbon Ltd., Great Britain, 1973.

O'Brien, Máire Cruise. An *tOileánach*: Tomás Ó Criomhthain (1856–1937). In: John Jordan ed. *The Pleasures of Gaelic Literature*. Cork: Mercier Press, 1977, pp. 25–38.

Ó Cadhain, Máirtín. *Páipéir Bhána agus Páipéir Bhreaca*. Baile Átha Cliath: An Clóchomhar Tta., 1969.

Ó Cadhain, Máirtín. *Kirkegardsjord: genfortaelling i ti mellemspil*. Translated by Ole Munch-Pedersen, Arhus: Husets Forlag, 2000.

Ó Coileáin, Seán. Tomás Ó Criomhthain, Brian Ó Ceallaigh agus An Seabhac. In: Seán Ó Mórdha eag. *Scríobh 4*. Baile Átha Cliath: An Clóchomhar, 1979, lgh. 159–87.

Ó Coileáin, Seán. An *tOileánach* – Ón Láimh go dtí an Leabhar. In: Máire Ní Chéilleachair eag. *Céiliúradh an Bhlascaoid 2: Tomás Ó Criomhthain 1855–1937*. Baile Átha Cliath: Coiscéim, 1998, lgh. 25–43.

Ó Coileáin, Seán. Réamhrá. In: Tomás Ó Criomhthain, An *tOileánach*. Seán Ó Coileáin a chuir in eag. Baile Átha Cliath: Cló Talbóid, (2002), lgh. xi–xliii.

Ó Coileáin, Seán. Preface. *The Islander*, by Tomás O'Crohan, translated by Garry Bannister and David Sowby. Dublin: Gill and Macmillan, 2012, pp. xii–xiii.

Ó Conaire, Brendán. Ómós do Tomás Ó Criomhthain, *Comhar*, 36, Márta (1977a): 15–16.

Ó Conaire, Brendán. Ómós do Tomás Ó Criomhthain (2), *Comhar*, 36, Aibreán (1977b): 19–23.

Ó Conaire, Brendán. Ómós do Tomás Ó Criomhthain (3), *Comhar*, 36, Meitheamh (1977c): 23–25.

Ó Conaire, Brendán. Tomás an Bhlascaoid, *Comhar*, 36, Lúnasa (1977d): 16–19.

Ó Conaire, Brendán. Tomás an Bhlascaoid, *Comhar*, 36, Meán Fómhair (1977e): 18–21, 27.

Ó Conaire, Brendán eag. *Tomás an Bhlascaoid*. Conamara: Cló Iar-Chonnachta, 1992.

Ó Conaire, Pádraic. *Emigrantliv*. Translated by Ole Munch-Pedersen, Arhus: Husets Forlag, 1999.

Ó Criomhthain, Seán. *Lá dár Saol*. Baile Átha Cliath: Oifig an tSoláthair, 1969.

Ó Criomhthain, Seán. Pádraig Tyers talking to Seán Ó Criomhthain. In: Pádraig Tyers ed. *Blasket Memories: the Life of an Irish Island Community*. Cork: Mercier Press, 1988, pp. 89–149.

Ó Criomhthain, Tomás. *Allagar na hInise*, An Seabhac a chuir in eagar. Baile Átha Cliath: Clólucht an Talbóidigh, 1928.

Ó Criomhthain, Tomás. *Allagar na hInise*. Pádraig Ua Maoileoin a chuir in eagar. Baile Átha Cliath: Oifig an tSoláthair, 1977.

Ó Criomhthain, Tomás. *Dinnsheanchas na mBlascaodaí*. Baile Átha Cliath: Oifig Díolta Foilseacháin Rialtais, 1935.

Ó Criomhthain, Tomás. *Seanchas ón Oileán Tiar*, Séamus Ó Duilearga a chuir in eagar. Baile Átha Cliath: Comhlucht Oideachais na h-Éireann, 1956.

O'Crohan, Seán. *A Day in Our Life*. Translated by Tim Enright. Oxford: Oxford University Press, 1992.

O'Crohan, Tomás. *Island Cross-Talk: Pages from a Diary*. Translated by Tim Enright. Oxford: Oxford University Press, 1986.

Ó Crualaoich, Gearóid. The Primacy of Form: A "Folk Ideology" in De Valera's Politics. In: J P. O'Carroll and John A. Murphy eds, *De Valera and His Times*. Cork: University Press, 1986: pp. 47–61.

Ó Fiannachta, Pádraig. An *tOileánach*/The Islandman, Tomás Ó Criomhthain. In: Proinsias Ó Conluain ed. *Islands and Authors: Pen-pictures of Life Past and Present on the Islands of Ireland*. Dublin: Mercier Press, 1983, pp. 44–58.

Ó Gaoithín, Mícheál. *Is Truagh ná Fanann an Óige*. Baile Átha Cliath: Oifig an tSoláthair, 1953.

Ó Giolláin, Diarmuid. *Locating Irish Folklore: Tradition, Modernity, Identity*. Cork: Cork University Press, 2000.

O'Guiheen, Mícheál. *A Pity Youth Does Not Last*. Translated by Tim Enright, Oxford: Oxford University Press, 1982.

Ó hÁinle, Cathal. Tomás Ó Criomhthain agus "Caisleán Uí Néill", *Irisleabhar Mha Nuad* (1985): 84–109.

Ó hÁinle, Cathal. Deformation of History in Blasket Autobiographies. In: James Noonan ed. *Biography and Autobiography*, 7, Ottawa: Carleton University Press, (1993), pp. 133–47.

O'Leary, Peter. *My Story*. Translated by Cyril Ó Céirín. Dublin and Cork: The Mercier Press, 1970.

O'Leary, Philip. *Gaelic Prose in the Irish Free State, 1922–1939*. Dublin: University College, 2004.

O'Leary, Philip. *The Prose Literature of the Gaelic Revival 1881–1921: Ideology and Innovation*. Pennsylvania: Pennsylvania University Press, 1994.

Ó Lúing, Seán. Robin Flower, Oileánach agus Máistir Léinn, *Journal of the Kerry Archaeological and Historical Society* 10 (1977): 111–42.

Ó Lúing, Seán. "To Be a German…" Oidhreacht Khuno Meyer. In: Seán Ó Mórdha eag. *Scríobh*, Baile Átha Cliath: An Clóchomhar, 1981a, lgh. 258–281.

Ó Lúing, Seán. Robin Flower (1881–1946), *Studies*, 70 (228–9), (1981b): 121–134.

Ó Lúing, Seán. Carl Marstrander (1883–1965), *Journal of the Cork Historical and Archaeological Society* 89 (248), (1984): 108–124.

O'Neill, Patrick. *Kennst du das Land?* Ireland and the German Literary Imagination. In: Gisela Holfter ed, *Irisches Tagebuch by Heinrich Böll*. Trier: WVT Wissenschaftlicher Verlag, 2010, pp. 79–88.

Ó Sé, Diarmuid. Léirmheas: Tomás Ó Criomhthain, *An tOileánach*, Eagarthóir Seán Ó Coileáin. *Éigse*, XXXV (2006): 127–33.

Ó Siochfhradha, Pádraig. Tomás Ó Criomhthain, Iascaire Agus Ughdar, *Bonaventura*, Samhradh (1937): 24–31.

Ó Siochfhradha, Pádraig. *Tríocha-Céad Chorca Dhuibhne*. Baile Átha Cliath: Cumann le Béaloideas Éireann, 1938.

Ó Siochfhradha, Pádraig. Tomás Ó Criomhthain agus Brian Ó Ceallaigh, *Irish Press*, December 21, 1956, 21.

Ó Súilleabháin, Muiris. *Fiche Blian ag Fás*. Baile Átha Cliath: Clólucht an Talbóidigh, 1933.

O'Sullivan, Carol. Retranslating Ireland: Orality and Authenticity in French and German Translations of Blasket Island Autobiography. In: Theo Herman ed.

*Translating Others:* Vol. 2. Manchester, UK & Kinderhook USA: St. Jerome Publishing, 2006, pp. 380–393.

O'Sullivan, Maurice. *Dwadziescia lat dorastania.* Translated by Ernest Bryll and Małgorzata Goraj. Warszawa: Ludowa Spoldzielnia Wydawnicza, 1986.

O'Sullivan, Maurice. *Inselheimat.* Translated by Elisabeth Aman. Zurich: Manesse Verlag, 1956.

O'Sullivan, Maurice. *Twenty Years A-Growing.* Translated by George Thomson and Moya Llewellyn Davies. London: Chatto and Windus, 1983, [1933].

O'Sullivan, Maurice. *Vingt ans de jeunesse.* Translated by Raymond Queneau, Paris, France: Gallimard, 1936.

O'Toole, Fintan. *A History of Ireland in 100 Objects.* Dublin: Royal Irish Academy, 2013.

O'Toole, Fintan. An Island Lightly Moored. *The Irish Times* March 29, 1997. Accessed September 29, 2017. https://www.irishtimes.com/sport/an-island-lightly-moored-1.57283

O'Toole, Fintan. *The Clod and the Continent: Irish Identity in the European Union.* Dublin: Irish Congress of Trade Unions, 2002. Available at: https://www.ictu.ie/download/pdf/essay1.pdf (accessed 14 October 2018).

Ó Tuama, Seán, *Repossessions: Selected Essays on the Irish Literary Heritage.* Cork University Press, 1995.

Pine, Richard. *The Diviner: the Art of Brian Friel.* Dublin: University College Dublin Press, 1999 [1990].

Porter, Joy. Primitive Discourse: Aspects of Contemporary North American Indian Representations of the Irish and of Contemporary Irish Representations of North American Indians, *American Studies* 49(3), (2008) https://journals.ku.edu/article/view/4004/3793. Accessed 23 October 2017.

Powers, William K. *Beyond the Vision: Essays on American Indian Culture.* Norman: University of Oklahoma Press, 1987.

Quigley, Mark. *Empire's Wake: Postcolonial Irish Writing and the Politics of Modern Literary Form.* New York: Fordham University Press, 2013.

Quigley, Mark. Modernity's Edge: Speaking Silence on the Blasket Islands, *Interventions*, 5(3), (2003): 382–406.

Radhakrishnan, Rajagopalan. *Theory in an Uneven World.* Blackwell, 2003.

Rapport, Nigel. Literary Anthropology. *Oxford Bibliographies Online.* Last modified: 11 January 2012. https://doi.org/10.1093/obo/9780199766567-0067

Rapport, Nigel. *Diverse World Views in an English Village.* Edinburgh: Edinburgh University Press, 1993.

Rapport, Nigel. *The Prose and the Passion: Anthropology, Literature, and the Writing of E. M. Forster.* Manchester: Manchester University Press, 1994.

Rapport, Nigel. Voice, History and Vertigo: Doing Justice to the Dead through Imaginative Conversation. In: Carol Smart, Jenny Hockey and Allison James eds, *The Craft of Knowledge: Experiences of Living with Data*. Basingstoke: Palgrave Macmillan, (2014), pp. 112–27.

Redfield, Robert. *Tepoztlan – A Mexican Village: A Study of Folk Life*. Chicago: University of Chicago Press, 1930.

Reed-Danahay, Deborah. Leaving Home: Schooling Stories and the Ethnography of Autoethnography in Rural France. In: Deborah Reed-Danahay ed, *Auto/Ethnography: Rewriting the Self and the Social*. Oxford and New York: Berg, (1997a), pp. 123–44.

Reed-Danahay, Deborah. Introduction. In: Deborah Reed-Danahay ed, *Auto/Ethnography: Rewriting the Self and the Social*. Oxford and New York. Berg, (1997b), pp. 1–17.

Ridgway, Keith. Review of *The Islander*, by Tomás O'Crohan, translated by G. Bannister and D. Sowby. *The Irish Times* Weekend Review, October 30, 2012. https://www.irishtimes.com/culture/books/a-blasket-bore-1.552077. Accessed: March 3, 2016.

Rosaldo, Renato. Imperialist Nostalgia. Representations, 26, Special Issue: Memory and Counter-Memory (1989a): 107–122.

Rosaldo, Renato. *Culture and Truth: The Remaking of Social Analysis*. Boston, MA: Beacon, 1989b.

Ross, Ciaran. Blasket Island Autobiographies: The Myth and Mystique of the Untranslated and the Untranslatable, *Translation and Literature*, 12(1), (2003): 114–43.

Rossi, Riika. Noble Savages and Human Beasts: The Primitive in Finnish Neo-Naturalism. In: Carolyn Snipes-Hoyt, Marie-Sophie Armstrong, Riikka Rossi eds, *Re-Reading Zola and Worldwide Naturalism: Miscellanies in Honour of Anna Gural-Migdalia*. Newcastle upon Tyne: Cambridge Scholars Publishing, 2013, pp. 399–413.

Rousseau, Jean-Jacques. *Discourse on the Origin of Inequality*. Oxford: Oxford University Press, 1999 (1755).

Said, Edward W. *Orientalism*. New York: Pantheon Books, 1978.

Said, Edward W, Representing the Colonized: Anthropology's Interlocutors, *Critical Inquiry* 15(2), (1989): 205–25.

Sapir, Edward W, *Selected Writings of Edward Sapir in Language, Culture and Personality*. Berkeley: University of California Press, 1985 [1949].

Sayers, Peig. *An Old Woman's Reflections*, translated by Séamus Ennis. Oxford: University Press, 1962.

Sayers, Peig. *Peig: A Scéal Féin*, edited by Máire Ní Chinnéide. Dublin: Talbot 1936.

Sayers, Peig. *So Irisch wie ich. Eine Fischersfrau erzählt ihr Leben*. Translated by Hans-Christian. Göttingen: Oeser, 1996.

Sayers, Peig. *Peig. Autobiograpie d'une grande conteuse d'Irlande*, translated by Joëlle Gac. Brittany: An Here, 1999.

Sayers, Peig. *The Autobiography of Peig Sayers of the Great Blasket*, translated by Brian McMahon. Dublin: The Talbot Press, 1972.

Sayers, Peig. *Labharfad le Cách/I Will Speak to You All*, edited by Bo Almqvist and Pádraig Ó Héalaí. Dublin: New Island Press, 2010.

Sayre, Robert. Vision and Experience in *Black Elk Speaks. College English*, 32(5), (1971): 509–35.

Scheper-Hughes, Nancy. *Saints, Scholars and Schizophrenics: Mental Illness in Rural Ireland*. Anniversary edition revised and expanded. Berkeley: University of California Press. 2001 [1979].

Seanad Éireann debate, Wednesday, 18 Nov 1942. Accessed June 15, 2018, https://www.oireachtas.ie/en/debates/debate/seanad/1942-11-18/6/

Sergel, Christopher. *John G. Neihardt's Black Elk Speaks*. Chicago: The Dramatic Publishing Company, 1996.

Shea, Thomas F. The Islander: A More Provocative Tomás O'Crohan, *New Hibernia Review* 18(3), (2014): 93–109.

Shepherd, Nan. *The Living Mountain*. Edinburgh: Canongate Books, 2011 [1977].

Shostak, Marjorie. *Nisa: The Life and Words of a !Kung Woman*. London: Vintage Books, 1983 [1981].

Sjoestedt, Marie-Louise. *La littérature qui se fait en Irlande, Études Celtiques*, 2, (1937): 334–46.

Sjoestedt-Jonval, Marie-Louise. *Description d'un Parler Irlandais de* Kerry. Paris: F. Champion, 1938.

Skelton, Robert, *The Writings of John M. Synge*. California: University of California Press, 1971.

Smith, Barry. *The Island in Imagination and Experience*. Salford: Sarabande, 2017.

Smith, Sidonie and Watson, Julia. *Reading Autobiography: A Guide for Interpreting Life Narratives*, 2nd edition. Minneapolis: University of Minnesota Press, 2010.

Solnit, Rebecca. *A Book of Migrations. Some Passages in Ireland*. London and New York: Verso, 1997.

Spivak, Gayatri Chakravorty (1973) Can the Subaltern Speak? In: Bill Ashcroft, Gareth Griffiths, and Helen Tiff eds, *The Post-Colonial Studies Reader*. London and New York: Routledge, (1998), pp. 28–37.

Spivak, Gayatri Chakravorty. The Rani of Sirmur: an Essay in Reading the Archives, *History and Theory* XXIV, no. 3 (1984): 247–72.

Stafford, Fiona J. *The Last of the Race: The Growth of a Myth from Milton to Darwin*. Wotton-under-Edge: Clarendon Press, 1994.

Stanley, Nick *Being Ourselves for You: the Global Display of Cultures*. Middlesex: University Press, 1998.

Stasch, Rupert. Primitivist Tourism and Romantic Individualism: on the Values in Exotic Stereotypy about Cultural Others, *Anthropological Theory*, 14(2), (2014): 191–214.

Stewart, James. An *tOileánach* – More or Less, *Zeitschrift für Celtische Philologie*, 35. (1976): 234–263.

Stocking, George Jr. *A Franz Boas Reader: The Shaping of American Anthropology 1883–1911*. New York: Basic Books, 1974.

Stover, Dale. A Postcolonial Reading of Black Elk. In: Clyde Holler ed. *The Black Elk Reader*. Syracuse: University Press: 2000, pp. 127–146.

Swann, Brian and Krupat, Arnold. Introduction to the Bison Books edition. In: Brian Swann and Arnold Krupat eds *Autobiographical Essays by Native American Writers*. Winnipeg: Bison Books (2005), pp. ix–xvi.

Synge, John Millington. *In Wicklow and West Kerry*. Gloucester: Dodo Press, 1912.

Synge, John Millington, *Collected Works 111: (Plays 1)*. Edited by Ann Saddlemyer, Oxford, 1968.

The Republican. *The Irish Legacy: A History of the Irish in Western Massachusetts*. Canada: Pediment Publishing, 2012.

Thomson, George. *Island Home: The Blasket Heritage*. Dingle: Brandon Book Publishers, 1988.

Thomson, George. *Studies in Ancient Greek Society: The Prehistoric Aegean*. New York: International Publishers, 1949.

Titley, Alan. Foreword. In: O'Crohan, Tomás. *The Islander: A Translation of an tOileánach*. Edited by Garry Bannister and David Sowby. Dublin: Gill & Macmillan, 2012, vii–xi.

Tolton, C.D.E. *André Gide and the Art of Autobiography: A study of Si le grain ne meurt*. Toronto: Macmillan, 1975.

Tracy, Honor. *The Straight and Narrow Path*. New York: Vintage, 1956.

Tuan, Yi-Fu. *Topophilia: A Study of Environmental Perception, Attitudes and Values*. New York: Columbia University Press, 1990 [1974].

Tyers, Pádraig ed. *Leoithne Aniar*. Baile An Fheirtéaraigh: Cló Dhuibhne, 1982.

Tyers, Pádraig, eag. *Blasket Memories: The Life of an Irish Island Community*. Cork: Mercier Press, 1998.

Tylor, Edward Burnett. *Primitive Culture*. Volume 1. London: John Murray. 1871.

Tymoczko, Maria. *Translation in a Postcolonial Context: Early Irish Literature in English Translation*. Manchester: St. Jerome Publishing, 1999.

Ua Laoghaire, Peadar. *Séadna*. Baile Átha Cliath: Bernard Doyle, 1898.

Ua Maoileoin, Pádraig. *Na hAird Ó Thuaidh*. Baile Átha Cliath: Sáirséal Agus Dill, 1960.

Ua Maoileoin, Pádraig. *De Réir Uimhreacha*. Baile Átha Cliath: Muintir an Dúna, 1969.

Ua Maoileoin, Pádraig. Réamhrá, In: Tomás Ó Criomhthain, *An tOileánach*, Pádraig Ua Maoileoin a chuir in eagar, Baile Átha Cliath, Cló Talbóid, 1973, lgh. 7–9.

Ua Maoileoin, Pádraig. An Criomhthanach. In: Breandán Ó Conaire eag. *Tomás an Bhlascaoid*. Indreabhán: Cló Iar-Chonnachta, 1992, lgh. 149–65.

Ua Maoileoin, Pádraig. *Na Blascaodaí: The Blaskets*. Baile Átha Cliath: Oifig na nOibreacha Poiblí, 1996.

Underhill, James W. *Humboldt, Worldview and Language*. Edinburgh: Edinburgh University Press, 2009.

Urry, John and Larsen, Jonas. *The Tourist Gaze 3.0*. Los Angeles: Sage, 2011 [1990].

Velie, Alan R. Black Elk Speaks, Sort Of: The Shaping of an Indian Autobiography, *Revue LISA/LISA* e-journal 2(4) (2004): 147–161. Accessed September 28, 2017. http://lisa.revues.org/2937;

Walsh, Ciarán. Charles R. Browne, the Irish 'Headhunter', *Irish Journal of Anthropology*, 16(1), (2013): 16–22.

Waterston A and Vesperi M D eds *Anthropology off the Shelf: Anthropologists on Writing*. Oxford: Wiley-Blackwell, 2009.

White, Michael. *Maps of Narrative Practice*, New York: Norton, 2007.

Whorf, Benjamin Lee. *Language, Thought, and Reality: Selected Writings*, Vol. 5, edited by John B. Carroll. Cambridge, MA: MIT Press. 1956.

Wiles, Ellen. Three Branches of Literary Anthropology: Sources, Styles, Subject Matter. *Ethnography*, 2018. https://doi.org/10.1177/1466138118762958.

Worster, W.W. Introductory Note. In: Knut Hamsun, *Dreamers*. CreateSpace Independent Publishing Platform, 2013, pp. 2–7.

Wulff, Helena. *Dancing at the Crossroads: Memory and Mobility in Ireland*. *New York:* Berghahn, 2003.

Wulff, Helena. An Anthropological Perspective on Literary Arts in Ireland. In: Ullrich Kockel, Máiréad Nic Craith and Jonas Frykman eds., *Blackwell Companion to the Anthropology of Europe*. Oxford: Wiley-Blackwell, 2012, pp. 537–50.

Wulff, Helena. Anthropologist in the Irish Literary World: Reflexivity through Studying Sideways. In: Thomas Hylland Eriksen, Christina Garsten and Shalini Randeria eds, *Anthropology Now and Next: Essays in Honor of Ulf Hannerz*, New York: Berghahn, 2014, 147–161.

Wulff, Helena. *Rhythms of Writing: An Anthropology of Irish Literature*. London, New York: Bloomsbury, 2017.

Wylie, Lawrence. Foreword. In: Hélias, Pierre-Jakez. *The Horse of Pride: Life in a Breton Village*. Yale: Yale University, (1978), pp. xi–xvii.

Žagar, Monika. *Knut Hamsun: The Dark Side of Literary Brilliance (New Directions in Scandinavian Studies)*. Seattle: University of Washington Press, 2011.

# INDEX

© The Author(s) 2020
M. Nic Craith, *The Vanishing World of* The Islandman,
Palgrave Studies in Literary Anthropology,
https://doi.org/10.1007/978-3-030-25775-0

Druck:
Customized Business Services GmbH
im Auftrag der KNV-Gruppe
Ferdinand-Jühlke-Str. 7
99095 Erfurt